STRATIFICATION IN COGNITION
AND CONSCIOUSNESS

ADVANCES IN CONSCIOUSNESS RESEARCH

ADVANCES IN CONSCIOUSNESS RESEARCH provides a forum for scholars from different scientific disciplines and fields of knowledge who study consciousness in its multifaceted aspects. Thus the Series will include (but not be limited to) the various areas of cognitive science, including cognitive psychology, linguistics, brain science and philosophy. The orientation of the Series is toward developing new interdisciplinary and integrative approaches for the investigation, description and theory of consciousness, as well as the practical consequences of this research for the individual and society.

Volume 15

Bradford H. Challis and Boris M. Velichkovsky (eds)

Stratification in Cognition and Consciousness

STRATIFICATION IN COGNITION AND CONSCIOUSNESS

BRADFORD H. CHALLIS

University of Tsukuba and Organon, Inc.

BORIS M. VELICHKOVSKY

Technical University, Dresden

JOHN BENJAMINS PUBLISHING COMPANY
AMSTERDAM/PHILADELPHIA

The paper used in this publication meets the minimum requirements of
American National Standard for Information Sciences — Permanence of
Paper for Printed Library Materials, ANSI z39.48–1984.

Library of Congress Cataloging-in-Publication Data

Stratification in cognition and consciousness / edited by Bradford H. Challis, Boris M.
Velichkovsky.
    p.   cm. -- (Advances in consciousness research, ISSN 1381-589X ; v. 15)
    Includes bibliographical references and index.
    1. Information processing. 2. Categorization (Psychology) 3. Visual perception. 4. Recollection
(Psychology) 5. Memory. I. Challis. Bradford H. II. Velichkovsky, B.M. (Boris Mitrofanovich) III.
Series.
BF444.S73   1999
153--dc21   99-29157
ISBN 90 272 5135 5 (Eur.) / 1 55619 195 2 (US) (Pb; alk. paper)   CIP

John Benjamins Publishing Co. • P.O.Box 75577 • 1070 AN Amsterdam • The Netherlands
John Benjamins North America • P.O.Box 27519 • Philadelphia PA 19118-0519 • USA

Table of Contents

Contributors

William P. Banks
Department of Psychology
Pomona College
Claremont, CA 91711
USA

David J. Bennett
Department of Psychology
Simmons College
Boston, MA 02115
USA

Bruce Bridgeman
Department of Psychology
University of California, Santa Cruz
Santa Cruz, CA 95064
USA

Bradford H. Challis
Institute of Psychology
University of Tsukuba
Tsukuba, Japan
and
Organon Inc.
Clinical Development Department
West Orange, NJ 07052
USA

Yung-Pin Chen
Department of Mathematics
Smith College
Northampton, MA701063
USA

Martin A. Conway
Department of Psychology
University of Bristol
Bristol, BS81TN
UK

Fergus I.M. Craik
Department of Psychology
University of Toronto
Toronto, Ontario
Canada M5S 1A1

Sarah H. Creem
Psychology Department
University of Virginia
Charlottesville, VA 22903
USA

John Gardiner
Psychology Department
City University
Northampton Square
London EC1V 0HB
UK

James E. Hoffman
Department of Psychology
University of Delaware
Newark, DE 19716
USA

Vanessa M. McKinney
Department of Psychology
University of South Florida
Tampa, FL 33620
USA

A. David Milner
School of Psychology
University of St Andrews
St Andrews, Fife KY16 9JU
Scotland, UK

Douglas Nelson
Department of Psychology
University of South Florida
Tampa, FL 33620
USA

Dennis R. Proffitt
Department of Psychology
University of Virginia
Charlottesville, VA 22903
USA

Matthew W. Prull
Department of Psychology
Stanford University
Stanford, CA 94305-2130
USA

Suparna Rajaram
Department of Psychology
SUNY at Stony Brook
Stony Brook, NY 11794-2500
USA

Henry L. Roediger III
Department of Psychology
Washington University
St. Louis, MO 63130-4899
USA

Boris M.Velichkovsky
Department of Psychology
Dresden University of Technology
D-01062 Dresden
Germany

An introduction to stratification, cognition and consciousness

Boris M. Velichkovsky   Bradford H. Challis

Do we really need a new word in our psychological vocabulary, like one in the title of this volume? What do we mean by stratification? Turning to the dictionary, one finds that stratification refers to a description of some structure as characterized by a succession of tabular layers or strata, from earth's crust or sky to people. As well, one finds that stratification as a research strategy has, sometimes, an obvious heuristic value. For instance, geologists infer the origin and age of substances from their relative localization in layers of some congregation. In social sciences, placement of people according to some criterion level, such as education or wealth, is used to predict attitudes and behavior. Now it is only one step to explain what sense it makes to use this term in hard core experimental psychology and neurosciences.

As the matter of fact, this understanding fits a number of approaches in contemporary cognitive research. Quite straightforward, this is the levels of processing approach by Craik & Lockhart (1972) which postulates several kinds of processing that can be ordered along the dimension of "depth" of respective activities: from "shallow" physical processing to "deep" semantic. Clearly, Craik and Lockhart emphasize a variation of encoding in their approach. In other conceptions of memory, the emphasis is rather on a variation of retrieval tasks. Still, we would place Tulving's (1985) memory systems view (procedural, perceptual, semantic, episodic) under the same general umbrella. The memory systems have different characteristics in terms of their cognitive structure and function, development, and associated brain systems, in keeping with the idea of stratification. In addition, different states of consciousness (anoetic, noetic, autonoetic) are associated with different memory systems, again reflecting the notion of stratification. In this vein, stratification is where Craik and Lockhart meet Tulving and Schacter (e.g., Schacter & Tulving, 1994) — as far as the lasts speak about hierarchical relationships among subsystems of human memory.

Not only memory is suspected to be stratified in one or another sense (see Velichkovsky, 1990). Some generic information processing models may be interpreted in a hierarchical way as they often presuppose "bottom-up" and "top-down" interactions among layers of representation such as features, letters, words, and concepts (LaBerge, 1995; Posner, 1978; Shiffrin & Schneider, 1977). Similar ideas can be found in studies of consciousness and higher-order cognition, especially if they are considered in the neuropsychologhical context of frontal lobes functions (Stuss, 1991). On the other end, stratification may be helpful to elucidate organization of "sensorimotor intelligence": there is a long and fruitful tradition of hierarchical explanations with respect to motor control (Bernstein, 1996) and the notion of stratification has been already used in connection with action mechanisms (de Jong & Sanders, 1990).

Thus, closer inspection reveals that the notion of stratification plays a role in various models and theories related to experimental psychology and neuro-science, although to date, this role has not been well articulated and identified. Indeed, stratification does not appear to be an integral part of some prominent paradigms in cognitive research. Two major paradigms easily come to mind.

One is based on the computer metaphor of the 60s. It treats cognitive architecture as a closed circuit of memory stores, in an analogy with the relationship of parts of a conventional computer. All parts are necessary for the fluent functioning of the device, and any history of developmental or evolutionary stages is hardly conceivable in the case. The only meaningful context of stratification would be a weak one, in terms of the temporal succession of information processing; for instance, any input information should be registered in some form of sensory stores before it eventually reaches a more durable internal container. Interestingly, consciousness is not of primary interest within this paradigm either, perhaps only as a synonym for selective attention, i.e. as a hypothetical mechanism with limited processing capacity (a view that creates difficulties and paradoxes in the explanation of even the simplest phenomena such as masking or stroboscopic motion, see Dennett, 1991).

The second paradigm is that of modularity of mind or domain specificity of cognitive mechanisms, spelled out as a new manifesto by Fodor (1983) and others. Double dissociations are at the focus of interest for the proponents of this approach and such dissociations have been looked for with vigor awarded by editors of major journals (see Goldberg, 1995). Processing capacity was itself partitioning, as for example in the model of Wickens (1984) who postulated several parallel systems with their own independent capacities. In a similar vein, many idiosyncratic forms of consciousness, so-to-say "incommensurable" and isolated from each other, have been postulated. The whole stratification issue however does not make much sense here because there are no layering in a random mosaic of presumably autonomous modules.

Taking the modularity approach as an example, we wish to argue that it would benefit from incorporating the notion of stratification. There is increasing evidence that in many cases the relationships between cognitive modules are not as symmetrical as they should be in a perfect parallel architecture. A well-known case is the distinction of two visual systems, the focal one and the ambient one. Both can be neurologically separated but developmentally they show a clear temporal primacy of (partially subcortical) ambient vision over (cortical) focal vision system (Trevarthen, 1968; Velichkovsky, 1982). Similar conclusion is valid also for a more recent distinction of stimulus-driven and conceptually-driven memory processes. In place of clear-cut double dissociations, one finds here an asymmetrical pattern of interdependencies: some variables that are expected to influence only the stimuli-driven tasks have an impact on the conceptual processing as well (see Roediger, Buckner, & McDermott, 1998).

The current trend seems to be away from the early ideas based on computer metaphor but also away from the rigid modularity view of the last decade. In sum, we see the notion of stratification as an overlooked but potentially important component on many theoretical perspectives in cognitive psychology. This is why we decided that it is time for stratification to receive more explicit consideration by the cognitive community, which was the prime motivation for this book. With this goal in mind, we solicited articles from researchers with a range of interests from eye movements and perception to episodic memory and consciousness. In other respects this was an almost random sample — participants of our book project certainly do not belong to any "believers-in-the-hierarchical-order" sect. We asked authors to contribute an article on their current research endeavors, and to the extent possible, broach the notion of stratification. Of course, we tried to explain what we meant by stratification, with the hope that after reading the contributions of the authors, we would have a better understanding of stratification.

In our opinion, and we hope you agree, a reading of the nine articles in the book provides important exposure to and insights into the role stratification in cognition and consciousness. While different authors emphasize different notions such as levels, stages, gradients or vertical modularity, the common idea which is addressed in supportive but also in critical ways is that of vertical organization as a feature of both cognition and consciousness. The contributions build three clusters of chapters, around the topic of visual processing, microstructure of memory tasks and varieties of subjective experience. Every part is commented by a distinguished colleague — David Milner, Fergus Craik and Henry Roediger.

The first chapter by Bruce Bridgeman examines a vertical (rather than horizontal) division of conscious and unconscious components in visual processing. He considers two examples of vertical organization, saccadic scanpath adaptation in reading and isomorphically controlled motor activity; this contrasts vision as probed with symbolic responses and vision probed with isomorphic motor activity (pointing). Both lines of research reveal an unconscious level of sensory processing responsible for sophisticated information management, including some kinds of adaptation and control of behavior. The inputs, "central" processing and output are all unconscious in the sense that the observer is unaware of their functioning, cannot describe the outputs of the systems and has no explicit memory of the operations or their results. The conscious system is what remains after the unconscious component is accounted for, or in a practical sense, it contains the information that is communicated. The stratification of consciousness is context-dependent, with a conscious record being left if an interaction with episodic memory is necessary.

James Hoffman analyzes the stages of processing in visual search and attention, elaborating on a traditional model that assumes two separate processing stages. A wealth of empirical findings, ranging from visual search and automaticity to physiological evidence, are discussed in the context of the model. The first, preattentive stage of processing serves to locate interesting objects in the visual world, for examination by a second stage of processing that may be associated with conscious awareness. This second stage is assumed to operate on one or a few objects at a time and forms a bottleneck in visual processing. The view of full and immediate access to the identities of all objects in view may reflect our ability to extract the gist of scenes, to quickly recognize attended objects and to derive an overall sense of the spatial layout. Preattentive vision knows about the visual world but objects identification may be limited to the subsequent processing stage associated with conscious awareness.

The chapter by Sarah Creem and Dennis Proffitt examines the role of time and place in performing perceptual judgments and visually guided actions. Dissociations between conscious awareness of objects in the environment and visually guided actions made towards these objects imply that visual system is segregated into distinct paths mediating these two activities. Experiments on memory for geographical slant provide important information about the nature of memorial visual guidance. Authors used egocentric judgment of the incline of hills with different time delays and responses measures (verbal, visual, haptic). The results suggest a stratification in memory similar to vision. In the short term and in the presence of the stimulus, a separate visual guidance memory and explicit memory inform action and phenomenal awareness, respectively. With a longer delay or when the observer is removed from the presence of the hill, communication between systems is apparent; visual guidance memory is not preserved and actions must rely on an explicit visual representation.

The second part of the book begins with Challis' analysis of memory tests with perceptually impoverished cues such as word fragment completion. The chapter calls into question the popular view that implicit (unconscious) AND explicit (conscious) retrieval processes provide two separate and independent sources of studied words on these tests. Rather, on perceptually-cued tests, studied items are retrieved only from implicit memory. The theoretical perspective is engendered in a generation–selection (G–S) model, in which G is an implicit process that resolves the degraded stimulus and S (i.e. selection) acts on the information provided by G to meet the test requirements. The author presents a range of findings showing that the G–S model explains and predicts performance on word fragment cued tests with different instructions (completion, inclusion, cued recall, exclusion). This perspective implies that implicit memory and explicit memory are stratified, with implicit preceding explicit retrieval, at least on perceptual tests.

William Banks, Yung-Pin Chen, and Matthew Prull examine conscious and unconscious components of memory with a detailed analysis of the process dissociation procedure. The authors develop signal detection models of process dissociation to address criticisms of the procedure. Their first model, a common intuitive model of decision processes in process dissociation, makes predictions that are not confirmed. The second model assumes a single memory representation based on memory strength and their source in recognition and does make a distinction between conscious and unconscious information: this model can predict recognition (inclusion), source discrimination and exclusion performance. According to their analysis, stratification of memory into conscious and unconscious is not a simple matter. Their best model suggests that subjects combine conscious and unconscious information continuously, with these two sorts of information best conceived as a single representation.

Douglas Nelson, Vanessa McKinney and David Bennett discuss the idea that known and novel information contribute independently to remembering, with their relative contribution determined by the retrieval cues. The research builds on their knowledge about extralist cued recall and recognition obtained over many experiments, and Nelson's PIER (processing implicit and explicit representations) model. The PIER2 model predicts, among other things, that connectivity among the associates of a studied word (like set size) will affect conscious and automatic influences of memory. The reported experiments examine various predictions using the process dissociation procedure to examine conscious and automatic influences on cued recall and recognition tests (Jacoby, 1991). The discussion considers consciousness and stratification. PIER2 implies automatic and conscious processing of a known word can occur simultaneously; this processing is stratified in that each kind of processing can serve different purposes, such as encoding what is known versus what is new.

Velichkovsky examines the stratification of cognitive processing in three domains, eye movement studies, brain imaging and traditional memory research. The central theme is the levels-of-processing approach to memory proposed by Craik and Lockhart (1972), and its continued value in understanding cognition. Memory experiments with a large matrix of encoding and test conditions produce findings compatible with the view of multiple levels of processing, with integration across levels dependent on the conscious status of memory test (see also Challis, Velichkovsky, & Craik, 1996). Similar issues are considered with neuroimaging studies involving various encoding and test conditions, with results implying a correspondence of functional and structural mechanisms in the multiple levels of processing. Research on eye movements provide independent measures and further insights into the multiple levels of processing view. The integration of theory and data from various domains (e.g., cognitive, developmental, neuro-psychological) points to stratification in consciousness and cognition.

The last two chapters discuss recent developments in an experiential approach to investigating memory. In the popular but controversial approach, subjects report the kinds of experiences that occur during memory retrieval, especially whether they remember or know that the stimulus occurred in the study phase of the experiment.

John Gardiner and Martin Conway, elaborating on Tulving's (1983) approach, assume that these two subjective states of retrieval reflect two kinds of consciousness, autonoetic and noetic consciousness, which in turn reflect functioning episodic and semantic memory systems. They review empirical support for the functional independence of remembering and knowing, and recent research that includes additional responses of "guessing", "just know", and feeling of familiarity. The findings show that know responses do not merely reflect a more lenient response criterion, but rather, know responses imply an additional source of memory. They suggest that just know responses, as do familiarity responses, reflect the semantic memory system and are manifestations of noetic consciousness. In line with the general stratification perspective, the states of consciousness and their associated memory systems can be viewed as organized hierarchically.

Suparna Rajaram evaluates the recent flurry of research on the Remember/ Know paradigm and how the procedure provides an elegant tool to quantify at least two different types of conscious experience. The author provides an excellent evaluation of the strengths and weakness of the various theoretical accounts proposed to explain dissociations and factors and processes that influence conscious experiences. A critical distinction among accounts is whether the model assumes that two (or more) different processes underlie remember and know responses, or the operation of a single process reflecting high and low confidence. Rajaram presents a variety of findings to substantiate the psychological reality of the distinction between remembering and knowing. This includes research on states of remembering with different subject groups (e.g., amnesics and elderly), with different test situations, and with a false memory paradigm (Roediger & McDermott, 1995).

The chapters reveal similarities but also differences. While some authors tend to an unitary view of representation, others argue for a dichotomic or even a multiple levels view of underlying mechanisms. These differences should not be overstated however provided the different scope of phenomena under consideration. Thus, even without (much) conspiracy on the part of editors, the bulk of the chapters give a rather coherent view on the importance of the stratification perspective.

One commonality is how naturally the stratification perspective integrate the consideration of consciousness — as something varying along the vertical dimension of mental functioning and not just among otherwise equal, parallel domains. Different forms of awareness, from protopathic sensitivity and sensory vigilance to reflective consciousness, may mirror these changes in processing capacities and integrative control on the way from low level mechanisms to higher-order structures. Also, the heuristic value of stratification comes to view in consideration of the relationship of consciousness and attention. They could well be different entities from the point of view of stratification paradigm. In a hierarchical architecture, conscious experience corresponds to the goals of the level currently dominating in the solution of a task (Bernstein, 1947; Bridgeman, this volume; Marcel, 1988). The effects of attention can be explained in terms of the control exerted by the upper on the lower levels whereby these influences may clearly be followed through to the bottom structures, as in the case of postural components of the motor or perceptual sets. Because several levels can be at work simultaneously, attentional control and monitoring should mostly proceed without conscious reflection.

The emerging picture is that of a shift in the dominate paradigm, from the search for double dissociations to a more systematic analysis of possible asymmetries with such dissociations revealing interactions among subsystems of cognitive mechanisms. Perhaps the future is in a combination of different approaches. An exiting issue may be that some of the modules, for example that for (varieties of) visual perception (Miener & Goodale, 1995; Rock, 1997), language processing (Deacon, 1997), or theory of mind (Lesley, 1994), have their own evolutionary and developmental history and a kind of tacit hierarchical or heterarchical architecture. However, the early evolutionary dream, in the spirit of John Hughlings Jackson (see Taylor, 1931/1932) and Nicholai Bernstein (1947), about a unitary hierarchical architecture of progressively evolving mind/brain mechanisms that take control over the older structures is not passé. In any case, data summarized on the following pages teach us one lesson: though all modules may be equal, some modules certainly are more equal than others.

In closing this introduction, it is our pleasure to thank all the contributors for their collaboration. Preparation of the book benefited from the support (to BV) of the Konrad Lorenz Foundation for Evolution and Cognitive Research (Vienna-Altenberg, Austria) and the support (to BC) of a University of Tsukuba Research Grant. As well, we would like to thank the John Benjamins Publishing House and editors of the series, particularly Bertie Kaal and Maxim Stamenov, for valuable guidance over all stages of this book project.

References

Bernstein, N. A. (1947). *O postrojenii dvizhenij [On the construction of movements]*. Moscow: Medgiz.

Bernstein, N. A. (1996). *Dexterity and its development*. Mahwah, NJ: Lawrence Erlbaum Associates.

Challis, B. H., Velichkovsky, B. M., & Craik, F. I. M. (1996). Levels-of-processing effects on a variety of memory tasks: New findings and theoretical implications. *Consciousness and Cognition, 5,* 142–164.

Craik, F. I. M. & Lockhart, R. (1972). Levels of processing: A framework for memory research. *Journal of Verbal Learning and Verbal Behavior, 11,* 671–684.

Deacon, T. W. (1997). *The symbolic species: The co-evolution of language and the brain*. New York: Norton.

Dennett, D. C. (1991). *Consciousness explained*. Boston: Little, Brown and Company

de Jong, H. L. & Sanders, A. F. (1990). Stratification in perception and action. *Psychological Research, 52,* 216–228.

Fodor, J. A. (1983). *The modularity of mind*. Cambridge, MA: MIT Press.

Goldberg, E. (1995). The rise and fall of modular orthodoxy. *Journal of Clinical and Experimental Neuropsychology, 17,* 193–208.

Jacoby, L. L. (1991). A process dissociation framework: Separating automatic from intentional uses of memory. *Journal of Memory and Language, 30,* 513–541.

Jacoby, L. L., Yonelinas, A. P., & Jennings, J. M. (1997). The relationship between conscious and unconscious (automatic) influences: A declaration of independence. In J. Cohen & J. W. Schooler (eds.), *Scientific approaches to the question of consciousness.* Mahwah, NJ: Lawrence Erlbaum Associates.

LaBerge, D. (1995). *Attentional processing: The brain's art of mindfulness.* Cambridge, MA: Harvard University Press.

Lesley, A. M. (1994). ToMM, ToBy, and Agency: Core architecture and domain specificity. In L. A. Hirschfeld & S. A. Gelman (eds.), *Mapping the mind: Domain specificity in cognition and culture.* New York: Cambridge University Press.

Marcel, A. J. (1988). Phenomenal experience and functionalism. In A. J. Marcel & E. Bisiach (eds.), *Consciousness in contemporary science.* Oxford: Claredon Press.

Milner, A. D. & Goodale, M. A. (1995). *The visual brain in action.* Oxford, UK: Oxford University Press.

Posner, M. I. (1978). *Chronometric explorations of mind.* Hillsdale, NJ: Lawrence Erlbaum Associates.

Rock, I. (1997). *Indirect perception.* Cambridge, MA: MIT Press.

Roediger, H. L., Buckner, R., & McDermott, K. B. (1998). Components of processing. In J. K. Foster & M. Jelicic (eds.), *Unitary versus multiple systems accounts of memory.* New York: Oxford University Press.

Roediger, H. L. & McDermott, K. B. (1995). Creating false memories: Remembering words not presented in the lists. *Journal of Experimental Psychology: Learning, Memory, and Cognition, 21,* 803–814.

Schacter, D. L. & Tulving, E. (1994). What are memory systems of 1994? In D. L. Schacter & E. Tulving (eds.), *Memory systems 1994.* Cambridge, MA: MIT Press.

Shiffrin, R. M. & Schneider, W. (1977). Controlled and automatic human information processing: II. Perceptual learning, automatic attention and general theory. *Psychological Review, 84,* 127–190.

Stuss, D. T. (1991). Self, awareness, and the frontal lobes: A neuropsychological perspective. In J. Strauss & G. R. Goethals (eds.), *The Self: Interdisciplinary approaches.* New York: Springer-Verlag.

Taylor, J. (ed.) (1931/32). *Selected writings of John Hughlings Jackson. Vol. 2 Evolution and dissolution of the nervous system.* London: Hodder and Stoughton, Reprinted (1959) by Basic Books, New York.

Trevarthen, C. (1968). Two visual systems in primates. *Psychologische Forschung, 31,* 321–337.

Tulving, E. (1983). *Elements of episodic memory.* New York: Oxford University Press.

Tulving, E. (1985). How many memory systems are there? *American Psychologist, 40,* 385–398.

Velichkovsky, B. M. (1982). Visual cognition and its spatial-temporal context. In F. Klix, Hoffmann, J., & Van der Meer, E. (eds.), *Cognitive research in psychology.* Amsterdam: North Holland.

Velichkovsky, B. M. (1990). The vertical dimension of mental functioning. *Psychological Research, 52,* 282-289.

Wickens, C. D. (1984). Processing resources in attention. In R. Parasuraman & D. R. Davies (eds.). *Varieties of attention.* New York: Academic Press.

PART I

Vertical dimension of visual processing

Seeing and doing

Two selective processing systems in vision

A. David Milner

Until very recently, there has been a near-universal tendency in psychology and neuroscience to think of visual processing as a means of constructing a single all-purpose perceptual representation that can then serve us in all of our dealings with the world, whether motor, mnemonic, aesthetic or social. It seems intuitively obvious that "what we see is what we get". But this view of vision has become increasingly untenable, and we are currently in the midst of a remarkable sea-change in the way that visual scientists conceptualize their field of study.

It is now increasingly recognized that there are quasi-independent visual subsystems in the primate brain each serving a different motor domain — saccadic eye movements, ocular pursuit, locomotion, reaching with the arm, grasping with the hand. These vertical systems for visuomotor control appear to operate with consummate indifference to any benefits that might be conferred by visual consciousness, although their efficient operation undoubtedly depends on selective spatial gating (part of what we mean by "attention"). Furthermore, these vertical visuomotor systems are themselves quasi-independent from the perceptual system that furnishes our visual awareness of the world and provides the raw materials for storing our visual memories of the world. Current evidence indicates that even this perceptual system is at least partially modular, with dedicated neural hardware devoted to the analysis of biologically important stimuli such as the faces, bodies, and movements of humans and other animals. (It seems reasonable to assume that the reason for this may be to enable our brains to give high priority to such stimuli: in effect they are routed through a neural "hot line" that does not get occupied by less urgent messages. The price we pay for this prioritization may be our proclivity to see a man in the moon, human shapes in the clouds, and waving arms when the wind blows through trees.).

The evidence for such verticality in the visual system is assembled in a recent book (Milner & Goodale, 1995), but the ideas are far from new. In 1909, Rudolf Bálint described a now-famous patient whose parietal lobes were damaged bilaterally, and who suffered from three main visually-related symptom clusters (Harvey, 1995). One of these three disorders was exemplified by an inability to reach out accurately to take hold of objects placed in front of him, a failure that Bálint named "optic ataxia" (*optische Ataxie*). The curious thing was that the patient only experienced this misreaching problem when he used his right hand. Clearly therefore there was no generalized failure of visuospatial localization, since that would have affected his left hand as well as his right. But neither could the reaching disorder be attributed to a motor impairment of the right hand, since the patient could point accurately under proprioceptive control, whichever hand he used. Thus Bálint concluded from his experiments that optic ataxia was *visuomotor* in nature. This important conclusion was ahead of its time, and did not receive general acceptance. We now know that patients with optic ataxia not only show visual misreaching, but also often have problems with other actions that depend on visual guidance. Thus when reaching to grasp objects, they typically fail to make appropriate turning movements of the wrist (Perenin & Vighetto, 1988) and opening movements of the hand (Jeannerod et al., 1994) in anticipation of contact with the object. Yet their *perception* of the same object properties can remain broadly unaffected.

In experimental psychology, the approach of J.J. Gibson (1950, 1966) represented a reaction away from the classic notion of perception as an all-purpose system that could be studied using pictures presented to static observers in the laboratory. Gibson argued that perception had to be studied within its practical ("ecological") context, as an integral part of our active interactions with the world. He was the first to draw attention in print to the importance of the optic flow field in guiding an organism's movements through space, a prime example of a dedicated system for providing visual guidance of action. The work of Gibson's successors (notably David Lee: see Lee, 1976; Lee & Thomson, 1982) has played a major role in the new way that vision is conceptualized. They have demonstrated incontrovertibly that vision can not be understood simply as a means of furnishing us with a rich subjective representation of the world. Our senses evolved through conferring increased efficiency upon our ancestors' behavioural transactions with the world, not through enhancing their subjective experience.

Perhaps because of Gibson's dismissal of the brain from his scientific world-view, it was not until the late 1960s that neuroscientists began to think seriously in terms of vertical visual processing systems in both animals and man. But neurobehavioural data began to suggest more and more strongly that such systems might be at work to provide visual information tailored for particular categories of motor acts (Held, 1970; Humphrey, 1970; Ingle, 1967, 1973; Schneider, 1967; Trevarthen, 1968). The work of these and other authors soon led to the discovery of "blindsight" — residual visual abilities in the subjectively "blind" hemifield of human subjects with damage to the primary visual cortex (Pöppel et al., 1973; Weiskrantz et al., 1974; Perenin & Jeannerod, 1975). Reviewing these and other data, Goodale (1983) argued explicitly that "the visual system ... evolved in vertebrates and other organisms as a network of independent sensorimotor channels."

Blindsight for stimulus location was initially observed with the use of visuomotor tasks, i.e. saccadic eye movements and manual pointing, and although it can be demonstrated in some patients even when verbal ("guessing") responses are elicited, it still appears to be most readily expressed through motor responses (Marcel, 1993). This differential between verbal and motor expression is especially clear when blindsight for intrinsic visual dimensions of objects like width or orientation is examined (Perenin & Rossetti, 1996; Rossetti, 1998). These authors have described hemianopic patients who, when reaching for objects placed in their blind field, can turn their wrist and open their grip appropriately in anticipation, even when quite unable to give verbal responses that are correlated with the relevant visual qualities of the stimulus.

Bruce Bridgeman, as is eloquently evident in his chapter in the present volume, has been a major player over the past 20 years in building up the empirical and theoretical foundations of this new approach to visual processing in human subjects (Bridgeman et al., 1979; Bridgeman, 1992). Bridgeman's work, along with that of Paillard (1987), Mack (e.g. Wong & Mack, 1981), and Goodale (Goodale et al., 1986) has shown convincingly that two distinct forms of encoding of visual space co-exist in the human brain. One system (which Paillard calls "representational") relates stimulus location to a contextual framework, and is consequently subject to various visual illusions, while the second (Paillard's "sensorimotor" system) relates stimulus location directly to the observer, and is therefore much less prone to systematic error. The egocentric system typically operates on a very short time-scale, while the representational system appears to take over at delays of more than a second or two (Rossetti, 1998).

There is accumulating evidence (Milner & Goodale, 1995) that these parallel spatial systems are each associated with comparable systems for processing other stimulus features, including size, shape and orientation, so that there is a cluster of visuomotor modules for visuomotor control within the brain that is quite separate from the visual processing systems that yield our perceptual experience. The chapter by Creem and Proffitt in the present volume makes the case that while the time-scale of visual processing for actions like reaching, grasping and saccadic eye movements may be limited to 1–2 seconds, other visuomotor systems may enjoy a longer visual "half-life".

The authoritative review by James Hoffman in the present volume provides food for thought as to whether and how "preattentive" representations may be available to nonconscious visuomotor mechanisms of the kind explored by Bridgeman in his chapter. For example, it may be that the "noisy identity" that these representations appear to provide corresponds to the pre-saccadic information that practised readers use when scanning printed text in experiments such as those described by Bridgeman. Increasingly, students of visual attention are also looking specifically at selection for action (Rizzolatti et al., 1994; Tipper et al., 1998) rather than only at selection for perception. (Selective perception may be expressed in motor terms such as a key-press, but the response is a symbolic, essentially arbitrary, one, which could just as well be verbal.) One example of this new development is that investigators are beginning to examine how visual priming can facilitate or interfere with pre-prepared actions to be directed to visual target objects (Craighero et al., 1998).

A strictly "vertical" conceptualization of visual processing might lead to the expectation that such priming would operate independently of, and in parallel with, priming related to the semantics of the target stimulus. In other words, that there should be little "cross-priming" between cognitive and visuomotor processing domains. Actually there is already some experimental evidence that there is such cross-talk (Deubel et al., 1998), leading its authors to argue for a possible master system for visuospatial selective attention within the visuomotor system which in turn exercises attentional control over perceptual processing (cf. Milner, 1995). But such studies are currently still in their infancy.

References

Bridgeman, B., Lewis, S., Heit, G., & Nagle, M. (1979). Relation between cognitive and motor-oriented systems of visual position perception. *Journal of Experimental Psychology (Human Perception and Performance), 5,* 692–700.

Bridgeman, B. (1992). Conscious and unconscious processes: The case of vision. *Theory and Psychology, 2,* 73–88.

Craighero, L., Fadiga, L., Rizzolatti, G., & Umiltà, C. (1998). Visuomotor priming. *Visual Cognition, 5,* 109–125.

Deubel, H., Schneider, W. X., & Paprotta, I. (1998). Selective dorsal and ventral processing: evidence for a common attentional mechanism in reaching and perception. *Visual Cognition, 5,* 81–107.

Gibson, J. J. (1950). *The Perception of the Visual World*. Boston: Houghton Mifflin.

Gibson, J. J. (1966). *The Senses Considered as Perceptual Systems*. Boston: Houghton Mifflin.

Goodale, M. A. (1983). Vision as a sensorimotor system. In T. E. Robinson (ed.), *Behavioral Approaches to Brain Research*. (pp. 41–61). New York: Oxford University Press.

Goodale, M. A., Pélisson, D., & Prablanc, C. (1986). Large adjustments in visually guided reaching do not depend on vision of the hand or perception of target displacement. *Nature, 320,* 748–750.

Harvey, M. (1995). Translation of 'Psychic paralysis of gaze, optic ataxia, and spatial disorder of attention' by Rudolph Bálint. *Cognitive Neuropsychology, 12,* 261–282.

Held, R. (1970). Two modes of processing spatially distributed visual information. In F. O. Schmitt (ed.), *The Neurosciences Second Study Program*. (pp. 317–324). Cambridge, MA: MIT Press.

Humphrey, N. K. (1970). What the frog's eye tells the monkey's brain. *Brain, Behavior and Evolution, 3,* 324–337.

Ingle, D. J. (1968). Two visual mechanisms underlying the behavior of fish. *Psychologische Forschung, 31,* 44–51.

Ingle, D. (1973). Two visual systems in the frog. *Science, 181,* 1053–1055.

Jeannerod, M., Decety, J., & Michel, F. (1994). Impairment of grasping movements following bilateral posterior parietal lesion. *Neuropsychologia, 32,* 369–380.

Lee, D. N. (1976). A theory of visual control of braking based on information about time to collision. *Perception, 5,* 437–457.

Lee, D. N. & Thomson, J. A. (1982). Vision in action: The control of locomotion. In D. J. Ingle, M. A. Goodale, & R. J. W. Mansfield (eds.), *Analysis of Visual Behavior*. (pp. 411–433). Cambridge, MA: MIT Press.

Marcel, A. J. (1993). Slippage in the unity of consciousness. In G. R. Bock & J. Marsh (eds.), *Experimental and Theoretical Studies of Consciousness*. (pp. 168–180). Chichester, UK: Wiley.

Milner, A. D. (1995). Cerebral correlates of visual awareness. *Neuropsychologia, 33,* 1117–1130.

Milner, A. D. & Goodale, M. A. (1995). *The Visual Brain in Action*. Oxford: Oxford University Press.

Paillard, J. (1987). Cognitive versus sensorimotor encoding of spatial information. In P. Ellen & C. Thinus-Blanc (eds.), *Cognitive Processes and Spatial Orientation in Animal and Man. Volume II: Neurophysiology and Developmental Aspects*. (pp. 43–77). Dordrecht: Martinus Nijhoff.

Perenin, M.-T. & Jeannerod, M. (1975). Residual vision in cortically blind hemifields. *Neuropsychologia, 13,* 1–7.

Perenin, M.-T. & Rossetti, Y. (1996). Grasping without form discrimination in a hemianopic field. *NeuroReport, 7,* 793–797.

Perenin, M.-T. & Vighetto, A. (1988). Optic ataxia: a specific disruption in visuomotor mechanisms. I. Different aspects of the deficit in reaching for objects. *Brain, 111,* 643–674.

Pöppel, E., Held, R., & Frost, D. (1973). Residual visual function after brain wounds involving the central visual pathways in man. *Nature, 243,* 295–296.

Rizzolatti, G., Riggio, L., & Sheliga, B. M. (1994). Space and selective attention. In C. Umiltà & M. Moscovitch (eds.), *Attention and Performance XV. Conscious and Nonconscious Information Processing.* (pp. 231–265). Cambridge, MA: MIT Press.

Rossetti, Y. (1998). Implicit short-lived motor representations of space in brain damaged and healthy subjects. *Consciousness & Cognition, 7,* 520–558.

Schneider, G. E. (1967). Contrasting visuomotor functions of tectum and cortex in the golden hamster. *Psychologische Forschung, 31,* 52–62.

Tipper, S. P., Howard, L. A., & Houghton, G. (1998). Action-based mechanisms of attention. *Philosophical Transactions of the Royal Society of London, B353,* 1385–1393.

Trevarthen, C. B. (1968). Two mechanisms of vision in primates. *Psychologische Forschung, 31,* 299–337.

Weiskrantz, L., Warrington, E. K., Sanders, M. D., & Marshall, J. (1974). Visual capacity in the hemianopic field following a restricted occipital ablation. *Brain, 97,* 709–728.

Wong, E. & Mack, A. (1981). Saccadic programming and perceived location. *Acta Psychologica, 48,* 123–131.

CHAPTER 1

Vertical modularity in the visual system

Bruce Bridgeman

Vision, to its user, seems to be a conscious activity — we see and recognize objects, surfaces and events, and can remember and act on visual perceptions and experiences. Yet what seems like a seamless, unified sense has now been shown to be fragmented into many components, both physiologically and functionally. Some of the functions of vision, and much of its machinery, operate in an unconscious mode, hidden from both memory and experience.

As a working definition, conscious aspects will be those that are verbally reported, or that could potentially be verbally reported. This definition fits the origin of the word, con/scious or with/knowing, those aspects of mental life that can be shared with others, internally verbalized, and used in planning future behavior. The etymologies of words for consciousness in several other languages, including Russian, share the concept of knowing-with. In contrast, unconscious aspects of vision are those that leave no direct trace in experience, cannot be described, and remain unknown until the indirect methods of science reveal them.

Psychology began as the study of human experience, on the assumption that the mental components that constitute it could be explicated by carefully examining one's experience. Unresolvable disputes using this methodology made it clear that this program was impossible — there were aspects of what we now call biological information processing that were inaccessible to verbal report, and remained forever hidden. These inaccessible domains included not only 'early' vision, such as retinal information processing, but also the algorithms and strategies by which sensory information is interpreted in the brain. Eventually it was discovered that the inaccessible parts of mental life dwarfed the accessible parts; most of the brain's work remains forever separate from verbal reportability. Psychology needed other methods than introspection, and eventually it found them.

A confirming line of evidence that most of mental life is at a level inaccessible to language comes from neurophysiology. Since the 1950s it has been possible to record with microelectrodes from a wide range of brain areas, seeking single-cell correlates of sensory processing, motor processing, memory, and other functions. The results have been fascinating but difficult, for hardly any of the thousands of published reports are easily related to conscious experience. The brain's great mass of neurons seems almost exclusively bent on aspects of biological information processing that have no direct correlates in human experience. No one could have guessed the properties of spatial organization of visual receptive fields, for example, or of the hierarchies of visual information processing, and theories of the nature of the processing benefit very little from insight achieved with everyday experience.

There are two ways to divide conscious from unconscious components in visual processing. One, the more conventional, is a 'horizontal' division in which unconscious early processes feed into later, conscious processes in a hierarchy of image analysis. A complementary organization will be introduced here: the idea that some visual systems are unconscious from start to finish. The inputs to these systems, the information processing, and the output are all unconscious in the sense that the observer is unaware of their functioning, cannot describe the outputs of the system even if pressed, and has no explicit memory of the operations or of their results. This is a 'vertical' division of conscious from unconscious systems. Following the definitive work of Howard and Rogers (1996), a system will be defined here as a coherent set of functions elaborated by a distinct neuronal machinery. Two examples of such vertical organization will be described in this chapter: saccadic scanpath adaptation in reading, and isomorphically controlled motor activity.

1. Unconscious visual functions I: Scanpath adaptation

An unconscious system within the visual modality that meets the above criteria has been encountered in my laboratory, in experiments on reading under intermittent presentation of text. Introducing the system will require some background on the practical issues theoretical implications of reading from video display terminals.

Video Display Terminals (VDTs), the dominant display devices for almost all computers, are normally refreshed at rates above the flicker fusion rate, so that the displays appear continuous. Yet reading from VDTs is about 30% slower than from hard copy (Muter, Latremouille, Treurniet, & Beam, 1982). Also, proofreading is 20–30% slower on VDTs (Gould & Grischkowsky, 1984). Extended use of VDTs has been associated with discomforts ranging from eye strain and headaches to musculoskeletal discomfort (Rossignol, Morse, Summers, & Pagnotto, 1987). Kennedy and Murray (1991) found with a lexical decision task that flicker resulted in saccadic irregularities. In addition, some VDT operators may be susceptible to such visual symptoms as accommodative error (Schleifer, Sauter, Smith, & Knutson, 1990; Jaschinski-Kruza, 1991) and horizontal heterophoria (Dain, McCarty, & Chan-ling, 1988).

Comfort and performance limitations have been ascribed to a myriad of physical characteristics of VDTs such as image quality, resolution, display stability, color, display polarity, luminance, and contrast (Nishiyama, 1990). While inadequacies in these properties may contribute to visual discomfort and slower reading speed, the refresh rate of the display has not been addressed as a potential problem for VDT users. Evidence for distortion of visual spatial processing by the temporal discontinuity of displays comes from studies of eye movements and of the detectability of target displacements during saccades. Even the pulsations of fluorescent lights, with their very long duty cycle, affect eye movement patterns (Wilkins, 1986).

Commonly used raster refresh rates of 60–75 Hz generally have been assumed not to affect vision, since the rates are well above flicker-fusion thresholds where the display appears to be continuous. In continuous illumination, the relative direction of eye and target motion does not affect displacement thresholds. Yet refresh rates between 30 and 260 Hz interfere with space constancy across saccadic eye movements (the perception that the world remains in the same place following a saccade). At lower refresh rates the visual system misjudges the extent of target displacements that take place during saccades, in the direction of a breakdown in space constancy (Macknik, Fisher, & Bridgeman, 1991). Specifically, a rapidly refreshed target tends to be seen as jumping in the direction opposite the saccade even when it is objectively standing still. The target must be moved slightly in the same direction as the eye and simultaneously with the saccade to be perceived as stable under these conditions.

Some of the observed deficits in reading rates on VDTs may be due to these continual small adjustments in space constancy that are necessary for uninterrupted perception. Wilkins (1993) has also described this mechanism. Kennedy and Murray (1993) found deficits in eye movement control that became more severe at a 100 Hz refresh rate than at a 50 Hz rate; while the dependency on refresh rate seems anomalous compared to the other studies reviewed here, the studies are not strictly comparable because Kennedy and Murray measured eye movements rather than reading speed.

On VDT screens the perception of displacement during saccades continues to be distorted up to refresh rates of 980 Hz (Bridgeman, 1995), indicating that screen refresh interacts with visual processing even at very high rates. Further, the distortion (in the direction of a breakdown in space constancy) is similar from 980 Hz to 60 Hz, increasing further only at refresh rates below 60 Hz. The latter result suggests that the presence of on- and off-transients interferes with visual processing, with an additional effect of slow refresh rates.

1.1 *Screen refresh and reading rate*

Another parameter that might interfere with VDT reading is based on a simpler hypothesis. Following a period of saccadic suppression (Bridgeman & Fisher, 1990; Bridgeman & Stark, 1979), when sensitivity to visual stimuli is greatly reduced, the visual system is ready for a new sample of textual information at the start of each fixational pause.

Very little semantic information is available from material not yet fixated, so that the visual system must begin processing nearly from scratch for each successive fixation position (McConkie, Zola, Blanchard, & Wolverton, 1982). Text in advance of the fixation point informs the reader about word length and shape, guiding the next fixational saccade, but it provides little semantic information. Rayner and Pollatsek (1989, p. 140) conclude that "While readers can identify words that they do not fixate, the more usual circumstance is that no word beyond the fixated word is fully identified." In the end, of course, readers would not fixate a new sample of text if they already had high-quality information about what was there.

Normally, readers nearly always fixate each word in a text (except for very short words), even if they pick up partial information about letters not yet fixated. In a raster-scanned field, however, the reader must wait until a usable image is displayed on the screen before reading can continue. At lower refresh rates there is more time on average when there is nothing on the screen for the eye to fixate after a saccade (see Figure 1). These longer dead times might account for some of the time lost in reading at lower refresh rates.

The flying spot of a raster scan spends most of its time illuminating pixels (except for the short durations of the horizontal refresh pulses and the vertical refresh pulse), but any single pixel is illuminated only once in each scan, for less than a microsecond. The exact duration depends on refresh rate and the size of the screen in pixels, and on the decay rate of the phosphor. A word will be refreshed during a few horizontal sweeps of the raster, normally requiring a few 10s of microseconds. Thus the duty cycle for any single word or fixation region is very brief compared to the refresh rate.

Reading stimulus conditions

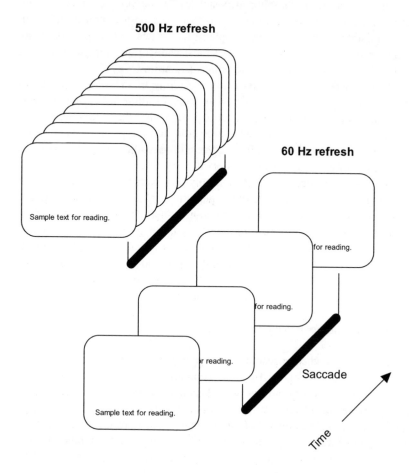

Figure 1. *Stimulus sampling in a reading experiment. At a refresh rate of 500 Hz (top left), the eye will meet a new sample of text in 2 msec or less after the end of a saccade. At 60 Hz (bottom right), the eye will have to wait up to 16 msec for a new sample. Timing of the saccade is uncorrelated with the synchronization of the display. At 500 Hz the sampling delay of 2 msec is negligible compared to a small reading saccade, with a minimum duration of about 20 msec. At 60 Hz the saccade is likely to end between stimulus samples, and the visual system must wait for a screen refresh before reading can proceed.*

At a 60 Hz refresh rate, there are 16.67 ms of dead time after every screen write (neglecting a short phosphor persistence). Since refresh times are un-correlated with eye movements, after the average saccade the subject must wait for half of this interval before a new sample of text appears at the fixation point. Following a saccade, therefore, the subject must wait for an average of 8.33 ms for usable information to appear at the point of fixation.

At 500 Hz there are 2 ms of dead time, resulting in an average of wait of 1 ms before a stimulus appears at a new fixation location, a negligible delay. Subjects cannot make use of the 8.33 ms wait time that the stimulus requires. Because saccadic suppression prevents perception during the saccades, subjects cannot begin pattern processing until the curtain of saccadic suppression is lifted at the beginning of each new fixation interval.

An ideal-observer theory predicts that only this average 8-ms wait time will delay reading on VDTs, with no other penalties. When the image appears, reading continues on in the normal way without further abnormalities in process-ing speed or quality. As the refresh rate is slowed, the system must wait longer and longer, on average, for text to appear, the average wait time always remain-ing half of the maximum wait. Thus reading speed should follow a hyperbolic function. At 60 Hz, the 8 ms delay will occur 4 times per sec (with a 250 ms fixation time), for a predicted total delay of about 3%.

1.2 *Comparing reading at two refresh rates*

We have investigated whether reading is adversely affected by the relatively low refresh rates of standard VDTs. Here we compare reading speeds and saccade patterns at two different refresh rates while keeping the appearance of the display constant. Because the ideal-observer sampling theory outlined above predicts only small changes in reading speed due to changes in refresh rate, we devoted all of our experimental resources to a contrast between two refresh rates. We use 60 Hz refresh for our low frequency because it is the standard used in many computer monitors, and 500 Hz for our upper boundary because it provides nearly constant presentation while allowing us to display an image that is identical to the low-frequency image in brightness, contrast, and appearance.

We did not use refresh rates below 60 Hz because flicker begins to become visible at lower rates, and visible flicker would mean that the subjects would no longer be blind to the refresh conditions of the experiment. Visible flicker might also introduce attentional distractions that are not present with refresh rates above the flicker fusion frequency. We invested all of our experimental effort on the 60 Hz and 500 Hz points to improve the reliability of data, for reading performance is always highly variable. This maximizes the probability of finding a statistically reliable difference between reading at faster and slower refresh rates.

At the high refresh rate the text was presented 8.33 times more frequently on the screen than it was at the low refresh rate. To compensate for the more frequent brightening of the phosphor, the text in the two conditions was brightness-compensated so that the time-averaged intensity of the text in both conditions was the same. Text appeared identical to the subjects under the two conditions, without visible flicker in either case.

The phosphor in the vector display was a green P31 with a medium short persistence, decaying exponentially to 1% of peak brightness in 0.02–2 ms (Keller, 1983). Under some conditions phosphor persistence can be visible with this phosphor (DiLollo, Bischof, Walther-Müller, Groner, & Groner, 1994), but the problem is lessened at low phosphor luminance (Bridgeman & Mayer, 1983). In the current experiments the phosphor is repeatedly reexcited, so that the visual system has no opportunity to adapt to very low-contrast image persistence. The width of the characters averaged 0.37° of visual angle. The text buffer software generated a proportional sans-serif font with constant line widths.

An eye movement monitor directly in front of the eye used an array of photocells to detect the image of the eye in two dimensions under infrared illumination. The head was restrained to allow accurate eye movement recording. The eye monitor recorded from the right eye, with binocular viewing of the text. Subjects were seated in front of the vector display on a height-adjustable chair. Each subject was at the same eye height relative to the screen; chair and chinrest were adjusted to make this height comfortable. In front of the subject was a one-key response box.

Reading material was from the first chapter of an introduction to physiological psychology (Bridgeman, 1988), standardized to a Kincaid readability grade of 13.2. The Kincaid scale is roughly equivalent to a grade level, so that our subjects were reading at or slightly below their grade level.

Subjects were told that they were in an experiment on reading and that all they had to do was read at a normal pace while maintaining adequate comprehension of the material. They pressed the key on the response box when they were finished reading a line of text, and it was immediately replaced by another line. They were given 50 lines of practice to asymptote their performance on the line-advancing procedure. Pilot experiments had shown that automatizing was poor if several lines of text were displayed at once, presumably because subjects had to decide at the end of each line whether to perform a return saccade only or to advance the text; our apparatus limits the high-speed display buffer to about 3 lines of text.

Following the practice lines and a one minute break, subjects were given four trial sets, each of 140 lines, with each successive set alternating between 60 Hz and 500 Hz display formats. These conditions were counterbalanced for order between subjects. Subjects were given 2 minute breaks between trial sets, and the eye monitor was re-calibrated before the each trial set began. The dependent measures were the reading rate (words/minute) and the eye movements for each line of text. Because a subject could read a given text only once, the design could not be balanced within subjects. The design was balanced between subjects, and combined data for all subjects are given here.

Eye movements were broken down into several groups. Scanning (or large forward) saccades were defined as any eye movements in the rightward direction larger than the size of the longest word in the text (4.8°). Look backs (or large reverse saccades) were movements of the same size range in the leftward direction. Normal reading (or small forward) saccades were defined as movements in the rightward direction that were 4.8° or less. Corrective (or small reverse) saccades were saccades in the leftward direction of 4.8° or less.

We recorded over 105,000 saccades from 20 subjects. The subjects averaged about 45 minutes to read the entire text sample. Data were divided into first and second halves of the experiment (i.e. first and second trial sets, and third and fourth trial sets) and analyzed independently. All of the distinctions in the results described below are statistically significant ($p < 0.05$); details, as well as another reading experiment not related to issues of conscious vs. unconscious processing, are given in Montegut and Bridgeman (1997).

In the first two trial sets there was a reliable difference in reading rate between the refresh frequency conditions, from 262 words/min at 60 Hz to 270 words/min at 500 Hz. Thus reading at 60 Hz is 3.05% slower than at 500 Hz, agreeing nicely with our prediction of a slowing of about 3% from the ideal-observer theory. The pattern of saccadic eye movements was typical of normal reading, with the most frequent saccade magnitudes about the length of a typical word of text. Perceptual span (the average number of words read per fixation) was 1.13, very close to the 1.11 words/fixation that Taylor (1965) found for college students. The result can be used to make quantitative predictions from a model based on the ideal-observer theory.

A Model: With 500 Hz reading rate data, and a hypothesis about the subjects' need to sample a new stimulus at the start of each fixation, we can construct an ideal-observer model of reading under intermittent illumination. The model can predict quantitatively the reading speed at any raster refresh rate, with the 'ideal' assumption that refresh rate causes no disturbance in subject performance beyond that caused by display delays. We begin by defining the relevant variables and their empirically derived values, where f is refresh frequency in samples/sec and S is reading speed in words/min.

Empirically derived values:

W = words/fixation = 1.13
P = processing time = 250 ms (at 500 Hz), including the saccade time.

The model makes the following assumptions:

D = delay/fixation = 1/2 (1000/f) = 500/f
T = time/fixation = P + D

Combining these parameters into the definition of reading speed,

$$S = \frac{W}{T}$$ (1)

we obtain

$$S = \frac{W}{P+D}$$ (2).

Substituting our empirically derived values and converting to minutes,

$$S = \frac{1.13}{250 + \dfrac{500}{f}} \times 60,000 \text{ ms/ min.}$$ (3).

This function is plotted in Figure 2. Values are calculated every 20 Hz, and intermediate values are interpolated. The curve in Figure 2 was plotted by combining the stimulus sampling model with empirical data that we obtained at the 500 Hz refresh rate. Processing time P includes the fixation interval and about 30 ms of saccade duration.

Equation (3) can be further characterized by evaluating S after substituting important values for f. The function has some intuitively appealing characteristics: its y-axis asymptote occurs at a maximum reading level defined by infinite refresh rate, i. e. continuous illumination. When f is infinite the term 500/f drops out, resulting in a predicted asymptote of 271.1 words/min under continuous illumination. The minimum of the function occurs when f = 0. Then the 500/f term becomes infinite, S = 0, and reading ceases. The Figure shows that reading at 500 Hz is very close to asymptotic levels, only 1.2 words/min below the predicted optimum.

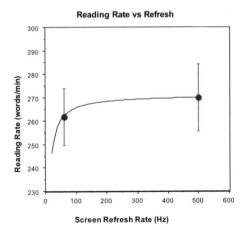

Figure 2. *Predictions of an ideal-observer model for reading speed. The curve is based on the theory described above and the empirically derived reading rate described below. The 60 Hz data point is confirmatory, and was not used in plotting the curve. Error bars on each data point are between-subjects standard deviations.*

The ideal-observer theory predicts that reading rates will drop precipitously at low refresh frequencies, but that there will be little change at rates above about 200 Hz. Our results have led us to recommend a minimum refresh rate of 120 Hz in computer displays (Bridgeman & Montegut, 1993), fast enough to capture most of the reading rate advantage of rapid refresh while remaining within the capability of commercially available raster-scan technology. Of course our data do not prove the validity of the model, but the high precision of quantitative agreement between data and theory is an encouraging sign that we are on the right track.

In addition to the overall differences in reading speed between the two refresh rates, there were differences in saccade frequency and type. The small standard reading saccades were by far the most common events throughout the study, with large look-backs comprising the smallest number of eye events. Subjects made about the same number of small reverse saccades regardless of display frequency. The small reverse saccade frequencies are measures of the refixations of McConkie, Kerr, Reddix, Zola and Jacobs (1989), and are probably due to non-central fixation within a word. The number of saccades per line was almost exactly equal in the two conditions: 9.985 saccades/line at 60 Hz, and 9.970 saccades/line at 500 Hz. There were 3% fewer saccades/sec in the 60 Hz condition, reflecting the difference in reading speed.

1.3 *Adaptation in reading rate*

In the 60 Hz condition, reading rate increased significantly from the first half to the second half of the reading session, from 262 to 276 words/min. But reading rate did not change significantly in the 500 Hz condition. At the end of the sessions, reading rate was the same for the two refresh conditions. If reading rate is limited by the refresh rate of the text, an increase in reading rate in the 60 Hz condition up to the 500 Hz reading rate would seem impossible. Results reviewed below show that subjects accomplished this speedup by adaptively altering the frequencies of the four types of saccades (Figure 3).

Large Forward Saccades: More large forward saccades were made at 500 Hz than at 60 Hz in the first half of the experiment, but this difference disappeared in the second half of the reading period. The number of large forward saccades increased in both conditions, but the frequency of these saccades increased more in the 60 Hz condition.

Small Forward Saccades: Of all the classes of eye movement, these seem the most stable. There was always a difference between 500 Hz and 60 Hz, and this difference remained consistent across the two halves of the study. In addition, in both conditions there was a significant and similar decrease in frequency of small forward saccades from the first to the second half of the study.

Small Reverse Saccades: In the first half of the experiment subjects made the same number of small reverse saccades at both refresh frequencies, but this number increased in the 500 Hz condition and decreased in the 60 Hz condition from the first to second half of the experiment. This resulted in significantly fewer small reverse saccades at 60 Hz in the second half of the experiment.

Large Reverse Saccades: There were more of these saccades with text refreshed at 500 Hz than at 60 Hz in the first half of the experiment, but this difference decreased in the second half. This is coupled with a decrease in the number of large reverse saccades made in the 500 Hz condition from the first to second half of the experiment. There were so few of these saccades, however, that differences in their frequencies had little effect on the overall results.

After the data collection, none of the subjects expressed any knowledge of the purpose of the experiment or the conditions. In fact, none of them had any idea that the refresh rate was changing during the experiment. And of course none was aware that reading rate had adapted over the course of the session.

What does it all mean?

The maximum wait for a new stimulus sample at 60 Hz is 16.67 ms (neglecting phosphor persistence), so that the average wait is 8.33 ms. This will occur 4 times

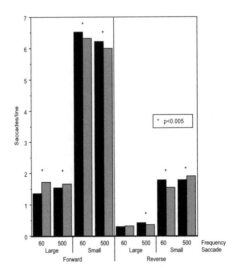

Figure 3. *Changes in saccade frequencies with adaptation. Black bars: trial sets 1 and 2. Gray bars: trial sets 3 and 4. Forward saccades (left to right on the screen) are on the left, and reverse saccades (right to left) are on the right of the figure. The most important changes with adaptation are an increase in large forward saccades at 60 Hz and a decrease in small reverse saccades at 60 Hz, compared to the 500 Hz condition, both of which make faster reading possible. Subjects remain unaware of the adaptation, or indeed of any other properties of their saccadic scanpaths.*

per second, the frequency of saccadic eye movements during reading. So the expected delay is $8.33 \times 4 = 33.33$ ms for each 1000 ms, or a slowdown of 3%. This agrees well with the 3.05% slowdown that we obtained empirically at 60 Hz, confirming the predictions of the ideal-observer model and suggesting that the delay of text samples is the only factor that differentiates the 500 Hz and the 60 Hz reading behavior. Other screen characteristics, such as blur and contrast, may decrease reading speed further, but these remained the same at both refresh rates.

The intermittent samples displayed on a VDT can be interpreted as brief displays interrupted by blank masks. Morrison (1984) found differences in fixation behavior in reading that depended on the duration of post-saccadic masks varying from 25 to 300 ms; we show more subtle differences at even shorter durations, up to 16 ms.

Differences in the way subjects read depending on the refresh rate were evident at the start of the session by the small but consistent differences in the types of saccades they made in the two conditions. This could be an indication of an active and immediate response of the visual system to different levels of information quality.

The goal that drives these differences could be efficient information uptake. The visual system, sensing a good deal of dead time in the 60 Hz condition (due to the 8.33 ms average wait after a saccade), might attempt to compensate by bringing in more information with each fixation. Since the mean fixation duration does not change, this means that the perceptual span of reading (Rayner & Pollatsek, 1989) increases. This would explain both the increased number of large forward saccades at 60 Hz relative to 500 Hz, and the decrease in small reverse saccades. It also accounts for the higher frequency of small forward saccades in the 60 Hz condition: subjects concentrate more on normal reading saccades. The higher frequency of these normal reading saccades in the slow-refresh condition is maintained throughout the experimental sessions.

Slow refresh also leads to fewer large saccades at the start of the sessions, possibly because the degraded image cannot at first support many larger saccades. The eye movement evidence suggests then that subjects work harder, but the reading rate data show that they read more slowly, unable at first to overcome the disadvantage of a slow refresh rate. Though statistically significant in our large sample, the small difference in saccade frequencies across refresh rates at the start of the sessions appears to have had little effect on reading speed.

1.4 *Unconscious oculomotor adaptation*

At the beginning of the reading period, subjects read faster at 500 Hz than at 60 Hz refresh, as the stimulus sampling theory predicts. By the end of the experiment, however, subjects had accelerated their 60 Hz reading until it was as fast as reading with text refreshed at 500 Hz. The stimulus sampling theory alone, unaided by consideration of other influences on reading rate, predicts that such an equalization of reading rates is impossible.

Adaptive changes in saccade patterns account for the apparent discrepancy. Such changes were found upon comparing the two halves of the experiment. A reason for the disappearance of difference in reading rates might be that subjects adapted to the lower frequency. Specifically, analyzing the saccade data, they seemed to be adjusting the microstructure of their saccadic scanpaths. Clearly there are small differences from the start in the way subjects read depending on the refresh rate, as evidenced by the differences overall in the types of saccades they made in the two conditions. This could be an indication of an active and immediate response of the visual system to different levels of information quality. The immediate differences are small, however, compared to the adaptive changes that occurred during the course of the experiment. Efficient information uptake could be the goal that drives these differences and changes.

The exception to this rule is the large reverse saccades, interruptions of normal reading. These saccades decrease with practice in the 500 Hz condition, but do not change in to 60 Hz condition. The frequency of the interruptions remains greater at the faster refresh rate throughout the experiment, however, suggesting that they have reached a minimum in the 60 Hz condition that is approached but not quite matched for the faster refresh rate. These movements are so infrequent, however, that their effect on overall reading speed is negligible.

How does the reader determine that reading, or information intake, is not optimal, as we all read at different speeds depending on the difficulty of the material? Also, if this is an adaptive mechanism, does it work like other adaptive mechanisms — for instance, is there some sort of negative aftereffect? The unconscious adaptation of saccade patterns might appear more quickly with increases in experience of VDT users, as Welch, Bridgeman, Anand and Browman (1993) found with practice in prism adaptation. Answers to these questions will enhance our understanding of the possible range of unconscious processing.

Raster refresh rate clearly cannot account for the entire 20–30% reduction in reading rate with reading from VDTs described in the literature. But the differences in pattern of saccadic eye movements we observe at low refresh frequency are in the direction of increased processing effort, perhaps explaining some of the fatigue effects that others have observed in reading from VDTs. In addition, these differences indicate that visual sampling processes operating on a millisecond time scale have predictable effects on behavior over extended periods.

Why does the subtle and complex information processing required for reading adaptation take place without conscious awareness? The fact that the adaptation found here remains unconscious may help to define what processes can be accomplished without consciousness, and by implication help to define the functions of consciousness itself. Adaptation to a slower stimulus refresh rate requires complex information processing, including an analysis of sensory delays, adjustment of saccadic eye movement generation patterns, and increasing the perceptual span in reading. None of these activities required adjustments in the readers' task or the goals, however. The implication is that interaction of sensory processing with goals, plans and episodic memories might require consciousness, but that sensory processing itself, no matter how elaborate, does not.

2.   Unconscious visual functions II: A motor visual system

This section reviews psychophysical evidence for the second example of a vertically organized unconscious system, revealing at least two neurological maps of the visual world, one conscious and the other unconscious. They have been labeled "cognitive" and "sensorimotor" respectively (Paillard, 1987; 1991). Under some conditions, the two maps can simultaneously hold different spatial values. The section also reviews some of the ways in which the representations communicate with one another.

Indications that cognitive and sensorimotor systems are separable in normal humans came originally from studies of eye movements. On one hand, subjects are unaware of sizable displacements of the visual world that occur during saccadic eye movements, implying that information about spatial location is degraded during saccades (Bridgeman, Hendry, & Stark, 1975; Brune & Lücking, 1969; Ditchburn, 1955; Mack, 1970; Wallach & Lewis, 1965). On the other hand, people do not become disoriented after saccades, implying that spatial information is preserved transsaccadically.

Some experimental evidence supports this conclusion, though many points remain controversial. For instance, an early report that the eyes can saccade accurately to a target that is flashed (and mislocalized) during an earlier saccade (Hallett & Lightstone, 1976) has been criticized because there were only a few target positions that subjects might have memorized. Others have failed to replicate the result (Dassonville, Schlag, & Schlag-Rey, 1992; Honda, 1990). Still others have found accurate pointing to targets flashed during saccades, however (Hansen & Skavenski, 1979), and hand-eye coordination remains fairly accurate following saccades (Festinger & Cannon, 1965; Honda, 1985). It would seem that under at least some conditions, accurate behavior is possible. How can loss of perceptual information and maintenance of visually guided behavior exist side by side? One possible answer is that information is lost to the cognitive system, but is preserved in an independent sensorimotor map that controls visually guided behavior.

Cognitive and sensorimotor functions have been dissociated by feeding the two systems opposite signals at the same time. The experiment involved stroboscopic induced motion; a small saccade target jumped in the same direction as a large inducing background frame, but the target did not jump far enough to cancel the induced motion (Wong & Mack, 1981). Although the target still appeared to jump in the direction opposite the frame, it actually jumped in the same direction. Saccadic eye movements followed the veridical direction even though subjects perceived stroboscopic target motion in the opposite direction. If a delay in responding was required, however, eye movements followed the perceptual illusion, implying that the motor system has a short-lived memory and must rely on information from the cognitive system if response is delayed.

These experiments involved stimulus motion or displacement, and reveal the complexity of the dynamics of several control systems and their real-time interactions. The dissociations between cognitive and motor responses might be related in some way to motion systems rather than to representation of visual space per se, however: subjects might simply confound motion and position, and the tests for cognitive and sensorimotor information make different demands on motion and position codes respectively.

A new method can test dissociations of cognitive and motor function without motion or displacement of the eye or the stimuli at any time during a trial. The dissociation is based on the Roelofs effect (Roelofs, 1935), a tendency to misperceive the position of the edge of a large pattern presented in an unstructured field. The pattern was presented so that one of its edges was in the subject's objective centerline. According to Roelofs, this edge of the pattern is perceived to be deviated to the side opposite the remainder of the pattern. A pattern with its right edge in the center, for instance, is perceived to have its right edge somewhat to the right of the center. The pattern as a whole tends to be mislocalized in the direction opposite its spatial bias, as though vision were calibrated on the object rather than on the objective straight ahead.

The principle of the Roelofs effect is elaborated here to measure the misperception of target position in the presence of a surrounding frame presented asymmetrically; this "induced Roelofs effect" will be called a Roelofs effect below. Locations of targets within the frame tend to be misperceived in the direction opposite the lateral offset of the frame.

2.1 *Differentiating conscious and unconscious pathways*

To investigate the contrast between cognitive and motor codes using the Roelofs method, subjects sat with stabilized heads before a hemicylindrical vertical screen that provided a homogeneous field of view. A rectangular frame $21°$ wide $\times 8.5°$ high $\times 1°$ in line width was projected, via a galvanic mirror, either centered on the subject's midline, $5°$ left, or $5°$ right of center. Inside the frame, an "x" could be projected via a second galvanic mirror in one of 5 positions, $2°$ apart, with the middle "x" on the subject's midline. Motor responses were recorded using an unseen pointer with its axis attached to a potentiometer mounted near the center of curvature of the screen and its tip near the screen. Subjects held the pointer with the forefinger on its tip, so that their arms were outstretched and most of the rotation came from the shoulder. Pointing data were recorded on a continuous scale.

Cognitive responses, or perceived target positions, were recorded from a keyboard placed in front of the subject as a 5-alternative forced choice. In both conditions, subjects were instructed to wait until the offset of the stimulus before responding.

One of the 5 targets and one of the 3 frames was presented with simultaneous onset on each trial, exposed for 1 sec, and simultaneously extinguished. Subjects were instructed to fixate the target, in accord with their spontaneous tendency. At stimulus offset, subjects heard a "beep" tone to indicate a judging trial or a longer "squawk" tone to indicate a pointing trial. Because they could not respond until offset of the stimuli, they were looking into a blank field at the time of their responses. Thus the task was a response to an internally stored representation of the stimulus, not a perceptual task.

With the cognitive measure, there was a significant effect of frame position in judging trials (statistics are given in Bridgeman, Peery, & Anand, 1997, who also describe several other experiments with the Roelofs effect). Thus, all subjects showed the Roelofs effect, a tendency to judge the target to be further to the left than its actual position when the frame was on the right, and vice versa. The mean magnitude of the Roelofs effect was a difference of 2.0° between judgments with the frame on the left and judgments with the frame on the right. This is a reliable effect, present in all subjects under all conditions.

The effect of frame position in pointing trials yielded a sharp division of the subjects into two groups: 5 subjects showed a highly significant Roelofs effect, while the other 5 showed no sign of an effect. The bimodal distribution shows that two qualitatively different results were obtained; the distribution of significances between subjects is not due to a small, normally distributed effect being significant in some subjects and not in others. That is, each subject showed either a large, robust effect or no sign of a frame influence.

Thus, responses on pointing trials were qualitatively different from responses on judging trials for half of the subjects; these subjects showed a Roelofs effect only for judging. The differences in performance among subjects were unrelated to their degree of psychophysical experience or knowledge of the experiment.

Why did only half of the subjects show a Roelofs effect in the motor measure? One possibility is that the sensorimotor system does not possess a memory for position that lasts long enough to control responses to targets no longer present. Some of the subjects may still have been able to use the motor representation of space to organize their responses, and therefore showed no Roelofs effect. Others might have already shifted to a mode where no spatial information was available in the motor map; to guide the response they would have to import information from the memory in the cognitive system, and the illusion would be imported along with the spatial information.

This theory predicts that all subjects should show a Roelofs effect in pointing if the motor response is delayed long enough. Therefore nine of the ten subjects were run with a delay between the stimulus and the auditory tone indicating the response mode. The delay forced the subjects to delay their responses. Procedures were the same as the No Delay condition except that a 4-sec delay was interposed between stimulus offset and the tone that indicated the type of response that the subject was to make (judging or pointing).

The major difference between the results in this condition and the no-delay condition was that 7 of the 9 subjects showed a significant Roelofs effect for the pointing task. Another subject showed a Roelofs effect when the delay was increased to 8 sec. These results confirmed the hypothesis that even those subjects who showed no Roelofs effects in the sensorimotor system with immediate response would show the effect when a long enough delay was interposed between stimulus offset and response. If the sensorimotor system has a memory, then, it can last for only a few seconds. This result implies that the bimodal distribution of Roelofs effects in pointing without delay had been due to the subjects using two different sources of information for pointing. One group had used a motor mode that was not sensitive to visual context, a 'privileged loop' between vision and motor activity. The other group imported spatial information from the cognitive system into the sensorimotor representation for use in pointing. One need not assume that the two groups of subjects followed different psychological laws, only that they switched from motor to cognitive modes at differing delays after stimulus offset.

Our results reinforce the conclusion that the normal human possesses two maps of visual space. One of them holds information used in perception: if a subject is asked what he or she sees, the information in this 'cognitive' map is accessed. This map can achieve great sensitivity to small motions or translations of objects in the visual world by using relative motion or position as a cue. The price that the cognitive system pays for gaining this sensitivity is that it loses absolute egocentric calibration of visual space. A useful model for this process is the process of differentiation in calculus. In calculating motion dx/dt by differentiation, the constant term (representing the egocentric spatial calibration) drops out of the equation.

The other visual map drives visually guided behavior, but its contents are not necessarily available to perception. This map does not have the resolution and sensitivity to fine-grained spatial relationships that the cognitive map has, but it is not required to: a small error in pointing, grasping or looking is of little consequence. The advantage of this map is its robustness; the "motor" map is not

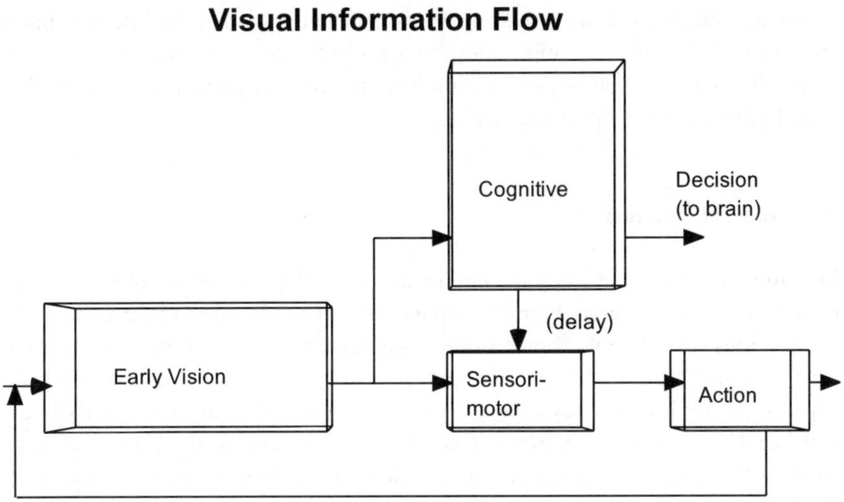

Visual Information Flow

Figure 4. *Information flow in two visual systems, formatted according to American engineering conventions. Revised from Bridgeman, Peery & Anand (1997).*

subject to illusions such as induced motion and the Roelofs effect. It also has only a short memory, being concerned mainly with the here-and-now correspondence between visual information and motor behavior. If a subject must make motor responses to stimuli no longer present, this system must take its spatial information from the cognitive representation, and brings any cognitively based illusions along with it. This is not to say that the sequence cannot be stored in memory and used to improve motor performance in the future; the current egocentric spatial values are lost, however. The relationships of information flow in the two systems are schematized in Figure 4.

Experiments using normal subjects do not form the only basis for the two visual systems distinction; others use clinical data from blindsight, where some visually guided motor capability remains despite lack of perception (Weiskrantz, Warrington, Sanders, & Marshall, 1974; Bridgeman & Staggs, 1982), or from other lesions (Goodale, Pelisson, & Prablanc, 1986; Goodale, Meenan, Bulthoff, Nicolle, Murphy, & Racicot, 1994). Goodale's group has differentiated one group of neurological patients who can recognize patterns, but cannot interact with them motorically, and another group that can handle objects appropriately but cannot recognize them cognitively.

We can conclude that the evidence for two distinct functional representations of visual space in humans is strong, but the interaction between the systems is not as simple as it once had seemed. The two systems do interact, but it appears that the flow of information can go only one way, from cognitive to motor. Influences in the other direction have not been observed, even when they would have improved performance.

3. General conclusions

The implications of the Roelofs experiments and other spatial orientation studies reviewed above are similar to the implications of the reading experiments. The unconscious level is not a horizontally organized 'early' preprocessor, for it can carry sensory information all the way through to the level of behavior. Its capabilities are limited, however, to isometrically coded actions where there is a consistent 1:1 mapping between position of a stimulus and position of a response. The cognitive spatial analyzer is also partly unconscious, for all of the resolution of retinally received information into a model of space in terms of objects and surfaces is already achieved before the conscious level is reached (Gibson, 1966). A conscious component becomes necessary at the level where a choice between several alternatives becomes involved, a choice based on goals and plans. At this point the decision is based on visual context, instructions, and motivation as well as the targeted stimulus array itself.

Both the spatial experiments and the reading experiments reveal an unconscious level of sensory processing that can perform very sophisticated tasks of information management, including some kinds of adaptation and control of behavior. This is a vertical organization that takes information from the sensory receptors all the way through to behavior without conscious intervention, as long as the behavioral 'rules of engagement' are not changed. The unconscious level cannot, however, interact with the level of planning of behavior; it works only within a context where the planned behavior is already specified. It can adjust parameters, but cannot reorganize them. The stratification of consciousness is context-dependent, a conscious record of activity not being left unless an interaction with episodic memory is necessary.

The conscious system is what remains after the unconscious component is accounted for. A practical definition is that it contains the information that is communicated, or can potentially be communicated to another. It constitutes only a small fraction of the brain's mental life, the part that puts things together, escaping the tyranny of the here-and-now by interacting with episodic memories and making plans. The unconscious can handle the present, but conscious mechanisms are necessary to fully exploit the past and the future.

Acknowledgments

The reading experiments were performed in collaboration with Dr. M. Montegut and J. Sykes. Supported by AFOSR grant #90-0095.

References

Bridgeman, B. (1988). *The biology of behavior and mind.* New York: Wiley.

Bridgeman, B. (1995). Direction constancy in rapidly refreshed video displays. *Journal of Vestibular Research, 5,* 393–398.

Bridgeman, B. & Fisher, B. (1990). Saccadic suppression of displacement is strongest in central vision. *Perception, 19,* 103–111

Bridgeman, B., Hendry, D., & Stark, L. (1975). Failure to detect displacement of the visual world during saccadic eye movements. *Vision Research, 15,* 719–722.

Bridgeman, B. & Mayer, M. (1983). Failure to integrate visual information from successive fixations. *Bulletin of the Psychonomic Society, 21,* 285–286.

Bridgeman, B. Peery, S., & Anand, S. (1997). Interaction of cognitive and sensorimotor maps of visual space. *Perception and Psychophysics, 59,* 456–469.

Bridgeman, B. & Montegut, M. (1993). Faster flicker rate increases reading speed on CRTs. *SPIE Proceedings, 1913,* 134–145.

Bridgeman, B. & Staggs, D. (1982). Plasticity in human blindsight. *Vision Research, 22,* 1199–1203.

Bridgeman, B. & Stark, L. (1979). Omnidirectional increase in threshold for image shifts during saccadic eye movements. *Perception and Psychophysics, 25,* 241–243.

Brune, F. & Lücking, C. (1969). Oculomotorik, Bewegungswahrnehmung und Raumkonstanz der Sehdinge. *Der Nervenarzt, 40,* 692–700.

Dain, S. J., McCarthy, A. K., & Chan-ling, T. (1988). Symptoms in VDU Operators. *American Journal of Optometry and Physiological Optics, 65,* 162–167.

Dassonville, P., Schlag, J., & Schlag-Rey, M. (1992). Oculomotor localization relies on a damped representation of saccadic eye displacement in human and nonhuman primates. *Visual Neuroscience, 9,* 261–269.

Ditchburn, R. (1955). Eye-movements in relation to retinal action. *Optica Acta, 1,* 171–176.

DiLollo, V., Bischof, W., Walther-Müller, P., Groner, M., & Groner, R. (1994). Phosphor persistence in oscilloscopic displays: its luminance and visibility. *Vision Research, 34,* 1619–1620.

Festinger, L. & Canon, L. K. (1965). Information about spatial location based on knowledge about efference. *Psychological Review, 72,* 373–384.

Gibson, J. J. (1966). *The senses considered as perceptual systems.* Boston: Houghton-Mifflin.

Goodale M. A., Meenan, J. P., Bulthoff, H. H., Nicolle, D. A., Murphy, K. J., & Racicot, C. I. (1994). Separate neural pathways for the visual analysis of object shape in perception and prehension. *Current Biology, 4,* 604–610.

Goodale, M. A., Pelisson, D., & Prablanc, C. (1986). Large adjustments in visually guided reaching do not depend on vision of the hand or perception of target displacement. *Nature, 320,* 748–750.

Gould, J. D. & Grischkowsky, N. (1984). Doing the Same Work with Hard Copy and with Cathode-Ray Tube CRT Computer Terminals. *Human Factors, 26,* 323–337.

Hallett, P. E. & Lightstone, A. D. (1976). Saccadic eye movements towards stimuli triggered during prior saccades. *Vision Research, 16,* 99–106.

Hansen, R. & Skavenski, A. (1977). Accuracy of eye-position information for motor control. *Vision Research, 17,* 919–926.

Honda, H. (1985). Spatial localization in saccade and pursuit-eye-movement conditions: A comparison of perceptual and motor measures. *Perception and Psychophysics, 38,* 41–46.

Honda, H. (1990). The extraretinal signal from the pursuit-eye-movement system: Its role in the perceptual and the egocentric localization systems. *Perception and Psychophysics, 48,* 509–515.

Howard, I. & Rogers, B. (1996). *Binocular vision and stereopsis.* New York: Oxford University Press.

Jaschinski-Kruza, W. (1991). Eyestrain in VDU Users: Viewing Distance and the Resting Position of Ocular Muscles. *Human Factors, 33,* 68–83.

Keller, P. (1983). Recent phosphor screen registrations and the worldwide phosphor type designation system. *Proceedings of the Society for Information Display, 24,* 323–328.

Kennedy, A. & Murray, W. S. (1991). The effects of flicker on eye movement control *Quarterly Journal of Experimental Psychology A: Human Experimental Psychology, 43,* 79–99.

Kennedy, A. & Murray, W. S. (1993). Display properties and eye-movement control. In G. D'Ydewalle and J. Van Rensbergen (eds.), *Perception and cognition* (pp. 251–263). Amsterdam: Elsevier Science Publishers.

Macknik, S. L., Fisher, B. D., & Bridgeman, B. (1991). Flicker Distorts Visual Space Constancy. *Vision Research, 31,* 2057–2064.

McConkie, G. W., Kerr, P. W., Reddix, M. D., Zola, D., & Jacobs, A. M. (1989). Eye movement control during reading: II Frequency of refixating a word. *Perception and Psychophysics, 46,* 245–253.

McConkie, G. W., Zola, D., Blanchard, H. E., & Wolverton, G. S. (1982). Perceiving words during reading: Lack of facilitation from prior peripheral exposure. *Perception and Psychophysics, 32,* 271–281.

Morrison, R. E. (1984). Manipulation of stimulus onset delay in reading: Evidence for parallel programming of saccades. *Journal of Experimental Psychology: Human Perception and Performance, 10,* 667–682.

Muter, P., Latremouille, S. T., & Beam, P. (1982). Extended Reading of Continuous Text on Television Screens. *Human Factors, 24,* 501–508.

Nishiyama, K. (1990). Ergonomic aspects of the health and safety of VDT work in Japan: a review. *Ergonomics, 33,* 659–85.

Paillard, J. (1987). Cognitive versus sensorimotor encoding of spatial information. In P. Ellen and C. Thinus-Blanc (eds.), *Cognitive processes and spatial orientation in animal and man* (Vol. 2, pp. 43–77). Dordrecht, Netherlands: Martinus Nijhoff Publishers.

Paillard, J. (1991). Motor and representational framing of space. In J. Paillard (ed.), *Brain and space* (pp. 163–182). Oxford: Oxford University Press.

Rayner, K. & Pollatsek, A. (1989). *The psychology of reading.* Englewood Cliffs, NJ: Prentice-Hall.

Roelofs, C. (1935). Optische Localisation. *Archiv für Augenheilkunde, 109,* 395–415.

Rossignol, A. M., Morse, E. P., Summers, V. M., & Pagnotto, L. D. (1987). Video display terminal use and reported health symptoms among Massachusetts clerical workers. *Journal of Occupational Medicine, 29,* 112–118.

Schleifer, L. M., Sauter, S. L., Smith, R. J., & Knutson, S. (1990). Ergonomic predictors of visual system complaints in VDT data entry work. *Behaviour Information Technology, 9,* 273–282.

Taylor, S. E. (1965). Eye movements while reading: Facts and fallacies. *American Educational Research Journal, 2,* 187–202.

Wallach, H. & Lewis, C. (1965). The effect of abnormal displacement of the retinal image during eye movements. *Perception and Psychophysics, 1,* 25–29.

Welch, R. B., Bridgeman, B., Anand, S., Browman, K. (1993). Alternating prism exposure causes dual adaptation and generalization to a novel displacement. *Perception and Psychophysics, 54,* 195–204.

Weiskrantz, L., Warrington, E., Sanders, M., & Marshall, J. (1974). Visual capacity in the hemianopic field following restricted occipital ablation. *Brain, 97,* 709–729.

Wilkins, A. J. (1986). Intermittent illumination from fluorescent lighting and visual display units affects movements of the eyes across text. *Human Factors, 28,* 75–81.

Wilkins, A. J. (1993). Reading and visual discomfort. In Willows, Kruk and Corcos (eds.). *Visual processes in reading and reading disabilities* (pp. 435–456). Hillsdale, NJ: Lawrence Erlbaum.

Wong, E. & Mack, A. (1981). Saccadic programming and perceived location. *Acta Psychologica, 48,* 123–131.

CHAPTER 2

Stages of processing
in visual search and attention

James E. Hoffman

Close your eyes, turn your head left or right, and briefly open and close your eyes. If your phenomenological experience is like mine, you may have the following impressions of this brief visual input. You can immediately see surfaces and shapes for all of the objects in your visual field and you seem to know their identities as well. This seems to be confirmed by your ability to arbitrarily pick out any one of the objects in your fading image of the scene and immediately name it, as if its identity had already been determined. Careful experiments, however, suggest that we have detailed information about only a handful of these objects at any one time, those that we happen to be "paying attention to", and that our visual experience of full knowledge of our visual surroundings must, in some sense, be a powerful illusion. The goal of this chapter is to lay out the evidence supporting this conjecture as well as specifying how visual attention provides a mechanism for explaining the origins of this illusion.

1.   Limited processing capacity in vision

It is easy to show that there is a limited capacity process involved somewhere in the processing and reporting of visual information. For example, Helmholtz (1924) illuminated a display of letters using an electric spark, guaranteeing an exposure duration too short to allow for changes in eye fixation. He found that he was able to direct attention to any one of the letters after the display was gone, suggesting the existence of a *covert* spatial attention system as well as a visual memory of the display that can outlast the physical stimulus. These suggestions were confirmed by Sperling (1960), who used a tone occurring after the display to indicate which subset of letters the subject was to report. He estimated that the entire contents of the display were available immediately after its termination and that this information "faded" over the subsequent half-second or so. At long cue delays, subjects were able to report approximately four characters, the same number they were able to report in *whole report* conditions in which they attempted to report as many letters as possible. Averbach and Coriell (1961) reported similar findings using a visual cue to indicate a single character for report. They also reported that performance continued to improve when the partial report cue *preceded* the display, suggesting that subjects can direct attention to a display location prior to the appearance of the display and that the contents of that location can be selectively "read-out" and reported. Eriksen and colleagues (Eriksen & Hoffman, 1972a,b) subsequently estimated that as long as a quarter of a second may be required to process a visual cue and direct attention to the cued location.

The implication is that somewhere in the performance of this task, there are one or more *limited capacity* processing mechanisms and an accompanying *selection* mechanism for dealing with these limitations. It should be noted that use of terms like "limited capacity" can be vacuous when they are merely used as substitutes for the observation that performance gets worse with increases in "processing load" (Allport, 1989; Pashler, 1998). The strategy pursued here will be to unpack this term by being specific about the nature of capacity limits and trying to specify where in the sequence of processing stages such limits have their effects. In the partial report experiments of Sperling and Averbach and Coriell, an obvious distinction can be made between processes involved in *recognizing* objects and those responsible for encoding and rehearsing object identities in *memory* long enough to report them.

Working memory is a potential source of limitations in any task which requires reporting multiple "chunks" of information (such as letter identities). Baddeley (1986) suggested that working memory can be fractionated into several different transient memory systems. The *phonological loop* can hold a limited number (approximately seven) of inner speech representations indefinitely as long as rehearsal is allowed. In addition, there is an active visual memory (the *visuo-spatial sketchpad*) which can hold a small number of "visual chunks" as long as the subject is allowed to pay attention to this information. This latter memory has been estimated to hold about four "objects" (Luck & Vogel, 1997). Either or both of these components of working memory could be responsible for the small number of objects reported in whole report experiments.

1.1 *Visual search*

Visual search is one of several tasks designed to reveal the nature of capacity limits that precede working memory. Memory requirements are reduced to a minimum by requiring subjects to simply indicate whether or not a target is present in a visual display. A consistent finding is that search time and errors increase with increases in the number of display items (*the display size effect*). Many models of visual search have been designed to account for the occurrence of the display size effect and how various factors such as target-distractor similarity affect its magnitide.

The most obvious explanation of display size effects is to assume that some process involved in search has a limited capacity so that objects in the display need to be examined one at a time (serial model) or several items are processed in parallel by a system that becomes less efficient with increasing load. Eriksen and Spencer (1969) provided a test of this account by comparing search performance under two different presentation conditions: a *simultaneous* mode, in which all display objects appeared simultaneously and a *sequential* mode in which the display objects appeared one-at-a-time with a variable interval separating them. They reasoned that if the display size effect was due to either serial or limited-capacity parallel processes, then it should be reduced by sequential presentation, which would allow this limited-capacity to be allocated to one object at a time. Surprisingly, they found a robust display size effect but found no difference in performance between sequential and simultaneous presentation modes.

Eriksen and Spencer (1969) pointed out that the equivalence of simultaneous and sequential presentation modes argues against the claim that limited capacity processes are involved in visual processing of the display items. How then could one account for the display size effect? They pointed out that even an ideal observer model with no capacity limitations whatsoever, would show a decrease in performance with an increase in distractors. Assuming that each object in the display has some probability of being mistaken as a target, increases in display size increase the probability that at least one nontarget object will be mistaken as a target. Therefore, even if *perceptual* processing of the display objects is not capacity-limited, display size effects would be obtained because of false alarms generated at the *decision* level. Models based on these and similar assumptions provided good accounts of display size effects in a variety of paradigms (Eriksen & Spencer, 1969; Kinchla, 1974).

The Eriksen and Spencer results and theoretical contributions are important because they indicate that the contributions of the decision process, as well as the limits of working memory, must be considered in trying to understand the nature of capacity limits in vision. Several investigators have tried to factor out the effects of decision noise to determine if there is any "residual" display size effect that could be attributed to "visual processing stages". For example, Shaw (1984) and Palmer (1994) both found that although the detection of luminance increments was not capacity-limited, certain other kinds of visual judgements were, including various letter search tasks (Shaw, 1984).

1.2 *Automaticity in search*

At least one factor that should be important in determining whether a task will be capacity limited at the visual processing level is the nature of training that is provided to subjects. Observers in the Eriksen and Spencer study searched for the same target in the same set of distractors for several hours (consistent mapping training or CM). Hoffman (1978) showed that when targets varied from trial to trial (varied mapping or VM), observers gained a large advantage with sequential presentation, as predicted by the limited capacity model. Other researchers have found sequential presentation advantages when larger numbers of distractors are used (Fisher, 1984) or when the targets and distractors are highly similar (Kleiss & Lane, 1986).

Although these results show that there are one or more limited-capacity processes at work in visual search that cannot be attributed to the decision stage, the nature of these processes is unclear. One possibility is that observers have to pay attention to each item in the display to determine whether it is a target. The time to shift attention, together with the time to compare the display item to memory, would establish the limits on how fast search could proceed. This model predicts a linear increase in search time with increases in display size and the slope of this function would then provide an estimate of the sum of the attention switching plus memory comparison times. Linear search functions have frequently been observed and their slopes are often quite small, with an average of 15 msec/item for target-present trials and 33 msec/item for target-absent (Wolfe, 1998). These times are faster than the time required to shift attention from one location to another which has been estimated to require a minimum of 50 msec (Hoffman, 1975) and a maximum of 250 msec (Colegate, Hoffman, & Eriksen, 1973). In addition, the attended item has to be compared to the target which can take a 100 msec or more depending on the number of items in the target set. These estimates are incompatible with a strictly serial search.

1.3 The two-stage search model

Hoffman (1978, 1979) proposed that these conflicting findings could be accommodated by assuming two separate processing stages. The first, *preattentive* stage, worked in parallel on all objects in the visual field to yield a measure of similarity of each object to the target set. Spatial attention was then allocated to the most similar object in order to transfer it to a second, slower comparison process that only dealt with one object at a time but had high accuracy. The effect of training was assumed to be on the accuracy of the similarity values provided by preattentive processing. If targets could be reliably discriminated from distractors by the preattentive stage, then targets would always reach the second stage first, regardless of the number of distractors; alternatively, the second stage could be dispensed with altogether. In either case, display size effects would disappear, particularly for discriminable target/distracter combinations (see Kleiss & Lane for supporting data).

A computer simulation of the two-stage search model provided a good account of the effects of display size and presentation rate on search speed and accuracy. In addition, several predictions of the model have been confirmed by subsequent research. Hoffman and Nelson (1981a) tested the prediction that spatial attention is preferentially allocated to search targets. They used a dual-task paradigm in which subjects searched for a target letter while also trying to determine the orientation of U-shaped figure that was presented just after the search display. When the target and the U occurred in different locations, increased accuracy on one task could be purchased only at the price of reduced performance on the other. In contrast, when the critical shapes occurred in adjacent locations, little trade-off in performance was observed.

A similar reliance on spatial attention was shown to hold for targets that had received extensive consistent mapping training (Shiffrin & Schneider, 1977). Shiffrin and Schneider (1977) found that at the end of training, CM targets were difficult to ignore when they appeared as distractors in a varied-mapping search task. They appeared to "pop-out" of the display and draw attention to themselves (the authors called this an "automatic attention response") which, in turn, prevented subjects from deploying their attention to find the VM targets. The spatial nature of this interference was confirmed by Hoffman, Nelson, and Houck (1983) who used a probe method similar to that employed by Hoffman and Nelson (1981a). Probes were discriminated better when they appeared in close spatial proximity to the CM targets, indicating that CM target detection is associated with a shift of attention to the target's location. In addition, detection of a CM target located in the parafovea was impaired when subjects also attempted a difficult visual discrimination located at the fovea. These results indicate that target detection continues to require access to spatial attention, even after extensive training has eliminated the display size effect.

Overall, the results are consistent with the claim that detection of a visual target is accompanied by allocation of spatial attention to the target's location and that preventing this process impairs detection. This holds even for extensively trained targets which gradually acquire the ability to call attention to their location, eliminating display size effects. One might go further and speculate that the second, serial stage of processing is associated with conscious awareness and that preventing an observer from attending to the *location* of a stimulus prevents awareness of that stimulus even when preattentive processes have extracted its identity (see also Rock, Linnett, Grant, & Mack, 1992). This point remains controversial as some researchers (Braun & Sagi, 1990) have reported that simple pop-out targets show no dual-task interference when spatial attention is allocated to other display locations (but see Joseph, Chun, & Nakayama, 1996).

Another prediction of the two-stage model is that detecting two targets arriving in close temporal proximity should be particularly difficult. A distracter will not interfere as much as another target because a target will generally win out over a distracter in the competition for access to stage-two processing. However, if two targets are present, one of them must wait until processing of the first target is complete, increasing the likelihood that it will be lost. Several experiments have confirmed this prediction. For example Ostry, Moray, & Marks (1976) had subjects detect targets in two separate streams of auditory digits. Performance in monitoring two streams was about as good as one stream except when targets occurred on both channels, in which case, one of the targets was likely to be missed. Duncan (1980) presents similar results from several visual and auditory detection experiments, all showing that it is mainly targets that compete for "limited-capacity".

Do targets from all modalities compete for the same limited-capacity system or should we think of stage two processing (and perhaps awareness in general) as modality-specific? Hoffman and Nelson (1981b) addressed this question by combining a visual CM detection task with another concurrent visual or auditory task. In different blocks of trials, subjects were given instructions regarding how much attention to allocate to each task. For example, in one block they would be instructed: "Pay 10% of your attention to discriminating the tone and the remainder to detecting the visual target". The results are shown in Table 1. Two major effects are of interest. First, as attention was withdrawn from the visual task (corresponding to smaller percentages) and allocated to the visual CM search task, performance of the visual task sharply declined. This replicates the earlier findings of Hoffman, Nelson, and Houck (1983) showing that CM search tasks require "attention". The effect of withdrawing attention from the auditory task was much smaller. Second, performance of the visual task was much worse when the CM target was present in the display, replicating the results reviewed above in showing that it is mainly *targets* that compete for processing capacity. Accuracy on the auditory task, however, was independent of whether the visual CM target was present or not, suggesting that the interference between simultaneous targets is modality specific. Duncan, Martens, and Ward (1997) reported an extensive test of this issue with similar results. Interference between simultaneous targets is largely modality-specific. We cannot tell from these experiments, however, whether the interference between targets is due to competition for visuo-spatial attention or the limited-capacity system associated with awareness. The latter possibility would imply that awareness is not a single "state" but differs depending on sensory modality.

Table 1. *d' on concurrent visual or auditory task as a function of attention allocated to that task and whether the CM target was present or absent.*

| | | Percent attention allocated to visual or auditory task | | | |
		10	50	90	100
Visual Task	Target Present	0.85	0.89	0.96	1.43
	Target Absent	1.20	1.40	1.48	1.54
Auditory Task	Target Present	0.85	0.98	0.91	1.05
	Target Absent	0.80	0.89	0.93	1.10

1.4 *Physiological evidence*

We could conduct a direct test of the two-stage search model if we could monitor the recognition process for each display item throughout a trial. We would expect to see that, initially, all the objects in the display would be processed in parallel but as the similarity of the target started to exceed that of the distractors, attention would be shifted to the target's position and processing of distractors would decline. Chelazzi, Miller, Duncan, and Desimone (1993) reported observations very close to these predictions. They recorded activity of cells in the inferior temporal (IT) area of monkeys in response to complex shapes. This is an area that appears to be important for recognizing objects and receives its principal input from the extrastriate visual areas whose cells seem to be concerned with fairly simple features such as line orientation, color, etc.. For each cell, they found a shape that activated the cell and another that had no effect. Each of these shapes then served as targets in a visual search task. Figure 1 shows the sequence of events on a typical trial. Following fixation, a cue object is presented (the target), followed by a display of two objects. The monkey's task is to move her eyes to the matching shape as quickly as possible.

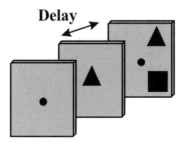

Figure 1. *Sequence of trial events in the Chelazzi et. al. 1993 study. A fixation point is followed by a cue stimulus. Following a delay, the array is presented and the monkey makes a saccade to the location whose shape matches the cue.*

Suppose that we are looking at the activity of a cell that responds to triangles but not rectangles. If the triangle is the target, then this cell should remain in an "active state" during the interval preceding the array. When the display appears, the triangle representation receives additional activation from the presence of the triangle in the display. In addition, cells that respond to rectangles would also be initially active but as spatial attention is drawn to the location of the triangle, this activity would decline while the activity of "triangle cells" would continue to increase.

The results are shown in Figure 2. The curve labeled "good cue" shows the activity of cells that respond to the target shape (a triangle). The curve labeled "poor cue" shows the activity of cells responding to the rectangle. The solid horizontal bars on the time line show the onset of the cue object and, following a delay, the onset of the array. Following the cue, cells that respond to the target object are maintained in an active state during the delay period, as if the monkey is holding in mind the target representation of a triangle. Beginning shortly after the onset of the array, cells responding to both objects in the display become active as they are matched to their corresponding representations in memory. However, the activity of the nontarget cell rapidly returns to baseline while target cell activity continues to grow. This is the pattern we would expect if search starts with a parallel recognition of all the display objects and is followed by attention to the target.

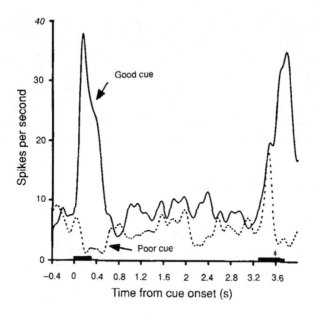

Figure 2. *Results of the Chelazzi at. al. (1993) study. The curve labeled "good cue" ("poor cue") represents the response of a cell tuned to the target (distracter).*

A couple of caveats are in order regarding these data. First, it is possible that the higher firing rate of the target cell may be due to the requirement to make a saccade to the target. Several recent experiments have shown that saccades are preceded by a shift of visuo-spatial attention to the location of the saccade goal (Hoffman, 1998; Hoffman & Subramaniam, 1995; Kowler, Anderson, Dosher, & Blaser, 1995). Second, there is no independent measure to indicate that the suppression of activity seen in cells responding to the distracter is due to spatial attention being allocated to the target. Previous research, has, however, shown that very similar effects occur in IT cells when attention is explicitly directed away from objects within a receptive field, so it seems likely that the suppression effects seen here do represent effects of spatial attention triggered by the target object.

It seems clear that some stage of vision has limited capacity, that is, it operates more slowly and less accurately with increases in the number of objects presented. This limited-capacity system is separable from working memory limits and decision level effects and seems to follow and be guided by a parallel, preattentive process that signals likely target locations. Access to this limited-capacity stage appears to depend on spatial attention so that observers may fail to detect even single objects when their spatial attention is allocated elsewhere. Of course, much of this picture still needs to be filled in. For example, the two-stage search model assumed that preattentive vision computed the similarity between each display object and the set of targets. How is this accomplished? Is matching done on the basis of features or "whole objects? To answer these questions, we need to inquire about the nature of preattentive visual representations.

2.   Preattentive representations

Why should the parallel routines of preattentive vision only be capable of providing "noisy identity" information about the objects in the visual field, as the two-stage model assumes? A possible answer is suggested by considering the "binding problem". Recording of neural activity from single cells located in "early" levels of the visual system such as V1, V2 and V4, suggests that these cells respond to specific "features" of the environment such as line orientation, color, direction of motion etc. (see Gazzaniga, Ivry, & Mangun, 1998 for a summary). Presumably, these cells are the building blocks of complex object representations at higher levels. For example, a yellow VW might be represented as a combination of various color and shape primitives, along with a specification of their spatial relationships (Biederman, 1987). We also need to recognize this object at any location in the visual field. If we solve this problem by replicating our VW recognition network at every location in the visual field, we end up requiring a huge number of neurons, and this need to be multiplied by the number of different objects we can recognize.

   A different approach to object recognition would be to have a set of basic feature detectors replicated over the visual field. These primitive detectors would all funnel into a single set of object detectors representing known objects. The yellow VW detector would receive inputs from all the cells coding yellow as well as various shape-primitives at all locations. The cells in IT cortex discussed earlier appear to have this property (Moran & Desimone, 1985). They have large receptive fields that can respond to their favored object when it is shown virtually anywhere in the visual field. This scheme achieves economy of representation but it would be susceptible to errors whenever it was presented with multiple objects. A yellow banana and a red VW, for example, would also trigger the "yellow VW detector". In order to eliminate these illusory conjunctions, we need a way of binding attributes together that come from the same object.

Treisman (1988) suggested a possible solution to the binding problem based on the observation that attributes that belong to a single object also usually occur in the same "location". If subjects focussed attention on a single object at a time, only those features would be matched against object representations and illusory conjunctions of features from different objects would be prevented. Her original model is shown in Figure 3. Individual spatiotopic feature maps represent dimensions such as color, shape etc. In addition, corresponding locations in each map are connected to a "master map of locations". Attending to a location is accomplished by activating a location in this master map which retrieves the various features that share that location. This integrated object representation can then be matched against known object representations.

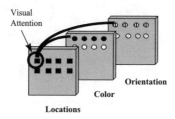

Figure 3. *Treisman's model in which features from different maps are combined into an object representation by attending to a location.*

This theory provides a solution to the feature binding problem and also makes some surprising predictions which have been explored by Treisman and colleagues in an extensive set of studies (Treisman & Gelade, 1980; Treisman & Gormican, 1988; Treisman & Schmidt, 1982). For example, in the absence of attention, unbound features may sometimes combine to produce illusory objects consisting of the color of one object and the shape of another (Treisman & Schmidt, 1982). In addition, search for objects that can be discriminated on the basis of a single feature such as color or shape shouldn't require attention (Treisman & Gelade, 1980) because feature integration is not required. In contrast, search for a conjunction of features will require the observer to attend to the location of each object in turn in order to integrate the features into a veridical object representation. Conjunction search should then be a linear function of the number of display objects and the slope of this function provides an estimate of the time to perform each conjunction. Figure 4 shows examples of feature and conjunction search and the reader can verify that the single feature target appears to "pop-out" of the display while search for a conjunction requires scrutiny.

Several findings appeared to argue against this strictly serial search for conjunctions. First, Egeth, Virzi, and Garbart (1984) reported that subjects were able to direct attention to just those objects that shared the target's color. For example, if the target was a red T embedded in red and green distracter letters, search time depended on the number of red letters and was unaffected by the number of green letters. Similar effects of segregating the display into subsets based on stereo depth and motion were reported by Nakayama and Silverman (1986). Further, Wolfe, Cave, & Franzel (1989) found that slopes for many conjunction searches were too small to be plausibly attributed to serial allocation of visual attention.

Feature Search   Conjunction Search

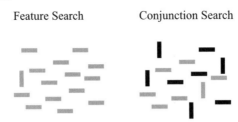

Figure 4. *The target is a gray vertical bar. In feature search, the target pops-out while in conjunction search, finding the feature is more difficult.*

To account for these anomalous findings, Wolfe and colleagues (Cave & Wolfe, 1990; Wolfe, 1994) proposed a "Guided Search Model" to explain their results. The guided search model is similar to the two-stage model proposed by Hoffman (1978, 1979) in assuming that a limited capacity mechanism is directed to likely targets by an initial, "noisy" parallel evaluation of the entire display. However, this model is more explicit about the nature of this preattentive stage. Consider the case in which a subject is searching for a red vertical line in a display of red horizontals and green verticals. Like Treisman, Wolfe assumes that preattentive vision reduces the objects to their component features, such as color and shape. Because the subject is searching for *red*, top-down processes result in high activation values in the color map for all the red objects. Similarly, activation of *vertical* results in high activation of all the locations with vertical lines. If these two activation maps are summed, then the most active location will usually index the target although noise in the activation process will sometimes produce higher activation values for distracters than targets. The subject is assumed to serially search the candidates in the activation map, starting with the highest activation value and working down. These are the same assumptions made by the two-stage model (Hoffman, 1978, 1979) except the guided-search model makes an explicit commitment to features as the basis for the preattentive similarity representation.

The guided-search model provides a clever solution to the binding problem. Rather than representing all possible combinations of features required to represent every object at every position, it separates features into separate spatio-topically organized maps, with each position in each map connected to a activation map, similar to Treisman's master map of locations. By sending a top-down signals to the feature maps representing the particular object being searched for ("red" and "vertical"), the activation map automatically indicates the likely location of the sought after object. This scheme doesn't work so well, however, in complex displays in which objects can occlude each other, and where perceiving the attributes of an object in different orientations and illuminations, depends on combining features. For example, to correctly perceive the *color* of a surface, one has to take into account the orientation of a surface in 3D space relative to the direction of the illuminant. Enns and Rensink (1990a,b; 1991) showed that subjects are sensitive to the 3D orientation of shapes and this information appears to depend on "T" and "Y" junctions where different surfaces of an object meet. The ability of preattentive vision to sort lines into these various classes of junctions is unexpected given the difficulty subjects have in searching for a "T" in a display of "L"s.

Similarly, He and Nakayama (1992) using displays like those shown in Figure 5, showed that subjects use stereopsis to group features into "surfaces" in which the identity of primitive edge features is no longer explicitly represented. This is an example of what Rensink and Enns (1995) call "preemption" in which a feature such as an oriented line, which might normally produce pop-out, becomes difficult to detect when embedded in a larger configuration. They showed that subjects can not efficiently search for the middle segment of a Mueller-Lyer figure, which ought to correspond to a "primitive feature", because this feature is preempted by the whole configuration of which it is a part.

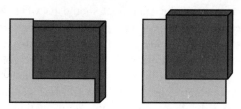

Figure 5. *Subjects are faster in searching for an "L" in displays like those on the left than on the right. The "L" shown on the right is difficult to detect because the visual system assumes it is part of a rectangular surface extending behind the occluding surface. After He and Nakayama (1992).*

Occlusion also would also pose difficulties for a visual search mechanism that only had access to simple features. Wolfe (1996) used stimuli like those in Figure 6 to show that preattentive visual processes "understand" occlusion (see also Rensink & Enns, 1998) and correctly assign ownership of edges to occluding and occluded objects. Search for a vertical, black line is not slowed by the presence of the vertical black line indicated by the arrow because the vertical feature is correctly assigned to the occluding white grid while the black color is assigned to the occluded black rectangle.

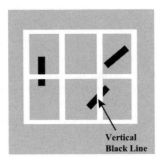

Figure 6. *Occlusion is understood by the preattentive system so it is not fooled by the vertical black line indicated by the arrow (after Wolf, 1996).*

Houck and Hoffman (1985) showed that even color and shape, which appear to be prototypes for separable features in visual search, might be integrated at early but not late levels. They looked at the effects of attention on the McCullough effect in which adaptation to a red-vertical grating results in an aftereffect in which a black and white, vertical grating appears green. This aftereffect depends on a conjunction of color and form and if these dimensions are kept separate in early vision, the strength of the aftereffect should be weak when the adapting gratings are unattended. The results showed that the *aftereffect* was independent of attention. In contrast, *visual search* for the same gratings showed the usual linear set-size function found in other studies of form and color conjunctions.

These findings, together with many others (Nakayama, He, & Shimojo, 1995), suggest that preattentive processes have access to conjunctions of features and in fact have already done some of the segmentation and integration of features that are necessary to form object representations. How can this conclusion be reconciled with the inability to use such information to guide visual search? Wolfe and Bennett (1997) propose that preattentive vision consists of "shapeless bundles of features", representations of separate objects but without any information about how features are bound together and with no representation of overall shape. For example, the letter "T" would be represented as an object having two features: vertical and horizontal line segments. The relationship between these two features would not be explicit, however, until attention arrives at the object's location.

3.   Object-based attention

In the previous section, I reviewed evidence indicating that preattentive representations consist of "unbound" features and that focal attention is required to correctly integrate the features into objects, determining, for instance, the spatial relationships between different line segments and assigning colors to their corresponding shapes. As stated, however, there are some obvious problems with this approach. If all the features in an attended area are integrated into an object representation and attention is simply allocated to spatial areas, then most of the objects we would experience would be a hopeless bundle of features, bearing little resemblance to the objects in the physical world. What is needed is some way of ensuring that attention is allocated to areas that have already been structured as objects. This presents something of a "chicken and egg problem" because one of the putative functions of attention is integration of features into objects. The solution proposed by Wolfe (1997), Rensink (1997) and others is to suppose that preattentive vision divides the world into "proto-objects" or "object files". In this context, an object file is a collection of features that belong to a single object but without specification of the interrelationships of the features or the identity of the object. Neither the spatial arrangement of the features nor the overall shape of the object is "known" until that object is attended. For example, a "plus" made up of a red vertical and green horizontal lines would give rise to the same object file as green vertical and red horizontal. These objects would not be distinguishable at the level of preattentive vision and, indeed, search through displays composed of these objects is "inefficient". Because attention is allocated to objects and not "empty space", these theories have become known as object-based models of attention.

Many different experiments suggest that attention is allocated to more than just space. A particularly good example is an experiment by Neisser and Becklen (1975). Subjects watched two different films superimposed on a video monitor. One film portrayed two pairs of hands engaged in a game in which one player tries to slap the other's hand. The second film showed a circle of people playing catch in a gym. Subjects were instructed to monitor one or the other film for target events and they could readily do this despite the fact that the films were superimposed, offering little in the way of location cues to guide attention. In addition, subjects were completely unaware of "oddball events" that sometimes occurred in the unattended film. For example, in the middle of the ball game, a man walked through the gym holding an open umbrella. None of the subjects who were attending to the "hand game" noticed this peculiar event even though all subjects spontaneously commented on it when they were monitoring the ball game.

Neisser and Becklen emphasize that perception was just as selective in their experiment as in other studies that used physical cues, such as location, to guide attention. They suggest that selection in this case reveals the "cyclical nature" of perception in which "schemas" guide the pick-up of information from the environment which, in turn, leads to activation of additional schemas, and so on. Selection, according to this model, depends on the observer's ability to perceive coherence in a dynamic event. The displays used by Neisser and Becklen are similar to the heads-up displays used in many military jets. Indicators of airspeed, heading, and so on are superimposed on the plane's windscreen allowing pilots to switch attention between the outside world and the instruments without changes in the direction of gaze. However, this arrangement doesn't allow perfect division of attention between these two sources of information. In fact, several experiments have confirmed that pilots attending to their instrument readings sometimes miss obvious objects visible through the windscreen, such as a passenger jet taxiing onto the runway (Wickens & Long, 1995).

Duncan (1984) suggested that all the features of an attended object are processed in parallel, without capacity limits, whereas, processing of features belonging to different objects is difficult and limited in capacity. He performed an experiment with stimuli like those shown in Figure 7. Subjects were presented with two overlapping objects with each object being composed of two "features". The box could vary in terms of the location of the gap, and the texture of its borders. The line could vary in tilt and texture. On different trials, subject were instructed to report the values of two features and these features could belong to a single object (e.g., location of gap and border texture for the box) or to different objects (e.g., the location of the gap for the box and the tilt of the line). He found that subjects could report two features of a single object as accurately as a single feature. However, reporting features belonging to different objects was more error prone. These results are consistent with the claim that attention is allocated to objects and that there is a cost to dividing attention between objects.

Further evidence for the distinction between object and space-based models of attention was provided by Egly, Driver, and Rafal (1994) using displays like those shown in Figure 8. They cued subjects to attend to one end of a vertical rectangle and on invalid cue trials, presented the target (a filled-in square) in

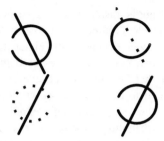

Figure 7. *Four different stimuli used in Duncan's (1984) experiment. Each display consisted of two overlapping objects, a line and circle.*

either the same rectangle (same object condition) or an adjacent rectangle (different object condition). The distance between the cued location and the target was the same in both conditions so any differences would be attributable to "object-based attention".

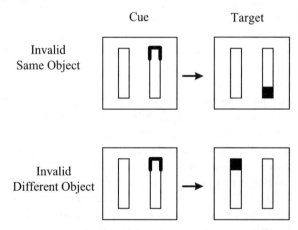

Figure 8. *Subjects are cued to the likely location of a target by a darkened rectangle. On invalid cue trials, the target (a solid square) can appear in a different location in the cued object (top row) or in the uncued object (bottom row) (after Egly, Driver, & Rafal, 1994).*

They found costs associated with the misleading cue for within-objects shifts of attention, as would be predicted by space-based models of attention. In addition, between-object costs were even greater, reflecting the additional costs of shifting attention between objects. They also performed this experiment with patients with damage to the left or right parietal areas of the brain and found some evidence implicating the right hemisphere in the control of object-based attention.

The Egly et. al. experiments indicate that attention can be allocated on the basis of separate systems which depend on either spatial location or object structure. One might try to rescue the space-based model by allowing object shape to modify the spatial distribution of attention. For example, spatial attention might be allocated to the contours or surfaces of objects (Nakayama, He, & Shimojo, 1995). In the case of Duncan's stimuli, for example, attention to the box would entail a distribution of attention over the contours of the box which would effectively exclude much of the overlapping line. Divided attention would involve spreading attention over a larger area with a resulting loss in resolution for each of the objects in its field.

Vacera and Farah (1994) attempted to distinguish these possibilities by employing the Duncan stimuli and presenting the two objects in one location at fixation (similar to Duncan's original experiment) or in separate locations to the left and right of fixation. They reasoned that if the object effect in Duncan's experiment was mediated by different distributions of spatial attention, then separated locations would increase the difficulty of dividing attention over greater spatial separations yielding greater costs associated with the separated objects condition. They reported equivalent costs for the separated and overlapping object conditions and concluded that subjects were performing the task by attending to object representations independent of their locations.

In a follow-up experiment, subjects made a speeded detection of a dot whose likely location was signaled by brightening one of the objects. When the two objects were separated, an invalid cue would cause subjects to attend to the wrong side of the display and a reallocation of attention to the opposite side would be required, resulting in a delay. In contrast, with overlapping objects, cueing the wrong object would still leave the subject attending to the location of the target. Vacera and Farah confirmed this pattern of results and suggested that attention may be allocated to location or objects depending on the task.

Recall that the key prediction for discriminating space and object-based models of attention made by Vacera and Farah was the greater costs associated with separated compared to overlapping objects. This prediction is based on the assumption that the time to switch attention from one location to another should be a function of their spatial separation. However, the majority of the evidence suggests that attention switching is discrete and independent of distance (Sperling & Weichselgartner, 1995). Kramer, Weber, and Watson (1997) sidestepped these methodological problems by using a "probe technique" similar to that used by Hoffman and Nelson (1981a) and Hoffman, Nelson, and Houck (1983) to study attention allocation. Suppose that subjects are reporting two features from one object in the separated condition. If attention is allocated to this location as part of making judgements about the objects, then subjects should be faster at responding to a probe dot occurring in this location compared to the "irrelevant object" location. Consistent with the probe results reported by Hoffman and Nelson (1981a) and Hoffman, Nelson, and Houck (1983) they found that judgements about object properties were accompanied by faster detection of other stimuli at the same location.

Where does the object based attention hypothesis stand? It seems unlikely that subjects ever rely solely on an object-based representation that is independent of location. Even pop-out search, which supposedly reflects the operation of preattentive visual processes, requires that attention be allocated to the location of the target for subjects to be aware of and report the presence of the target (Hoffman, Nelson, & Houck, 1983; Joseph, Chun, & Nakayama, 1996; however, see Braun, & Sagi, 1990). Selection based on object properties such as color, are mediated by the relevant color triggering a shift of spatial attention to the target (Shih & Sperling, 1996).

Attention to location appears to gate targets into conscious awareness but there must also be a role for object-based attention. Although it often difficult to disentangle object and space-based attention effects, it seems clear from a variety of different paradigms that both kinds of selection occur. Lavie and Driver (1996) have recently attempted to separate these two modes of attention. They asked subjects to judge the similarity of two features that could appear on same or different objects. In addition, they manipulated the spatial separation of these features. Consistent with the object-based theory, they found that performance was better in the same-object condition and that spatial separation had no effect. However when subjects were pre-cued to restrict their attention to one area of the display that did not include the entire object, the object advantage disappeared and performance depended on spatial separation. Thus, object and space-based effects were found with the same stimuli depending on the subject's state of attention.

These results are consistent with the claim that both modes of attention exist and they may mutually affect one another. In other words, the spatial extent of attention may help determine what features are combined into objects and the objects within the field of attention may determine how attention is allocated spatially. These results are reminiscent of early debates in the area of auditory attention on the adequacy of filter theory (Broadbent, 1958), which assumed that selection occurred on the basis of "early" sensory features such as pitch and location. Several experiments showed that unattended material that was semantically related to the attended message could "break through" the filter and cause subjects to begin shadowing the to-be-ignored material (Gray & Wedderburn, 1960). Such results are consistent with the claim that, at least sometimes, material that should be blocked on the basis of attention to location does get through to awareness because of "top-down effects" based on expectation. In addition, these stimuli affect the settings of the attentional mechanism based on location because the subject continues to shadow the to-be-ignored material once it has "captured" attention.

3.1 *Change detection*

Perhaps, one of the most compelling demonstrations that appears to support the view that preattentive vision knows little about object identity comes from a paradigm known as *change detection*. Rensink, O'Regan, and Clark (1997) presented observers with two alternating pictures of complex visual scenes. Each picture was shown for 240 msec. with an 80 msec. delay between onsets. The two images were identical except for a single object or feature. For example, the presence of an object, its location, or its color could change from one image to the other. The images alternated until the subject noticed the change and was able to indicate the location and identity of the object being changed. The average time to notice these changes was surprisingly long, ranging from 15 to 25 sec. for different changes. Detection of change appeared to rely on attention because changes to objects rated as being of "central importance" in the picture were detected faster than those rated as marginal. Some sense of the difficulty of this task can be appreciated by attempting to detect the differences (seven of them) in the two drawings shown in Figure 9. This evidence of a failure to represent the details of a visual scene is echoed by research in several other areas. For example, Pashler (1988) reported an early example of this type of experiment in which he showed that that an observer is quite poor at detecting changes to arrays containing more than 4-5 alphanumeric characters. The same limits appeared to apply to displays of characters reflected about their horizontal axis suggesting that what was being stored from one view to another was the visual form of the letter, not its identity. Similar results have been reported by Phillips (1974) and Luck and Vogel (1997) using geometric shapes and various controls to exclude naming strategies. Luck and Vogel reported that subjects could store about four "objects" in this visual memory, regardless of whether the objects are defined by one or four features.

Work on integration of information across saccades makes much the same point. Irwin (1996) showed observers one display at fixation and then following a saccade, a second display. He found that the ability (or inability) to integrate the two displays across the saccade was consistent with a visual short-term memory of limited capacity. As was the case in the change detection experiments,

Figure 9. *Try to detect the differences between the two drawings. Drawing by Stevie French.*

what observers preserve from one fixation to the next depends on attention. McConkie and Currie (1996) found that subjects were poor at detecting changes to objects in a scene that were made during a saccade, unless the changes occurred in the area that was the target of the eye movement. This is consistent with the claim that attention is required in order to detect changes in objects because subjects attend to a location prior to making an eye movement to it (Hoffman & Subramaniam, 1995; Kowler, Anderson, Dosher, & Blaser, 1995).

These results suggest that we "know" much less about the visual world before us than we think. That part of the scene that is currently of interest and engaging our attention is "known" and is stored in a limited-capacity visual memory that holds approximately four objects. After an eye movement is completed, the contents of this memory are available to be compared to the currently attended location. The rest of the visual world, currently unattended, is represented as "objects" but without specific information about shape, or arrangement of features. The claim is that preattentive vision, using information about line junctions, orientations, shading, etc. has produced a representation of surfaces; their colors, orientations, distance, etc. (Nakayama, He, & Shimojo, 1995). This surface representation is what is available to the attention system, and preempts any earlier representations constructed along the way. These surfaces may have even been segmented and grouped into "objects". But identification and recognition, the determination of whether this object has been seen before and in what context, is the exclusive domain of a limited-capacity system that is accessed through spatial attention.

However, we should be cautious about making strong claims on the basis of the evidence at hand. One might question whether the change-detection paradigm is diagnostic regarding the observer's knowledge of object identities. There are clearly change detection mechanisms built into the visual system which can capture attention and alert us to the arrival of new objects (Yantis, 1998). These new objects are usually associated with onset transients that indicate the location of a change in the scene or movement against a stationary background. The change-detection experiments have been designed to eliminate these physical cues to change (by swamping them with many onsets as each new image is presented) and they show that attention is not captured by changes in the *identity* of objects in these conditions. However, it is possible that the identities of *all* objects in the scene have been extracted but this knowledge is simply not represented in such a way as to generate change signals that can produce a shift of attention. Other, "indirect" methods might reveal information about object identity that is not picked up by the change detection measure. Some intriguing evidence along these lines was provided by a recent experiment by Rensink (1998) that required observers to indicate whether they had any sense of the presence of an object change even if they didn't know the identity or location of the object. Some observers could reliably indicate that an object change was occurring even when they were unsure about its details. If object change was always associated with attention to the changed object, and if attention to the object was related to conscious knowledge about that object, one wouldn't expect knowledge of change in the absence of conscious knowledge of identity.

4.   The attentional blink

There are other intriguing cases of dissociation between object identity and conscious knowledge of that identity. In the *attentional blink* paradigm (AB), shown in Figure 10, observers watch a stream of gray digits presented at the center of the screen at a rate of 10 digits/sec. The task is to report the identity of a single black digit (known as the first target or T1) embedded somewhere in the stream. In addition, subjects are told to indicate whether the letter "X" (the second target or T2) appeared in the stream (the "X" is gray and doesn't pop-out on the basis of color). Observers have trouble detecting T2 when it occurs approximately two positions after T1 (Raymond, Shapiro, & Arnell, 1992). This is not simply a case of T1 masking T2 because if observers are instructed to ignore T1, T2 is now readily detected. It appears that the interfering effects of T1 are due to its occupying the limited-capacity, stage-two processor for an extended period. When T2 occurs immediately after T1, both may gain access to stage 2. However, when T2 is delayed 2 positions, it appears that the "gate" admitting items to stage 2 (Sperling & Weichselgartner, 1995) has closed and items will be lost until this stage is free again.

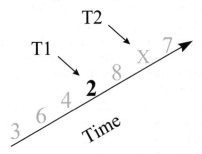

Figure 10. *Attentional blink paradigm.*

This explanation of the attentional blink (AB) assumes that the locus of interference is occurring at a "late stage of processing" when items are competing for access to stage 2 processing. All the items in the stream, including T2, might be completely identified but the presence of T2 would be missed because it never reaches conscious awareness. Luck, Vogel, & Shapiro (1996) evaluated this possibility using event-related brain potentials (ERPs), which reflect the electrical activity of the brain which is time-locked to a particular stimulus. The N400 component of the ERP is elicited by words or pictures (Nigam, Hoffman, & Simons, 1993; Nigam, Hoffman, Simons, & Gebhart, 1997) that violate a semantic context. Luck and Vogel established a semantic context by requiring subjects to determine whether T2 was related to a context word presented at the beginning of the trial. They found that when T2 was unrelated to the context word, it elicited an N400 and the amplitude of the N400 was unaffected by whether T2 was detected or not. In other words, when subjects responded to T1, causing T2 to be missed, the undetected T2 was processed to the semantic level. Vogel, Luck, & Shapiro (1998) further reported that although a "blinked" T2 elicited a normal N400, the P300 was essentially abolished. The P300 appears to be associated with conscious target detection, so this result suggests that subjects did not simply detect and forget T2; instead it appears they never "detected" it at all. Shapiro, Driver, Ward, & Sorensen (1997) reached similar conclusions using semantic priming to assess semantic processing of T2. They found that T2 produced normal semantic priming of subsequent words in the stream, even when it was undetectable because of the "blink" produced by T1.

Work on AB suggests that objects have to gain admission to stage-two processing to be consciously detected. Further, stage-two appears to have a limited capacity such that when it is occupied, newly arriving items have to queue and can be replaced by subsequent items arriving in close temporal and spatial proximity, causing them to go undetected. These items have nonetheless been processed to a semantic level. What implications does AB research have for understanding the nature of preattentive vision? That remains to be seen as the attentional blink paradigm differs in potentially important ways from search and directed attention experiments. In directed attention experiments, subjects are cued to a single location (Posner, 1980) or object. Processing of objects in the cued position appear to be enhanced (Luck, 1998) while unattended objects are suppressed (Milliken & Tipper, 1998; Moran & Desimone, 1985). In the AB paradigm, Vogel, Luck, & Shapiro (1998) showed that the "early" components of the event-related brain potential, which are known to be affected by spatial attention, are unaffected by the attentional blink, suggesting that the blinked item is undergoing more analysis than objects outside the focus of spatial attention. Nonetheless, the occurrence of semantic priming for items that cannot be reported raises the possibility that in visual search and change detection experiments, preattentive processing may result in deeper processing than is reflected in conscious reports.

5. Summary

The initial, preattentive stage of processing serves to locate interesting objects in the visual world to be examined by a second stage of processing that may be associated with conscious awareness. This second stage is thought to operate on one or a few objects at a time and forms a bottleneck in visual processing. This view of attention and perception is based on two assumptions: one is that it is impossible to identify all the objects in view (perhaps because of the binding problem discussed earlier); the other is that visual working memory is limited (Luck & Vogel, 1997) so that the world itself may be used as a memory (O'Regan, 1992). Our impression of full and immediate access to the identities of all objects in view may be based on our ability to rapidly extract the overall "gist" of scenes (Intraub, 1981), to quickly recognize attended objects, and to derive an overall sense of spatial "layout". These results are suggestive that preattentive vision knows quite a bit about the visual world but that object identification may be the exclusive province of a subsequent processing stage associated with conscious awareness. Further research on the nature of preattentive vision should aid in understanding the nature of the different stages participating in visual search.

References

Allport, A. (1989). Visual attention. In M. I. Posner (ed.), *Foundations of cognitive science*. (p. 631–682). Cambridge, MA: MIT Press.

Averbach, E. & Coriell, A. S. (1961). Short-term memory in vision. *Bell System Technical Journal*, 40, 309–328.

Baddeley, A. D. (1986). *Working Memory*. Oxford: Oxford University Press.

Biederman, I. (1987). Recognition-by-components: A theory of human image understanding. *Psychological Review, 94*, 115–147.

Braun, J. & Sagi, D. (1990). Vision outside the focus of attention. *Perception & Psychophysics, 52*, 277–294.

Broadbent, D. E. (1958). *Perception and Communication*. London: Pergamon Press.

Cave, K. R. & Wolfe, J. M. (1990). Modeling the role of parallel processing in visual search. *Cognitive Psychology, 22*, 225–271.

Chelazzi, Miller, Duncan, Desimone (1993). A neural basis for visual search in inferior temporal cortex. *Nature, 363*, 345–347

Colegate, R. L., Hoffman, J. E., & Eriksen, C. W. (1973) Selective encoding from multielement displays. *Perception and Psychophysics, 14*, 217–224.

Duncan, J. (1980). The locus of interference in the perception of simultaneous stimuli. *Psychological Review, 87*, 272–300.

Duncan, J. (1984). Selective attention and the organization of visual information. *Journal of Experimental Psychology: General, 113*, 501–517.

Duncan, J., Martens, S., & Ward, R. (1997). Restricted attentional capacity within but not between sensory modalities. *Nature, 387*, 808–810.

Egeth, H. E., Virzi, R. A., & Garbart, H. (1984). Searching for conjunctively defined targets. *Journal of Experimental Psychology: Human Perception & Performance, 10*, 32–39.

Egly, R., Driver, J., & Rafal, R. D. (1994). Shifting visual attention between objects and locations: Evidence from normal and parietal lesion subjects. *Journal of Experimental Psychology: General, 123*, 161–177.

Enns, J. T. & Rensink, R. A. (1990a). Scene based properties influence visual search. *Science, 247*, 721–723.

Enns, J. T. & Rensink, R. A. (1990b). Sensitivity to three-dimensional orientation in visual search. *Psychological Science, 1*, 323–326.

Enns, J. T. & Rensink, R. A. (1991). Preattentive recovery of three-dimensional orientation from line drawings. *Psychological Review, 98*, 335–351.

Eriksen, C. W. & Hoffman, J. E. (1972a). Some characteristics of selective attention in visual perception determined by vocal reaction time. *Perception and Psychophysics, 11*, 169–171.

Eriksen, C. W. & Hoffman, J. E. (1972b). Temporal and spatial characteristics of selective encoding from visual displays. *Perception and Psychophysics, 12*, 201–204.

Eriksen, C. W. & Spencer, T. (1969). Rate of information processing in visual perception: Some results and methodological considerations. *Journal of Experimental Psychology Monograph, 79(2)*, 1–16.

Fisher, D. L. (1984). Central capacity limits in consistent mapping, visual search tasks: Four channels or more? *Cognitive Psychology, 16*, 449–484.

Gazzaniga, M. S., Ivry, R. B., & Mangun, G. R. (1998). *Cognitive Neuroscience: The Biology of the Mind*. W. W. Norton, New York.

Gray, J. A. & Wedderburn, A. A. I. (1960). Grouping strategies with simultaneous stimuli. *Quarterly Journal of Experimental Psychology, 12*, 180–184.

He, J. J. & Nakayama, K. (1992). Surfaces vs. features in visual search. *Nature, 359*, 231–233.

Helmholtz, H. (1924). *Helmholtz's treatise on physiological optics*, translated from the 3d German Edition. Edited by James P. C. Southall. Rochester, NY: The Optical Society of America.

Hoffman, J. E. (1975). Hierarchical stages in the processing of visual information. *Perception and Psychophysics, 18*, 348–354.

Hoffman, J. E. (1978). Search through a sequentially presented visual display. *Perception and Psychophysics, 23*, 1–11.

Hoffman, J. E. (1979) A two-stage model of visual search. *Perception and Psychophysics, 25*, 319–327.

Hoffman, J. E. (1998) Attention and eye movements. In H. Pashler (ed.), *Attention* (pp. 119–154). Sussex, UK: Psychology Press.

Hoffman, J. E. & Nelson, B. (1981a) Spatial selectivity in visual search. *Perception and Psychophysics, 30*, 283–290.

Hoffman, J. E. & Nelson, B. (1981b). The nature and role of attentional resources in controlled and automatic detection: A final report. University of Delaware Research Report #8103.

Hoffman, J. E., Nelson, B., & Houck, M. R. (1983). The role of attentional resources in automatic detection. *Cognitive Psychology, 51*, 379–410.

Hoffman, J. E. and Subramanium, B. (1995). The role of visual attention in saccadic eye movements. *Perception and Psychophysics, 57*, 787–795.

Hoffman, J. E. (1998), Visual attention and eye movements. In H. Pashler (ed.), *Attention* (pp. 119–154). East Sussex, UK: Psychology Press.

Houck, M. R. & Hoffman, J. E. Conjunction of color and form without attention: Evidence from an orientation-contingent color aftereffect. *Journal of Experimental Psychology: Human Perception and Performance, 12*, 186–199.

Intraub, H. Rapid conceptual identification of sequentially presented pictures. *Journal of Experimental Psychology: Human Perception and Performance, 7*, 604–610.

Irwin, D. E. (1996). Integrating information across saccadic eye movements. *Current Directions in Psychological Science, 5*, 94–100

Joseph, J. S., Chun, M. M., & Nakayama, K. (1996). Attentional requirements in a "preattentive" feature search task. *Nature, 379*, 805–807

Kinchla, R. A. (1974). Detecting target elements in multielement arrays: A confusability model. *Perception & Psychophysics, 15*, 149–158.

Kleiss, J. A. & Lane, D. M. (1986). Locus and persistence of capacity limitations in visual information processing. *Journal of Experimental Psychology: Human Perception and Performance, 12*, 200–210.

Kowler, E., Anderson, E., Dosher, B., & Blaser, E. (1995). The role of attention in the programming of saccades. *Vision Research, 35*, 1897–1916.

Kramer, A. F., Weber, T. A., & Watson, S. E. (1997). Object-based attentional selection: Grouped arrays or spatially invariant representations? Comment on Vecera and Farah (1994). *Journal of Experimental Psychology: General, 126*, 3–13.

Lavie, N. & Driver, J. (1996). On the spatial extent of attention in object-based visual selection. *Perception and Psychophysics, 58*, 1238–1251

Luck, S. J. (1998) Neurophysiology of selective attention. In H. Pashler (ed.), *Attention* (pp. 257–298). Sussex, UK: Psychology Press

Luck, S. J. & Vogel, E. K. (1997). The capacity of visual working memory for features and conjunctions. *Nature, 390*, 279–281.

Luck, S. J., Vogel, E. K., & Shapiro, K. L. (1996). Word meanings can be accessed but not reported during the attentional blink. *Nature, 383*, 616–618.

McConkie & Currie, C. (1996). Visual stability across saccades while viewing complex pictures. *Journal of Experimental Psychology: Human Perception and Performance, 22*, 563–581.

Milliken, B. & Tipper, S. P. (1998). Attention and inhibition. In H. Pashler (ed.), *Attention* (pp. 191–222). Sussex, UK: Psychology Press

Moran, J. & Desimone, R. (1985). Selective attention gates visual processing in the extrastriate cortex. *Science, 229*, 782–784

Nakayama, K., He, Z. J., & Shimojo, S. (1995). Visual surface representation: a critical link between lower-level and higher level vision. In S. M. Kosslyn and D. N. Osherson (eds.), *Vision Cognition*, Vol.2 in *Invitation to Cognitive Science*. M. I. T. Press, p. 1–70.

Nakayama, K. & Silverman, G. H. (1986a). Serial and parallel processing of visual feature conjunctions. *Nature, 320*, 264–265.

Neisser, U. & Becklen, R. (1975). Selective looking: Attending to visually specified events. *Cognitive Psychology, 7*, 480–494.

Nigam, A., Hoffman, J. E., & Simons, R. F. (1992). N400 and semantic anomaly with pictures and words. *Journal of Cognitive Neuroscience, 4*, 15–22.

Nigam, A., Hoffman, J. E., Simons, R., & Gebhart, A. (1997). A comparison of N400s to objects and words in scenes. Paper presented at the 38th Annual meeting of the Psychonomics Society, Philadelphia, PA. November, 1997.

O'Regan, K. (1992). Solving the "real" mysteries of visual perception. The world as an outside memory. *Canadian Journal of Psychology, 46,* 461–488.

Ostry, D., Moray, N., & Marks, G. (1976). Attention, practice, and semantic targets. *Journal of Experimental Psychology: Human Perception and Performance, 2,* 326–336.

Palmer, J. (1994). Set-size effects in visual search: the effect of attention is independent of the stimulus for simple tasks. *Vision Research, 34,* 1703–1721.

Pashler, H. E. (1998). *The Psychology of Attention.* Cambridge, MA: MIT Press.

Pashler, H. (1988). Familiarity and visual change detection. *Perception & Psychophysics, 44,* 369–378.

Phillips, W. A. (1974). On the distinction between sensory storage and short-term visual memory. *Perception & Psychophysics, 16,* 283–290.

Posner, M. I. (1980). Orienting of attention. *Quarterly Journal of Experimental Psychology, 32,* 3–25.

Raymond, J. E., Shapiro, K. L., & Arnell, K. M. (1992). Temporary suppression of visual processing in an RSVP task: An attentional blink? *Journal of Experimental Psychology: Human Perception & Performance, 18,* 849–860.

Rensink, R. (1997). How much of a scene is seen? The role of attention in scene perception. *Investigative Ophthalmology & Visual Science, 38,* 707.

Rensink, R. A. (in press). Mindsight: visual sensing without seeing. *Investigative Ophthalmology & Visual Science, 39.*

Rensink, R. A. & Enns, J. T. (1998). Early completion of occluded objects. *Vision Research 38,* 2489–2505.

Rensink, R. A. & Enns, J. T. (1995). Pre-emption effects in visual search: evidence for low-level grouping. *Psychological Review, 102(1),* 101–130.

Rensink, R., O'Regan, J. K., & Clark, J. J. (1997). To see or not to see: The need for attention to perceive changes in scenes. *Psychological Science, 8(5),* 368–373.

Rock, I., Linnett, C. M., Grant, P., & Mack, A. (1992). Perception without attention: Results of a new method. *Cognitive Psychology, 24(4),* 502–534.

Shapiro, K., Driver, J., Ward, R., & Sorensen, R. E. (1997). Priming from the attentional blink: A failure to extract visual tokens but not visual types. *Psychological Science, 8,* 95–100.

Shaw, M. L. (1984). Division of attention among spatial locations: A fundamental difference between detection of letters and detection of luminance increments. In H. Bouma and D. G. Bouwhuis (eds.), *Attention and Performance X.* Hillsdale, NJ: Erlbaum.

Shih, S. I. & Sperling, G. (1996). Is there feature-based attentional selection in visual search? *Journal of Experimental Psychology Human Perception and Performance, 22(3),* 758–779

Shiffrin, R. M. & Schneider, W. (1977). Controlled and automatic human information processing: II. Perceptual learning, automatic attending and a general theory. *Psychological Review, 84,* 127–190.

Sperling, G. (1960). The information available in brief visual presentations. *Psychological Monographs: General and Applied,* Whole No. 498, 1–29.

Sperling, G. & Weichselgartner, E. (1995). Episodic theory of the dynamics of visual attention. *Psychological Review, 102(3),* 503–532.

Treisman, A. (1988). Features and objects: The fourteenth Bartlett memorial lecture. *The Quarterly Journal of Experimental Psychology, 40A(2),* 201–237.

Treisman, A. & Gelade, G. (1980). A feature-integration theory of attention. *Cognitive Psychology, 12,* 97–136.

Treisman, A. & Gormican, S. (1988). Feature analysis in early vision: Evidence from search asymmetries. *Psychological Review, 95,* 15–48.

Treisman, A. M. & Schmidt, H. (1982). Illusory conjunctions in the perception of objects. *Cognitive Psychology, 14,* 107–141.

Vecera, S. P. & Farah, M. J. (1994). Does visual attention select objects or locations? *Journal of Experimental Psychology: General, 123(2),* 146–160.

Vogel, E. K., Luck, S. J., & Shapiro, K. L. (1998). Electrophysiological evidence for a postperceptual locus of suppression during the attentional blink. *The Journal of Experimental Psychology: Human Perception and Performance 24,* 1656–1674.

Wickens, C. D. & Long, J. (1995). Object versus space-based models of visual attention: Implications for the design of head-up displays. *The Journal of Experimental Psychology: Applied, 1(3),* 179–193.

Wolfe, J. M. (1994). Guided Search 2.0: A revised model of visual search. *Psychonomic Bulletin and Review, 1(2),* 202–238.

Wolfe, J. M. (1996). Extending Guided Search: Why Guided Search needs a preattentive "item map". In A. Kramer, G. H. Cole, & G. D. Logan (eds.), *Converging operations in the study of visual selective attention* (pp. 247–270). Washington, DC: American Psychological Association.

Wolfe, J. M. (1997). Inattentional amnesia. In V. Coltheart (ed.), *Fleeting Memories.* Cambridge, MA: MIT Press.

Wolfe, J. M. (1998). What can 1,000,000 trials tell us about visual search? *Psychological Science, 9,* 33–39.

Wolfe, J. M., (1998). Visual Search. In H. Pashler (ed.), *Attention* (pp. 13–73). East Sussex, UK: Psychology Press.

Wolfe, J. M. & Bennett, S. C. (1996). Preattentive object files: Shapeless bundles of basic features. *Vision Research, 37,* 25–43.

Wolfe, J. M., Cave, K. R., & Franzel, S. L. (1989). Guided Search: An alternative to the Feature Integration Model for visual search. *The Journal of Experimental Psychology: Human Perception and Performance, 15,* 419–433.

Yantis, S. (1998). Control of visual attention. In H. Pashler (ed.), *Attention* (pp. 223–256). East Sussex, UK: Psychology Press.

CHAPTER 3

Separate memories for visual guidance and explicit awareness

The roles of time and place

Sarah H. Creem   Dennis R. Proffitt

Within the visual system, a dissociation is evident between an explicit awareness of objects in the environment and the on-line visually guided actions made towards these objects. For example, a hill appears steeper than it really is, but a person still ascends it without stumbling. A distance may seem shorter than its physical extent, but it is walked accurately. A brain-damaged patient may fail to recognize the size and form of an object, but shows remarkably accurate guidance of her hand when grasping this object.

Evidence from behavioral studies suggests that although explicit representations of objects or of the environment may be influenced by distortions or biases, direct action with the objects or the environment remains accurate. Moreover, neuropsychological studies find cases in which conscious representations of objects may exist without accurate visual guidance, as well as those in which accurate visual guidance exists without conscious perception. In the visual system, two functionally and anatomically distinct streams have recently been labeled as "what" and "how" visual processing systems (Goodale & Milner, 1992). These pathways have also similarly been named "cognitive" and "motor" (Bridgeman, Lewis, Heit, & Nagle, 1979), "semantic" and "pragmatic" (Jeannerod, 1994; Rossetti, 1998), and "representational" and "sensorimotor" (Paillard, 1991). In each case, these distinctions imply a dissociation between mechanisms mediating conscious awareness of objects in the environment and those subserving on-line visually guided actions.

The difference between the two visual systems lies in the transformations of the information taken in. It is not that different information is used, but rather that information is used in different ways for different purposes. In essence, the "how" system and the "what" system subserve different goals. The "how" system must accommodate actions to the observer's immediate perspective in the world, a perspective that changes with every change in posture or position. Because egocentric coordinates of a target can change rapidly, it is necessary to compute the coordinates for action on a momentary basis. This on-line computation requires the presence of the stimulus in the location in which it is perceived. The "what" system serves a different purpose. It represents the visual world in viewer-invariant frameworks that promote an awareness of the world's persistent structure. Conscious perception uses object- or environment-relative reference systems where attributes and meanings of objects are encoded in relation to themselves or external objects and do not involve momentary egocentric changes needed for action.

Two important issues must be considered given these functional differences between the two systems. The first issue is the role of time. Given that visually guided action is an on-line process dependent on the presence of the stimulus, a logical question arises as to the temporal characteristics of visual guidance. Does a visual guidance *memory* exist after the stimulus is no longer present? Recent research has examined visually guided action after implementing time delays (Bridgeman, Peery, & Anand, 1997; Creem & Proffitt, 1998; Haffenden & Goodale, 1997; Rossetti, 1998). The findings have suggested that accurate visually guided action degrades within a short amount of time. With a longer delay, actions become influenced by the conscious representation of the "what" stream. Because the action system must update information on a momentary basis allowing for changes in object position with respect to the observer, it is logical to predict that memorial visually guided actions would not show the accuracy seen in immediate responses. The question arises, how long does a visual guidance memory last? Recent research shows that the length of this memory is not constant across tasks. Because pointing to a target does not require the same amount of time as walking to that target, it may be the case that memories for these different actions do not persist for the same amount of time. It is useful to think about visual guidance memory in terms of the amount of time needed to execute an appropriate action.

A second concern is the role of place. We found (Creem & Proffitt, 1998) that accurate visual guidance is limited not only by temporal constraints but also by the physical location in which the stimulus is seen. We asked whether the nature of visual guidance as a direct act on the environment required the presence of the environment itself. We compared a motoric judgment of hills at the location of the hill with the same judgment made away from the hill, keeping the short time frame constant. Whereas accurate visual guidance is preserved within the hill location, responses made away from the hill are influenced by an explicit representation. The findings suggest that accurate visual guidance depends on both a short time frame and the presence of the same environment.

This chapter will illustrate the roles of time and place in memory for visual guidance and explicit awareness. Our work involving judgments of geographical slant shows that visual guidance memory for hills lasts for at least two minutes, longer than found in the research on pointing or saccades. Secondly, for judgments of the incline of hills, the response is tied to the location in which the hill was perceived. Our findings suggest that memories for visual guidance and explicit awareness are dissociated in the short term when in the presence of the stimulus. However, with the addition of longer time delays, or by removing the observer from the surroundings, communication between conscious awareness and visual guidance is necessary. Visual guidance memory is not preserved in these cases, and we find that actions are thus informed by the explicit visual representation stored in memory.

1.   Stratification in perception and memory

1.1   *Perceptual awareness and visual guidance*

In perception, a number of behavioral and neuropsychological studies have shown that conscious perception can be dissociated from visually guided actions. For example, Bridgeman and his colleagues asked participants to judge verbally and through pointing or saccadic eye movements whether a target was displaced (Bridgeman, Kirch, & Sperling, 1981; Bridgeman et al., 1979). In several experiments, participants were able to make saccades and point accurately to a displaced target, even though they did not verbally report that they detected the displacement. More recently, researchers have used pictorial illusions as stimuli to illustrate the perception/action dissociation. Haffenden and Goodale (1998) presented participants with the Ebbinghaus illusion in which two same-size disks appear to be different sizes depending on the size of the surrounding circles. Participants gave a perceptual estimation through a manual task of matching the distance between their thumb and index finger to the diameter of the target disk. They also responded with a visuomotor task in which they grasped the disk without the view of their hand. Haffenden and Goodale found that maximum grip aperture corresponded to the actual size of the disk, regardless of the appearance of the disk. In contrast, the manual estimations of disk size were influenced by the illusion. These results help support the dissociation between the mechanisms mediating conscious perception and visually guided action.

Using a more global task, Proffitt, Bhalla, Gossweiler, and Midgett (1995) illustrated a clear dissociation between perceptual and motoric judgments of the incline of hills. Participants judged the slant of a hill from the top or bottom with verbal, visual, and haptic measures. The verbal measure required participants to report the number of degrees that they perceived the hill to be. The visual measure was an adjustment of a disk to equal the perceived cross-section of the hill. In the haptic measure, the participants gave a motoric judgment by adjusting a tilting board with their unseen hand until they felt the slant was equal to the slant of the hill. Proffitt et al. found that participants greatly overestimated the incline of the hill using the verbal and visual measures, but were much more accurate when using the haptic adjustment. These findings were interpreted to be consistent with the previous research on anatomical and functional dissociations between conscious awareness and visually guided actions.

There are numerous other examples of studies performed with both normal participants and neuropsychological patients showing similar dissociations (e.g. Goodale, Jakobson, & Keillor, 1994; Jakobson, Archibald, Carey, & Goodale, 1991; Pelisson, Prablanc, Goodale, & Jeannerod, 1986). These behavioral dissociations correspond to the two streams of visual projections identified in the primate cortex. One stream projects ventrally from the primary visual cortex to the inferotemporal cortex and a second stream projects dorsally from the primary visual cortex to the posterior parietal cortex (Goodale & Milner, 1992). Both non-human primate research and human patient studies support the distinction between the ventral "what" stream and the dorsal "how". However, these systems are clearly dissociated functionally and anatomically only in the short term. When we consider changes in the time course or place of response, interdependence between the systems is seen. When visual guidance is not preserved, actions are influenced by what is consciously perceived.

1.2 *Frames of reference*

The dissociation between conscious awareness and visual guidance lies not only in the type of response, but in the frame of reference utilized to process spatial information. Frames of reference provide a locational structure within which the spatial position of objects and events is specified (Wraga, Creem, & Proffitt, in press). The egocentric frame locates the position of an object relative to a reference frame centered on the observer's body. Object- and environment-relative frames relate the location of things to reference frames that are independent of the observer. The two processing streams utilize different frames of reference in accordance with the different purposes they serve. The "what" system mediates conscious recognition of objects and their characteristics, and thus, may use a viewer-invariant frame of reference. Within this system, object representations last over time and must not be dependent on an ever-changing frame of reference tied to the observer. Thus, the processing of information is predominantly object- or environment-relative.

On the other hand, the "how" stream serves quite a different purpose. A visually guided action requires the updating of spatial information on a momentary basis. The action is dependent on the spatial relationship of the object to the observer. Unlike a task of identity recognition, a visually guided action requires constant updating of the spatial properties of the object in egocentric coordinates. This egocentric coding allows for the direct transformation of information for action.

1.3 A role for time and place

The concepts of both time and place are important in the dissociation between conscious awareness and visual guidance. The temporal influence on perceptual and motor responses has been studied much more than the influence of physical location. However, in terms of distinctions between the two visual systems, both play an important role. The conscious judgment, in terms of time, is semi-permanent. Awareness of object characteristics does not change quickly. As we have described, the conscious system processes attributes of objects with object- or environment-relative frames of reference for long-term representation. In contrast, visual guidance is short-lived. Because of the nature of momentary coordinates needed for accurate visually guided action, visual guidance persists for only a short amount of time. In addition, the length of a visual guidance memory appears to be relevant to the task itself. Just as the amount of time required to point to a target is less than that required to walk to that target, visual guidance memories for more global tasks should last longer than those directed at specific, fleeting ones.

In terms of place, few studies have investigated the effect of the environment in performing conscious perceptual judgments and visually guided actions. For conscious judgments, place, as with time, has little importance. The object-relative frame of reference used to represent the information is unconcerned with the location in which the stimulus was seen. On the contrary, place is very relevant for visual guidance. A visually guided action is performed directly on the object itself. Thus, the guidance is tied to the environment in which the object is perceived.

2. Memory for action and awareness

A number of recent studies have explored the role of time on visually guided actions, most involving egocentric motoric tasks such as directing saccades, pointing, or blind walking. Most recently, Creem and Proffitt (1998) have used an egocentric judgment of the incline of hills. The research together establishes the importance of time and its different relations to conscious awareness and visual guidance. For the conscious perception system, time is not as crucial. The function of this system, one of recognition and identification, uses properties of objects that are long lasting. For example, the size of most objects does not change within a matter of minutes, however the position of the object may change momentarily with respect to the observer. For this reason, time is very important in performing visually guided action. Visuomotor coordinates are computed on-line before each action.

A number of recent neuropsychological studies have looked at temporal factors and visual guidance. Rossetti (1998) showed evidence with a blindsight patient, that visually guided action is constrained by time. Most blindsight patients can direct an action to a stimulus in their blind hemifield without being able to consciously see the stimulus. Rossetti tested a blindsight patient, N.S., on a pointing task by measuring her movement latency. He found that the patient was better at performing the action when her actions were faster. These results suggest that information needed for action is only available for a short time. In all, Rossetti showed that visually guided action degrades rapidly with time and that actions after a delay require information from awareness.

Other patients with damage to either the "what" or "how" systems have been studied to further understand the dissociation. Recently, experiments involving time delays have been incorporated into their testing. An agnosic patient, D.F. has been extensively studied by Goodale and Milner (Goodale, Milner, Jakobson, & Carey, 1991; Milner & Goodale, 1995). As a result of carbon-monoxide poisoning, she experiences severe deficits in conscious perception of object attributes such as size and shape. Areas of her brain that are most damaged are the ventrolateral regions of her occipital lobe. Although she can not recognize objects, she reaches and grasps for them accurately. After establishing her abilities to perform visually guided actions and her disabilities in phenomenal awareness, Goodale et al. (1994) tested her pantomimed reaching actions. She was presented with an object and then was asked to reach for the object two seconds later, with opaque glasses preventing vision of the object. Although she would have no trouble reaching for the object without a delay, her performance was remarkably poor after the two-second delay. The study showed that D.F.'s reaching from memory was completely different from her normal reaching. D.F.'s grasp did not accommodate to the target in any way. These findings are strikingly different from D.F.'s performance with the stimulus present. She, like normal participants, shapes her hand to the size and dimensions of the target object as it approaches the object. However, in memory, all anticipatory hand shaping disappeared.

Interestingly, normal participants were also tested in this task. An analysis of their performance showed differences in the kinematics of reaching from memory, compared to those in the sighted reaching task. In a second condition, the object came back into sight at the end of the two-second period and the participants reached as they had with normal visually guided action. In this condition, the return of the stimulus ensured their accurate action toward the object. This result suggests that visuomotor coordinates are computed immediately before each action. The difference between D.F.'s and the normal participants' behavior is not surprising. D.F. did not have the object in front of her to drive the visuomotor system acting in real time. Unlike normal participants, she also could not refer back to a stored representation of the object because she had no conscious 'percept' of the object from the beginning. Thus, D.F. had no representation to drive her action, as a normal subject would do from memory.

Several studies involving normal participants have examined the distinction between visual awareness and visually guided action with tasks involving a delay between perception and response. Wong and Mack (1981) asked participants to make saccades to a displaced target immediately and then to look back to the original position of the target. Immediately after the presentation of the target, saccades were accurately directed to the actual displacement of the target even though the perceived displacement differed. The performance in the delay condition, however, supports the notion of the influence of time. When participants were asked to look back to the original location of the target, the saccades were made to the perceived location rather than the actual location. These memory-driven saccades were based on the participant's conscious perception of the displacement, in sharp contrast to the immediate saccades that were driven by actual displacements in retinocentric coordinates. Thus, in memory, a stored perceptual representation informs the action from an environmental rather than an egocentric frame of reference.

Bridgeman, Peery, and Anand (1997) recently concluded that visual guidance memory is short-lived and that conscious perception influences motoric responses after a delay. Using the Roelofs effect, in which people tend to misperceive the position of a target in an unstructured field, they created both an immediate and delay condition. They presented participants with a rectangular frame centered on either their midline or 5° left or right of center, with an 'x' placed inside the frame in one of five positions. Participants responded with both a 'cognitive' response, which involved estimating target position with the keyboard, and a motor response, which was made with a hand-held pointer. Without a delay, all participants showed the Roelofs effect in the cognitive judgment, a bias to judge the target to be farther in the opposite direction of the offset of the frame. However, with the motor response, half of the participants did not show the effect. After a four second delay, all participants were biased by the frame position in the motoric task. Bridgeman et al. concluded that introducing a long enough delay before the response required participants to use the cognitive information biased by the frame position.

Visual illusions have become a helpful tool for exhibiting the dissociation between awareness and visually guided action. The nature of illusions, perceiving something different from its physical reality, allows for creative investigation into the separation and communication of the two visual streams. Gentilucci, Chieffi, Daprati, Saetti, and Toni (1996) tested participants with the Muller-Lyer illusion, introducing several different conditions involving variations in time and visual feedback. In this illusion, a line is judged to be shorter or longer depending on the open or closed characteristic of the arrows on each end. The study included four experimental conditions in which participants were asked to point to an endpoint of the line without paying attention to the surrounding scene. The first was a full-vision condition in which both the stimulus and the hand could be seen. The second was no-visual-feedback condition that involved an open-loop response, meaning that participants could see the stimulus but not their hand. The last two conditions were completed without vision (lights were turned off) with either a 0 or 5 second delay. Although the illusion affected all conditions, the illusion effect differed between conditions. Participants overshot the endpoint with the open characteristic and undershot with the closed characteristic. More importantly, the effect of the illusion on pointing position increased in the memory (no-vision) conditions. The largest effect of the illusion was seen in the no-vision 5-second delay condition. Gentilucci et al. proposed that in no vision conditions, the efficiency of egocentric cues is reduced, and environmental or contextual information interacts to guide movement.

Another recent study has been conducted using time delays and the Ebbinghaus illusion. As mentioned earlier, Haffenden and Goodale (1998) showed a dissociation between a manual response of the perceived size of the disk, matching the distance between thumb and index finger, and a measure of grip aperture when grasping the disc. The manual estimates of size were biased by the illusion, although the grip aperture was dependent on the physical, not the perceived, size of the target. Haffenden & Goodale (1997) also compared a no-delay condition with a two-second delay. Without a delay, grip aperture was highly correlated with physical size, but after the delay, grip aperture was strongly influenced by the illusion.

The task of walking to a target without vision has also been used to illustrate accurate visual guidance and the duration of a visual guidance memory. Thomson (1983) asked participants to walk to targets ranging from 3 to 21 meters away with eyes open or closed. He found that they were accurate in both conditions up to 9 meters. An increase in variability for eyes closed was found at 12 meters or greater. Thomson then introduced a delay between sight of the target and the walking action. He found that with increasingly longer delays, only shorter distances could be walked accurately. He concluded that 8 seconds was the maximum length of a memory for walking. However, other studies did not find evidence supporting these conclusions.

For example, Steenhuis and Goodale (1988) conducted a study that investigated short-term memory for spatial location, also using blindwalking as their measure. They asked participants to walk to a target with their eyes closed, immediately after viewing the target, or with 2, 4, or 30 second delays. Unlike Thomson, they concluded that short-term memory of target locations decays slowly over periods of time. There was no difference in performance for 2 or 4 second delays compared with immediate walking. Even though participants were less accurate after a 30 second delay, the delay did not affect constant errors. Thus, they found more variability with time, but no systematic errors, suggesting that a memory for spatial location lasts over a short period of time of about 30 seconds. Further studies of goal-directed locomotion have replicated the findings of Steenhuis and Goodale (Elliot, Jones, & Gray, 1990), where 2 second delays had no effect on performance and more variable error resulted with a 30 second delay.

Furthermore, recent research involving both a spatial localization and blind-walking task found evidence for the persistence and slowly decaying function of visual guidance information (Tyrrell, Rudolph, Eggers, & Leibowitz, 1993). In a series of studies, Tyrrell et al. asked participants to position a light at a previously viewed target or walk down a previously viewed path after varying amounts of delay. They found that participants were able to perform on both tasks without the visual presence of the stimulus, and that their performance decayed gradually over 60 seconds.

2.1 *Two memories for geographical slant*

Although there are a good number of recent studies concerned with the temporal factors of visual guidance, Creem and Proffitt's (1998) study on memory for geographical slant addressed the importance of place, as well as time, in the interaction of conscious awareness and visual guidance. The action system does not only work in real-time, but depends on the stimulus to which it is directed. For this reason, the presence of the stimulus should be a necessary part of accurate visually guided action. Creem and Proffitt's studies examined the importance of both time and location in judging the incline of hills around the grounds of the University of Virginia.

Previous studies of geographical slant perception have shown that hills appear to be steeper than they really are (Bhalla & Proffitt, in press; Proffitt et al., 1995). These studies, as mentioned earlier, involved three response measures, verbal, visual, and haptic. The verbal measure was a verbal report of the participant's perception of the incline of the hill. The visual measure was a matching task, in which the participant was instructed to adjust a disk that represented the cross section of the hill. The disk consisted of an adjustable angle that could be set to the perceived inclination of the hill. The haptic measure was given on a tilt board, adjusted by the participant's palm without looking at the hand, until the participant felt the incline was equal to that of the hill.

These three measures can be differentiated by the frame of reference used, and thus, the visual processing system thought to mediate the response. The verbal and visual responses call for the participants to judge the slant of the hill with respect to the environmental horizontal, requiring an environmental reference frame supplied by the "what" system. In contrast, knowledge of the horizontal is completely unnecessary for the adjustment made on the tilt board. This task is purely egocentric. Participants need only to move their hand so as to make it parallel to the slant of the hill. Since the haptic response does not require participants to relate the incline of the hills to the horizontal, the response can be guided by underlying processes that need not represent geographical slant at all. The haptic response is, thus, represented in an egocentric framework provided by the "how" system.

The findings of the Proffitt studies illustrated that participants overestimated the incline of hills when giving a verbal or visual report, but were much more accurate when giving the haptic estimate. Furthermore, Bhalla and Proffitt (in press) found that conscious overestimations increased with manipulations of behavior potential such as fatigue, physical fitness, and age/health, but motoric judgments remained accurate. Proffitt et al. related the differences between verbal/visual and haptic responses to the different purposes of conscious awareness and motoric actions. The perceived exaggeration in conscious slant perception provides information to help inform us about the possibility of traversing a given hill. Long-term planning is a task of the conscious perception system.

However, the act of traversing an incline demands a veridical evaluation of the environment. The accuracy of the haptic measure suggests that visually guided actions are immune to slant overestimations. Although people may perceive a hill to be much steeper than it is, they do not stumble when walking over the terrain.

The studies of Proffitt et al. and Bhalla and Proffitt also involved a measure of internal consistency, showing communication as well as separation of phenomenal awareness and visually guided action. In this measure, participants made haptic estimates on the tilt board in response to verbal instructions. The haptic adjustment performed in response to a given verbal instruction was internally consistent with responses given while viewing hills. For example, when participants viewed a 10° hill, they called it 30° and adjusted the board to about 10°. When the participants were not looking at the hill, and were simply told to set the board to 30°, they set the board to 10° again. Thus, an internal consistency was found between verbal representations and the haptic adjustments.

Based on the dissociation seen in Proffitt et al. (1995) and knowledge of the importance of time from other studies of visual guidance, Creem and Proffitt (1998) asked what would happen when a hill judgment was given after time delay and/or a change of location. People were asked to judge the slant of familiar hills from memory giving both a verbal and motoric response. This task led to two important findings. First, verbal overestimations increased in memory beyond those given when viewing the hills. Second, motoric responses differed depending on the length of time delay and the location of the response. When participants were given a short time delay and remained at the location of the hill, their motoric responses remained accurate as in the perceptual conditions. However, when a longer delay was introduced, or the participant was taken to a new location away from the hill, motoric responses increased proportionately with the verbal responses from memory. Thus, hill judgments were made both in the presence of the hill and in a new location, quickly after viewing the hill, or with much longer delays. Each of these experiments will be described further as evidence for separation of memories for visual guidance and explicit awareness in the short term, and communication as a result of changes in time and place.

2.2 *Memorial judgments given in the presence of the hill*

As in the Proffitt et al. (1995) studies, participants viewed a real hill binocularly from the front while standing at the base of the hill. However, in the memory studies (Creem & Proffitt, 1998), they were not explicitly told that they would be making judgments about the slant of the hill. Instead, they were instructed to try to remember the environment that they saw in front of them. Three different hills

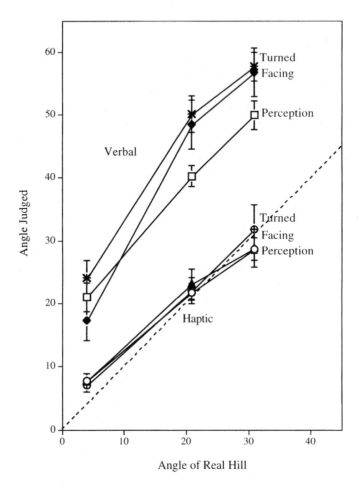

Figure 1. *Mean judgments (+/- SE) for Turned, Facing, and Perception conditions as a function of hill angle.*

around the grounds of the University of Virginia were used with inclines of 4°, 21°, and 31°. One hill was a sidewalk and the other two were grassy inclines. After looking at the hill for about 10 seconds, the participants performed in one of two conditions. They either remained facing the hill, closed their eyes, and performed the verbal and haptic response (on the tilting board as described earlier) or they turned around and with eyes closed made the same judgments. Participants performed one trial at only one of the hills and were given no feedback on their responses. The delay between sight of the hill and either method of response was no more than two minutes.

In this first experiment, slant judgments were made after a relatively short delay in the presence of the hill. As in all of the memory experiments we will describe, verbal responses increased beyond those given when viewing the hills. However, the haptic judgments remained the same as in the perceptual studies for both the facing and turned conditions. Interestingly, there was no difference between the haptic facing and turned responses. Figure 1 compares the facing and turned conditions with the perceptual condition taken from Proffitt et al. (1995). These results lead us to believe that visual guidance memory for geographical slant remains separate from a memory informing explicit awareness for a time frame of at least two minutes in the presence of the hill.

This experiment, however, leaves some questions unanswered. Based on the previous research involving time delays, we predicted that explicit awareness of the hill would influence visual guidance after a longer delay. Thus, the separation of memories for visual guidance and explicit awareness would no longer exist. In creating a longer time delay, we also implemented a change in location. Thus, the next set of experiments was conducted away from the original hills.

2.3 Memorial judgments given away from the hill

2.3.1 Long delay
We conducted several different experiments involving judgments made away from the hill location. The first involved a one-day delay between sight of the hill and response. Participants were taken to the three different hills and told to remember the layout of the environment, although hill slant was not mentioned. They were asked to return to the laboratory the next day for some questions about what they saw. The following day, participants were asked to imagine the place to which they had been taken, to picture the hill in front them, and to give the verbal and haptic judgments. Participants gave slant judgments about all three of the hills.

The results of this experiment differed from the two minute delay experiment. Once again, memorial verbal judgments increased compared those given in the perceptual condition. Most importantly, haptic judgments increased as well. Figure 2 shows these results. These findings support the conclusions of much of the literature on visual guidance memory. When the action system cannot operate on it's own (given time delays or a change of location), the conscious system works to inform the action.

It is important to note why the haptic response does not increase to match the verbal response, but rather increases proportionately. These results are

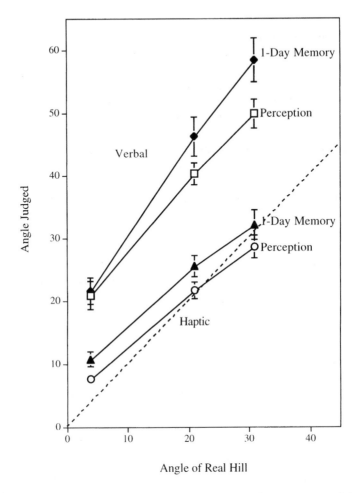

Figure 2. *Mean judgments (+/– SE) for 1-day Memory and Perception conditions as a function of hill angle.*

consistent with Proffitt et al.'s findings of internal consistency. They showed an internal mapping between the awareness of slant and visually guided action. A person looking at a 10° hill will report that it is 30°, but motorically respond on the tilt board at 10°. The same person, when verbally instructed to set the tilt board to 30° will set it to 10°. Thus, the motor adjustment of 10° corresponds to an explicit awareness of 30°, whether both are informed by direct perception of

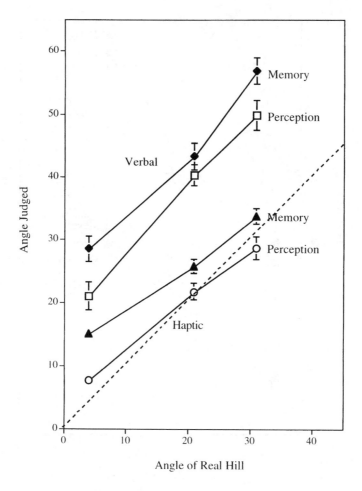

Figure 3. *Mean judgments (+/− SE) for Memory and Perception condition as a function of hill angle.*

the hill, or explicit verbal instructions. Following this reasoning, in the internal consistency measure, a verbal instruction to set the tilt board to 30° or 35° will lead a person to set it to about 10° or 12°, respectively. In memory, a person explicitly remembers a 10° hill to look 35° instead of 30°. If the explicit memory is informing both verbal and haptic responses, then we would expect a verbal report of 35° and a motoric response of about 12°.

Another study was conducted to assess memory for hills over the long-term.

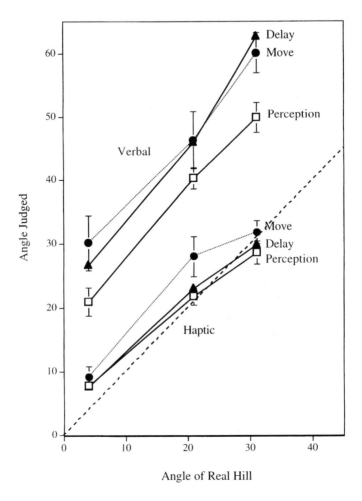

Figure 4. *Mean judgments (+/− SE) for Move, Delay, and Perception conditions as a function of hill angle.*

Because the hills used were familiar ones around campus, participants could be brought into the lab and asked to imagine these hills without having been shown them explicitly. In this way, we were able to determine the participants' long-term representation of the hills. In the laboratory, participants listened to descriptions of the locations of each hill. They were asked to imagine each particular hill and then to give a verbal and haptic judgment. If they were not certain of the hill we were describing, they were not included in the study. Figure 3 shows that the results of this experiment replicated the one-day delay experiment. Both verbal and haptic responses increased systematically in memory compared to perception. These findings suggest again the need for input from conscious awareness to guide action when time has been introduced.

2.3.2 Short delay

The experiments thus far show separate memories for visual guidance and awareness in the short term and the influence of explicit memory on visual guidance in the long term. However, in the former case, participants remained at the hill location and in the latter, participants gave their responses in a new location. It was necessary to create a situation with a short time delay but including a change in location. The fourth experiment was carried out for this purpose. After viewing a hill, participants either walked to a new location out of sight of the hill to give their responses (Move condition), or turned around to respond at the hill (Delay condition). Participants responded to only one of the three hills. Both conditions required no more than two minutes between viewing the hill and responding.

The design of this experiment stressed the importance of location of response in addition to time. The memorial verbal reports increased for both the Move and Delay conditions compared to the perception condition. As for the haptic response, only the Move condition increased along with the verbal reports (see Figure 4). These results suggest that the visual guidance memory system is tied to the spatial location in which it is formed. When the participants were present at the hill, their visual guidance remained accurate, separate from the increase in conscious awareness of the incline. However, within the same time frame, participants who left the hill site showed an increase in their visually guided response consistent with the increase in verbal report. A preservation of place is very important for accurate visually guided action.

The move/delay experiment clearly suggests the importance of the presence of the stimulus in guiding action. With a two minute delay, motoric responses increased when the participant was taken to a new location but stayed the same when the participant remained in the presence of the hill. One might suppose, however, that it was the act of walking, not the change in location, that disrupted the visual guidance memory. A last experiment was designed to test this possibility. Participants viewed one hill ($21°$) and then either walked to a new location (Move condition) or marched in place (March condition) for two minutes. In this way, the motor act performed between sight of the hill and

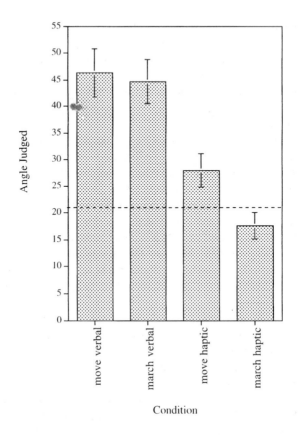

Figure 5. *Mean verbal and haptic judgments (+/- SE) for Move and March conditions for the 21° hill.*

response was the same. The only difference between the two conditions was a change in location for the response.

The findings of this experiment support the claim for the importance of location. Figure 5 indicates that for verbal reports, there was no difference between the Move and March conditions. However, haptic responses were greater for the Move condition compared to the March condition. Although the participants overestimated their motoric responses after walking to a new location, they remained accurate after walking in place. Thus, it was the change in location and not the walking movement which disrupted the visual guidance memory.

2.4 *Geographical slant conclusions*

In all, the memorial geographical slant experiments suggest two memory systems for hills that operate differently depending on the length of delay and the response location. Across all of the experiments, verbal reports increased beyond those given in the perception studies. The haptic responses, however, differed depending on the time and location components. With a short delay, motoric responses made at the hill remained accurate. Responses given away from the hill with the same delay, however, increased proportionately with the verbal response. Here, the importance of place as well as time is seen. These results suggest that the explicit representation of the hill informed the action because the action had been tied to the location in which the stimulus was seen. The experiments involving longer delays indicated similar findings. In the one-day delay and the general memory for hills studies, haptic responses increased as well. The studies together suggest that while the same explicit memory is informing verbal slant judgments in all experiments, different memory systems inform motor behaviors. With a short delay, in the hill location, the motoric response is guided by a visual guidance memory whereas the verbal response is guided by a separate explicit memory. With longer delays, or a change in response location, both motoric and verbal responses are guided by the same explicit representation.

3. Conclusions

The research discussed in this chapter suggests the importance of considering both time and place in the relationship between conscious awareness and visually guided action. It is evident that there is both separation and interdependence between the two systems. Although we experience one consistent visual world, there is clear evidence of a stratification of systems within visual processing *in the short-term*. Two streams projecting from the primary visual cortex can be differentiated by the purposes they serve. The ventral stream, leading to the inferotemporal cortex, transforms information of object identity for conscious awareness using environmental or object-relative frames of reference. The dorsal stream, projecting to the posterior parietal cortex, uses information in preparation for visually guided behavior based on an egocentric coordinate system.

All of the studies show that when time delays are introduced, memories for action and awareness remain separate for a brief amount of time. In studies involving saccades, pointing, or grasping, it is a matter of seconds. With blind-walking or hill judgments, the duration is as long as two minutes. After longer time delays, actions become dependent on conscious awareness. In the long-term, explicit memories inform both the visually guided action and phenomenal awareness. Thus, communication between the two systems is evident. Moreover, we have shown that the location of response is also quite important for accurate visually guided action. Without the presence of the environment in which the stimulus was seen, the action system again relies on input from awareness to guide its movements. Visual guidance memory remains separate from explicit memory in the short-term in the presence of the stimulus. However, visual guidance becomes dependent on explicit awareness with a longer delay or a change in location of response.

The frames of reference used by each of the systems also relate to issues of time and place. The action system's use of an egocentric coordinate system is much influenced by time. It works in real time to constantly update spatial information relative to the observer. For similar reasons, location of response is important to the visually guided response. An on-line action must be directed toward an object present in a specific environment. When that environment changes, the visual guidance is not preserved. On the contrary, time and observer-relative place are somewhat irrelevant to the system mediating conscious awareness. Tasks involving object recognition and phenomenal awareness do not depend on momentary updating of spatial information. They are centered on the properties of the object itself, and not its relation to the observer.

In all, the study of time and place in relation to the two visual systems allows for a greater understanding of the mechanisms each subserves. It becomes clear that two separate systems in perception and in memory function only under some circumstances. When time delays and location changes are introduced, interdependence between the two systems is a necessary occurrence.

References

Bhalla, M. & Proffitt D.R. (in press). Visual-motor recalibration in geographical slant. *Journal of Experimental Psychology: Human Perception and Performance.*

Bridgeman, B., Kirch, M., & Sperling, A. (1981). Segregation of cognitive and motor aspects of visual function using induced motion. *Perception & Psychophysics, 29,* 336–342.

Bridgeman, B., Lewis, S., Heit, G., & Nagle, M. (1979). Relation between cognitive and motor-oriented systems of visual position perception. *Journal of Experimental Psychology: Human Perception and Performance, 5*(4), 692–700.

Bridgeman, B., Peery, S., & Anand, S. (1997). Interaction of cognitive and sensorimotor maps of visual space. *Perception & Psychophysics, 59(3),* 456–469.

Creem, S. H. & Proffitt, D. R. (1998). Two memories for geographical slant: Separation and interdependence of action and awareness. *Psychonomic Bulletin & Review, 5(1),* 22–36.

Elliot, D., Jones, R., & Gray, S. (1990). Short-term memory for spatial location in goal-directed locomotion. *Bulletin of the Psychonomic Society, 28(2),* 158–160.

Gentilucci, M., Chieffi, S., Daprati, E., Saetti, M. C., & Toni, I. (1996). Visual illusion and action. *Neuropsychologia, 34(5),* 369–376.

Goodale, M. & Milner, A. D. (1992). Separate visual pathways for perception and action. *Trends in Neuroscience, 15,* 20–25.

Goodale, M. A., Jakobson, L. S., & Keillor, J. M. (1994). Differences in the visual control of pantomimed and natural grasping movements. *Neuropsychologia, 32,* 1159–1178.

Goodale, M. A., Milner, A. D., Jakobson, L. S., & Carey, D. P. (1991). A neurological dissociation between perceiving objects and grasping them. *Nature, 349,* 154–156.

Haffenden, A. M. & Goodale, M. A. (1997). Temporal properties of the mechanisms underlying visually guided prehension. *Investigative Ophthalmology & Visual Science Abstracts, 38,* S988.

Haffenden, A. M. & Goodale, M. A. (1998). The effect of pictorial illusion on prehension and perception. *Journal of Cognitive Neuroscience, 10(1),* 122–136.

Jakobson, L. S., Archibald, Y. M., Carey, D. P., & Goodale, M. A. (1991). A kinematic analysis of reaching and grasping movements in a patient recovering from optic ataxia. *Neuropsychologia, 29,* 803–809.

Jeannerod, M. (1994). The representing brain: Neural correlates of motor intention and imagery. *The Behavioral and Brain Sciences, 17,* 187–245.

Milner, A. D. & Goodale, M. A. (1995). *The Visual Brain in Action.* Oxford: Oxford University Press.

Paillard, J. (1991). Motor and representational framing of space. In J. Paillard (ed.), *Brain and Space.* Oxford: Oxford University Press.

Pelisson, D., Prablanc, C., Goodale, M. A., & Jeannerod, M. (1986). Visual control of reaching movements without vision of the limb. *Experimental Brain Research, 62,* 303–311.

Proffitt, D. R., Bhalla, M., Gossweiler, R., & Midgett, J. (1995). Perceiving geographical slant. *Psychonomic Bulletin & Review, 2(4),* 409–428.

Rossetti, Y. (1998). Implicit short-lived motor representations of space in brain damaged and healthy subjects. *Consciousness an Cognition, 7,* 520–558.

Steenhuis, R. E. & Goodale, M. A. (1988). The effects of time and distance on accuracy of target-directed locomotion: does an accurate short-term memory for spatial location exist? *Journal of Motor Behavior, 20(4),* 399–415.

Thomson, J. A. (1983). Is continuous visual monitoring necessary in visually guided locomotion. *Journal of Experimental Psychology: Human Perception and Performance, 9(3),* 427–443.

Tyrrell, R. A., Rudolph, K. K., Eggers, B. G., Leibowitz, H. W. (1993). Evidence for the persistence of visual guidance information. *Perception & Psychophysics, 54(4)*, 431–438.

Wong, E. & Mack, A. (1981). Saccadic programming and perceived location. *Acta Psychologica, 48*, 123–131.

Wraga, M., Creem, S. H., & Proffitt, D. R. (in press). Spatial frames of reference in perceiving and acting. In M. K. McBeath, S. Fountain, & J. Banks (eds.) *Navigational principles in humans, animals, and machines*. Thousand Oaks, CA: Sage Publ.

PART II

Stratification of memory tasks

PREFACE

Levels of encoding and retrieval

Fergus I.M. Craik

In what sense might memory tasks be "stratified"? This is the question posed in the present section, and addressed in a variety of ways by authors of the following four chapters. Thinking about the question myself, it seemed useful to first divide memory tasks into those aspects concerned with encoding and those concerned with retrieval. The encoding question brings me back to familiar ground — the work stemming from the Craik and Lockhart (1972) paper — and I will discuss these issues for the most part in this preface. But "levels of retrieval"? How might retrieval tasks be stratified?

In his chapter, Challis gives one answer to this question; the suggestion is that implicit sources of represented information first generate potential solutions to the current memory query, then explicit processes act on this generated information to select, edit, and check for relevance. Banks and his colleagues address a similar point by asking whether memory may be stratified into unconscious and conscious realms, with conscious processes again acting to edit information drawn from the unconscious component. They ultimately reject this version of the model, suggesting instead that information from conscious and unconscious sources are combined continuously into a single memory representation. The chapters by Velichkovsky and by Nelson and his colleagues talk more about the *interaction* of encoded representations (which may be stratified in various ways) with the different uses of these representations as exemplified by the combination of the person's goals and different retrieval tasks.

The point that observed memory performance reflects an interaction between the nature of the stored representation and the nature of the retrieval task is undeniable. Further, the nature of the stored representation will be determined largely by the processes operating during encoding, and the retrieval task can be understood in terms of the cues provided, the instructions to the subject, and the subject's ostensible goals — to complete a word fragment, for example, or to recollect an episodic event. These necessary interactions between encoding and retrieval processes were stressed by Tulving in his encoding specificity principle (Tulving & Thomson, 1973), by Kolers in his ideas on repetition of operations (Kolers, 1973), and by proponents of transfer-appropriate processing (Morris, Bransford, & Franks, 1977; Roediger, Weldon, & Challis, 1989). But do these arguments necessarily imply that no one form of encoding is inherently superior to any other form, that we cannot make any statement about the potential memory performance associated with a specific type of encoding without knowing the precise details of the retrieval test?

This goes too far in my opinion. The influential article by Morris et al. (1977) demonstrated that rhyme-related encoding was superior to semantic encoding when the retrieval test was one of rhyme recognition; but it is also worth noting that when encoding and retrieval were compatible, the semantic-semantic combination led to substantially higher levels of recognition than the rhyme-rhyme combination, .68 vs. .40 averaged over Experiments 1 and 2. In my opinion it is useful to speak about different levels of encoded representations, and to maintain that some types of representation have the potential to yield higher levels of memory performance than others, assuming that the optimal retrieval cue is provided (Moscovitch & Craik, 1976). In the remainder of this short essay I will outline some current thoughts on levels of processing (LOP) as we approach the new millennium! (see also a review by Lockhart & Craik, 1990).

1.1 What is depth of processing?

One of the main criticisms of the LOP viewpoint has been the vagueness of the shallow-deep dimension. What is meant by "deep processing" exactly? The notion of a continuum of processing types running from "shallow" sensory analyses to "deep" analyses of meaning and implication is readily grasped at an intuitive or common sense level. Seamon and Virostek (1978) demonstrated that point by having subjects rate the depth of 12 different encoding operations, then showing that these subjective ratings correlated highly with later memory performance. But can we characterize deep processing in a more objective manner?

Part of the problem of doing this in a satisfactory way is that "deep" signifies "meaningful", and there does not appear to be a relevant theory of meaning that we can buy into. Until such a theory is formulated we may have to content ourselves with a description of some characteristics of depth of processing that the theory will have to incorporate. First, the phrase "deeper levels of processing" implies the involvement of abstract, schematic, conceptual information, whose representations have been formed from the common features of a large number of individual instances; in this sense deeper levels of processing correspond to higher levels of abstraction. Presumably such representations capture the essence of categories and concepts, and the gist of statements and narratives. Incoming stimuli can therefore be categorized and understood in terms of these distillates of past experience, and new examples can be generated from the existing prototypes. In this sense schematic representations can serve both to 'compress' and classify novel inputs, and also to 'expand' and create new outputs that embody the essential features of the concept in question. In turn, this means that such schematic representations must involve rules that may be used both for analysis and for creative reconstruction.

Other necessary features of schematic representations include their ability to draw inferences and make implications that go beyond the information presented. Thus a deeply processed pattern is meaningfully enriched on the basis of past experience. It also seems likely that deeper-level representations are more interconnected than are shallow-level representations. That is, surface characteristics such as color, shape, and texture do not predict each other in shallow representations, whereas a higher-level concept such as "fruit-orange" incorporates a specific set of surface features. This aspect of deeper-level processing enables a perceived stimulus to be elaborated in terms of a prototype, while also being specified in terms of the current sensory input. In a sense, then, deeper-level representations function in a way that is analogous to a theoretical framework in science — a coherent set of interconnected principles that enable us to interpret and understand sensory data.

Higher-level (or deeper) processing is often associated with language, but as we have pointed out previously (Lockhart & Craik, 1990) deeper-level concepts are not necessarily linguistic. A grand master in chess can process a complex pattern deeply, as can a professional wine-taster or a skilled musician. In this sense deep processing is a product of expertise (Bransford, Franks, Morris, & Stein, 1979), and indeed there is a great deal of evidence that experts have phenomenal memories for events and patterns in their specific domain of expertise.

So why is deeper-level processing associated with higher levels of memory in subsequent tests? Our previous answer to this central question still seems reasonable: First, deeper processing yields a record of the original event that is *distinctive* in terms of the relevant, meaningful, schematic operations. Second, the interconnected schematic structure of such deeper representations facilitates the processes of reconstruction at the time of retrieval (Lockhart & Craik, 1990).

1.2 Circularity and the elusive "independent index"

Critics of the depth-of-processing framework have justifiably pointed to the circularity inherent in our arguments. That is, there has been a tendency to define deep processing as 'that type of processing associated with high levels of memory performance'. The previous section attempted to describe some general characteristics of deeper processing separated from the memory consequences of such processing, but clearly it would be more satisfactory to have an objective index of depth. At first it seems as if processing time, or processing effort, or the amount of attentional resources required to carry out the processing, should be suitable candidates; but in my view these measures all fail because of the confounding factors of practice and expertise. That is, a highly meaningful, familiar type of stimulus will be processed deeply (and be well remembered) with a minimal expenditure of time, effort, and attentional resources. Good examples are board positions to a chess expert, novel melodies to a skilled musician, and pictures of scenes to normal adults. In fact it may be difficult to *prevent* deep processing of highly meaningful stimuli such as pictures. In his critical review of the LOP work, Baddeley (1978) complained that levels of processing appeared to be relevant to verbal stimuli only, given that pictures were only slightly affected by different orienting tasks. My answer to this criticism is that meaningful pictures are processed deeply *regardless* of the nominal orienting task, and this assertion is borne out in data reported by Grady, McIntosh, Rajah, and Craik (1998).

It seems to me, therefore, that any valid independent index of depth must reflect the final representation achieved by the processing sequence, and not simply measure the ease or difficulty of achieving that representation. Velichkovsky (Chapter 7) reports interesting data linking longer visual fixations to deeper processing; it is a nice suggestion that a greater *proportion* of longer fixation times indicates a mental set to process items more deeply. In fact, with the *same items* (e.g., words of a given frequency class) longer fixation times, as well as longer decision times, more attention and more effort, may all index deeper processing of these specific items. The difficulty comes when items of a different type are compared.

Other contenders for the "independent index" prize include a reduction in heart-rate variability when deeply-processed words are retrieved (Vincent, Craik, & Furedy, 1996), and changes in evoked potentials (Sanquist, Rohrbaugh, Syndulko, & Lindsley, 1980). Perhaps specific measures of brain function hold out the greatest hope for a universally satisfactory measure; some initial work in this domain is described in a final section.

1.3 *Are levels of processing truly "stratified"?*

One of our early critics (T.O. Nelson, 1977) suggested that the term "levels" was misleading, in that there was no convincing evidence for a fixed single sequence of levels from shallow to deep as was implied in the Craik and Lockhart paper. Nelson maintained instead that "types of processing" was a more appropriate term. This point had already been partly acknowledged by Lockhart, Craik, and Jacoby (1976). In that article we suggested that the term "domains of processing" might capture the undeniable differences between the types of processing necessary for words, pictures, melodies, faces, mathematical equations, etc., etc. However *within* a particular domain of processing the notion of a stratified series of levels of analysis still seems quite reasonable, with early analyses concerned with the sensory characteristics of the stimulus, and later (deeper) analyses concerned more with the meaningful implications of the stimulus in terms of the perceiver's past experience and accumulated knowledge and expertise in that specific domain. This "levels of analysis" formulation was proposed originally by Anne Treisman (1964, 1979) in her theory of attention, and extended to the study of memory by Craik and Lockhart (1972).

In our 1972 paper Lockhart and I stressed that the "levels" we were talking about were not "levels of memory" but rather levels of general cognitive processing, running from early data-driven sensory analyses to later conceptually-driven analyses of meaning and implication. By this view there is no self-contained "memory module"; rather, memory is a by-product of the general processes of perception and comprehension. Attention and memory are intimately linked in this model, since it is attentional processes that largely determine how deeply a stimulus is processed. Given that early sensory analyses are typically run off in a parallel, automatic fashion, compared to the serial, controlled processing of deeper semantic analyses, it follows that attentional resources (and attentional control) play an increasingly large part as processing moves from shallow to deep.

In summary, the LOP viewpoint strongly endorses a stratified view of cognition and memory. As processing progresses from early/shallow to later/deeper analyses, the qualitative nature of processing changes from sensory to semantic, the type of processing changes from parallel to serial, and the role of explicit conscious control becomes progressively more dominant.

1.4 *Levels of processing and the brain*

Shortly after the Craik and Lockhart paper came out I met Brenda Milner briefly in Montreal. She was complimentary, but had an awkward question: "How is it that my amnesic patients can perceive and comprehend meaning perfectly well, yet they cannot remember?" Presumably the answer must be along the lines that deep processing is necessary but not sufficient for later episodic memory. Since amnesia is often associated with damage to hippocampal and medial-temporal areas of the brain, it seems necessary to acknowledge that structures in this region carry out some crucial function of consolidation or binding. The details of this function are still under active debate (see for example Nadel & Moscovitch, 1997; Squire, 1992), although empirical findings from neuroimaging, animal, and human lesion studies are accumulating rapidly. In one interesting recent paper Tulving and his colleagues reported a meta-analysis showing that encoding was associated with PET activations in anterior regions of the hippocampus, whereas retrieval processes were associated with activations in posterior regions (Lepage, Habib, & Tulving, 1998).

More direct evidence linking LOP to specific brain functions comes from studies of the frontal lobes. In a positron emission tomography (PET) study, Kapur, Craik, and colleagues (1994) reported that deeper processing of verbal materials was associated with activation of the left prefrontal cortex. This association between the processing of meaning and activation of the left frontal lobe has also been reported by other groups of cognitive neuroscientists. However, it is quite unlikely that such activations represent the storage site for deeply processed items since *retrieval* of the same information is associated with activations in the *right* frontal lobe (Tulving et al., 1994). Rather, these frontal activations probably signal the control processes involved in encoding and retrieval respectively, with the products of processing operations being stored in material-specific regions in posterior regions of the cortex (e.g., Nyberg et al., 1995). In conclusion, it seems to me that the exciting new techniques of cognitive neuroscience can complement the existing evidence from cognitive science, experimental psychology, and neuropsychology to expand our understanding of the stratified nature of memory and cognition.

Acknowledgments

I would like to thank Jacob Ross for useful discussions of many of the issues covered in this preface.

References

Baddeley, A. D. (1978). The trouble with levels: A re-examination of Craik and Lockhart's framework for memory research. *Psychological Review, 85,* 139–152.

Bransford, J. D., Franks, J. J., Morris, C. D., & Stein, B. S. (1979). Some general constraints on learning and memory research. In L. S. Cermak & F. I. M. Craik (eds.), *Levels of processing in human memory* (pp. 331–354). Hillsdale, NJ: Erlbaum.

Craik, F. I. M. & Lockhart, R. S. (1972). Levels of processing: A framework for memory research. *Journal of Verbal Learning and Verbal Behavior, 11,* 671–684.

Grady, C. L., McIntosh, A. R., Rajah, M. N., & Craik, F. I. M. (1998). Neural correlates of the episodic encoding of pictures and words. *Proceedings of the National Academy of Sciences, U. S. A., 95,* 2703–2708.

Kapur, S., Craik, F. I. M., Tulving, E., Wilson, A. A. Houle, S., & Brown, G. (1994). Neuroanatomical correlates of encoding in episodic memory: Levels of processing effect. *Proceedings of the National Academy of Sciences, USA, 91,* 2008–2011.

Kolers, P. A. (1973). Remembering operations. *Memory and Cognition, 1,* 347–355.

Lepage, M., Habib, R., & Tulving, E. (1998). Hippocampal PET activations of memory encoding and retrieval: The HIPER model, *Hippocampus, 8,* 313–322.

Lockhart, R. S. & Craik, F. I. M. (1990). Levels of processing: A retrospective commentary on a framework for memory research. *Canadian Journal of Psychology, 44,* 87–112.

Lockhart, R. S., Craik, F. I. M., & Jacoby, L. L. (1976). Depth of processing, recognition and recall. In J. Brown (ed.), *Recall and recognition.* New York: Wiley.

Morris, C. D., Bransford, J. D., & Franks, J. J. (1977). Levels of processing versus transfer appropriate processing. *Journal of Verbal Learning and Verbal Behavior, 16,* 519–533.

Moscovitch, M. & Craik, F. I. M. (1976). Depth of processing, retrieval cues, and uniqueness of encoding as factors in recall. *Journal of Verbal Learning and Verbal Behavior, 15,* 519–533.

Nadel, L. & Moscovitch, M. (1997). Memory consolidation, retrograde amnesia and the hippocampal complex. *Current Opinion in Neurobiology, 7,* 217–227.

Nelson, T. O. (1977). Repetition and levels of processing. *Journal of Verbal Learning and Verbal Behavior, 16,* 151–171.

Nyberg, L., Tulving, E., Habib, R., Nilsson, L.-G., Kapur, S., Houle, S., Cabeza, R., & McIntosh, A. R. (1995). Functional brain maps of retrieval mode and recovery of episodic information. *NeuroReport, 7,* 249–252.

Roediger, H. L., III, Weldon, M. S., & Challis, B. H. (1989). Explaining dissociations between implicit and explicit measures of retention: A processing account. In H. L. Roediger & F. I. M. Craik (eds.), *Varieties of memory and consciousness: Essays in honour of Endel Tulving* (pp. 3–41). Hillsdale, NJ: Erlbaum.

Sanquist, T. F., Rohrbaugh, J. W., Syndulko, K., & Lindsley, D. B. (1980). Electrocortical signs of levels of processing: Perceptual analysis and recognition memory. *Psychophysiology, 17,* 568–576.

Seamon, J. G. & Virostek, S. (1978). Memory performance and subject-defined depth of processing. *Memory and Cognition, 6,* 283–287.

Squire, L. R. (1992). Memory and the hippocampus: A synthesis from findings with rats, monkeys, and humans. *Psychological Review, 99,* 195–231.

Treisman, A. (1964). Selective attention in man. *British Medical Bulletin, 20,* 12–16.

Treisman, A. (1979). The psychological reality of levels of processing. In L. S. Cermak, & F. I. M. Craik (eds.), *Levels of processing in human memory* (pp. 301–330). Hillsdale, NJ: Erlbaum.

Tulving, E., Kapur, S., Craik, F. I. M., Moscovitch, M., & Houle, S. (1994). Hemispheric encoding/retrieval asymmetry in episodic memory: Positron emission tomography findings. *Proceedings of the National Academy of Sciences, USA, 91,* 2016–2020.

Tulving, E. & Thomson, D. M. (1973). Encoding specificity and retrieval processes in episodic memory. *Psychological Review, 80,* 352–373.

Vincent, A., Craik, F. I. M., & Furedy, J. J. (1996). Relations among memory performance, mental workload and cardiovascular responses. *International Journal of Psychophysiology, 23,* 181–198.

CHAPTER 4

Stratification of memory retrieval processes on perceptual tests

Bradford H. Challis

The contemporary study of memory is marked by a controversy over the nature of consciousness and memory retrieval processes on priming tasks. The debate centers on this issue: Does priming reflect only implicit (automatic, unconscious) retrieval processes or do explicit (controlled, conscious) retrieval processes also contribute to priming?

In the majority of work on priming, subjects study words (e.g., elephant) and on a later memory test they resolve fragmented or perceptually-degraded stimulus with the first word that comes to mind. These "perceptually-cued" tests include word fragment completion (-l-ph--t), word stem completion (ele___) and masked word identification (tachistoscopic presentation of a word)[1]. Considerable research shows that a prior encounter with a target word facilitates or primes subsequent identification of its physically degraded form. The issue is whether priming is a pure measure of implicit memory or is priming "contaminated" by explicit memory. (For further discussion of the issue, see Richardson-Klavehn & Bjork, 1988; Roediger & McDermott, 1993; Reingold & Toth, 1996).

The controversy over priming reflects a basic and widely accepted assumption; namely, implicit memory and explicit memory are two separate and independent sources of studied words on perceptual tests. That is, a studied word may be retrieved directly from implicit memory or directly from explicit memory, with each being a source of studied items.

A related assumption is that test instructions affect the contribution of implicit and explicit memory on perceptually-cued tests. When subjects are told to complete a fragment with the first word that comes to mind (Completion), the studied items are assumed to be retrieved from implicit memory. When subjects are told to use the fragment to remember a studied word and to complete the fragment with a studied word (Cued recall), the studied items are assumed to be retrieved directly from explicit memory (like free recall and recognition).

Some researchers argue that both implicit and explicit memory contribute to performance on Completion and Cued recall. Motivated by this assumption, researchers have applied the process dissociation procedure to perceptually-cued tests (Jacoby, 1991). The procedure uses inclusion and exclusion instructions. In Inclusion, subjects are told to complete the fragment with a word from the study list, or failing that, with the first word that comes to mind. On this test, subjects are assumed to retrieve items from implicit memory, and failing that, from explicit memory. In Exclusion, subjects are told to complete the fragment with the first word that comes to mind, but to exclude any words that appeared in the study list. On this test, retrieval is assumed to involve only implicit memory. If we accept these assumptions, then the difference between Inclusion and Exclusion provides an estimate of the contribution of explicit processes. A basic assumption of the process dissociation procedure is that implicit (automatic) and explicit (controlled) retrieval process are two independent sources of studied words.

The present article calls into question the assumption that both implicit memory and explicit memory are independent sources of studied words on perceptually-cued tests. A central thesis of the article is that studied items are retrieved from only one source, implicit memory. Explicit memory is not a source for studied words on fragment tests, although explicit memory may influence performance because it is used to select studied items from those retrieved from implicit memory.

The idea that implicit memory is the only source of studied items on word fragment tests is engendered in a generation-selection model (hereafter referred to as the G–S model). When presented with a word fragment cue, regardless of test instructions, solutions are first generated by implicit memory processes. The probability of generating a target word is enhanced by the prior presentation of the target in the study phase. Explicit memory is not a source of studied items, but depending on test instructions, explicit memory is used to identify and select studied words from those items generated from implicit memory. Implicit and explicit memory are stratified or hierarchical, in the sense that implicit retrieval precedes explicit memory, with explicit memory acting on information provided by implicit memory.

The article begins with a discussion of the classic generation-recognition model, for it lays the foundation for the G–S model of performance on word fragment tests. The G–S model is developed and discussed in the context of empirical and theoretical issues. The broader implications of the G–S model are discussed.

0.1   The classic generation/recognition model

A venerable model of memory retrieval holds that recall of a studied item from memory involves two successive stages of information processing. The remember first implicitly produces "candidate targets" to the available cues, and then selects from the "candidates" the desired target item. The first stage is usually referred to as generation, and the second as recognition. Hence the designation of "generation/recognition" model of recall. (For reasons discussed later, our model uses "selection" rather than "recognition".)

The history of the model precedes Ebbinghaus' time. It was accepted into the 1970s because it could account for a variety of phenomena of recognition and recall. The model's popularity waned when it was found that the model, as then formulated, could not account for two basic facts: context effects in recognition and recognition failure of recallable words. Especially damaging to the model was the finding that, under a variety of conditions, experimental subjects frequently could not recognize studied items that they were capable of producing to cues other than copies of targets in subsequent recall tests. This kind of an outcome was precluded by the logic of the model, which required that the output of two successive processing stages (recall) could not exceed the output of just one of the two (recognition). Because many experiments produced just such results, the generation/recognition model lost much of its earlier luster. (For an extensive discussion and references on the classic generation /recognition model, see Tulving, 1983.)

Now, however, it looks as if the earlier wholesale rejection of the ideas engendered in the generation/recognition model may have been premature. Under certain conditions at least the model seems to describe the data as well as rival theories, and perhaps better. The critical feature of such conditions has to do with the relation between the cue and the studied target. If the cue represents a perceptually impoverished or degraded description of the target (e.g., word fragment cues), then performance seems to be determined by the processes comprising the sequence of stages very much envisaged in the generation/ recognition model, as noted by some researchers (e.g., Humphreys, Bains, & Pike, 1989; Jacoby & Hollingshead, 1990).

0.2   Modifying the classic generation/recognition model for word fragment tests

The classic generation/recognition model must be modified in four ways to account for performance on word fragment tests. These relate to the nature of the test cue, memory processes involved in generation, the probability of generating a target item, and criterion for the recognition stage.

1. *The nature of the test cue.* In a cued recall experiment, an experimenter selects targets and test cues, reflecting a relation between them. The relation may be a perceptual one, in that a target word (e.g., elephant) is cued at test by its fragmented or perceptually-degraded form, as with fragments (-l-ph--t) or stems (ele____). Or, the test cue may be conceptually related to the target word, in the absence of any perceptual similarity between them, as with category cues (animal ___). Research shows that perceptually-cued tests and conceptually-cued tests behave quite differently (e.g., Blaxton, 1989; Blaxton, Bookheimer, Zeffiro, Figlozzi, Gaillard, & Theodore, 1996; Challis, Chiu, Kerr, Law, Schneider, Yonelinas, & Tulving, 1993). The classic generation/recognition model did not distinguish between cues, but the G–S model is assumed to apply only to perceptual cues such as word fragments.

2. *Memory processes (or systems) involved in generation.* The classic model assumed that generation depends on a semantic system or network of interconnected associations. The G–S model for fragment cues assumes that generation involves primarily perceptual processes; generation is a data-driven process (e.g., Roediger, Weldon, & Challis, 1989) that depends on a perceptual memory system (e.g., Tulving & Schacter, 1990). Terms and concepts such as episodic, semantic and perceptual memory systems, and data- and conceptually-driven are defined and discussed elsewhere (e.g., Roediger & McDermott, 1993; Schacter & Tulving, 1994; Tulving, 1983).

3. *Probability of generating a target item.* In the classic model, the probability of generating an item was determined by pre-experimental associations that did not change during the experiment. The classic model said nothing about priming or strengthening previously established associations between potential cues and their targets (Tulving, 1983). In the G–S model, the probability of generating an item can be affected by a previous experimental event. Typically, a prior exposure to an item increases the probability of the item being generated, consistent with the phenomenon of priming.

4. *Criterion for the recognition stage and on a recognition test.* The classic model assumed that these criterion are the same. If these criterion are assumed to vary then the classic model can accommodate findings such as recognition failure of recallable words. In the G–S model for fragment cues, these criterion can vary. The criterion for selecting a generated word as studied word is not necessarily the same as selecting a word as studied on a recognition test. In a word fragment test situation, responses of nonstudied word provides an indication of criterion across tests.

1.   The G–S model

1.1   *The generation process (G)*

On a word fragment test, subjects see a stimulus that is a fragmented form of a word. Subjects have been told the fragment can be completed to make a word. When presented with the perceptually-degraded stimulus, the cognitive system automatically works on resolving the fragment into something meaningful, a word. The retrieval process is driven by the physical information in the test cue and is a characterized as a data-driven process. The degraded stimulus provides partial physical information and the cognitive system relies on processing of a perceptual representation.

Generation (G) is an implicit, unconscious cognitive process that resolves the degraded stimulus into a word. G is an automatic process that develops during the reading process because the physical form or surface features of normal text has some physical ambiguity. A word fragment is a more extreme case of a physically degraded stimulus that needs to be resolved into a meaningful stimulus.

For nonstudied items, the probability of generating the target word depends on the subject's preexperimental encounters with the word. Prior encounters with the word in the study phase of an experiment increase the probability of generating the solution (i.e., prior presentation facilities or primes G).

G conforms to the basic principles engendered in encoding specificity and transfer appropriate processing, whereby G and resolution of the degraded stimulus depend on the similarity of the stored information and information provided in the test cue (e.g., Roediger, Weldon, & Challis, 1989; Tulving & Schacter, 1990). So with a visually-presented fragment, G benefits most from prior visual encounters with the target word, as compared to hearing the word, generating it from a conceptual cue, or seeing its pictorial referent. Priming on Completion provides the clearest measure of G, in that generated words are output without any selection process. Subjects are instructed to respond with the first word that comes to mind, so they simply respond with the first word provided by G.

1.2   *The selection process (S)*

Selection (S) occurs after G has resolved the fragment cue into a meaningful stimulus (e.g., a word). S is not a source of studied items but rather S acts on the information provided by G and serves to meets the demands of the test instructions.

If subjects are told to complete the fragment with the first word that comes to mind (Completion), subjects output generated items and S does not play a role. If subjects are told to complete the fragment with a studied word (Cued recall) or a nonstudied word (Exclusion), then S is engaged to select an appropriate word from those items generated. In Cued recall, words identified as studied are output. In Exclusion, words identified as new are output. In Inclusion, subjects are instructed to output a studied word but are given the option of outputting any word so the role of S is less clear-cut. S may be engaged in some cases but not others, such that S may be used to select studied words from those generated (as in Cued recall), or words may be output without regard for their presentation history (like Completion).

The S process involves a decision about the status of a generated word, so the output of a word depends on selection criterion. In Cued Recall, a lenient criterion leads to greater output of generated words whether studied or non-studied. As the criterion becomes more lenient, responses of studied and nonstudied items are more similar to that of Completion, in that all generated items are output. In the extreme case, generated words are output without regard to their presentation history, so performance in Cued recall is the same as Completion. With a stricter response criterion, the output of studied and non-studied words drops in that generated items are more likely to be identified as new and not output. One indication of criterion in Cued recall is provided by a comparison of nonstudied responses in Cued recall and Completion; a similar nonstudied rate implies a more lenient criterion in Cued recall. In Exclusion, as in Cued recall, a more lenient criterion leads to greater output of generated items with no selection. In Inclusion, the affect of criterion depends on the extent that subjects treat the test as Cued recall.

S is a conceptually-driven process that operates on information provided by G. Selection is analogous to, but not synonymous with, processes on a recognition test (hence the use of "selection" rather than "recognition" in the G–S model). One obvious difference is that S acts on a mental representation of word provided by G, whereas words are physically presented by the experimenter on a recognition test. S may benefit from certain attributes of G (e.g., studied words are generated faster), whereas fluency of processing the physical stimulus may benefit the recognition process. Notwithstanding, conceptually-driven processes play a dominant role in S and recognition. The conceptually-driven nature of S means that the process is sensitive to study manipulations in much the same way as performance on tests of recognition and free recall, which have been well documented (e.g., Roediger & McDermott, 1993). For instance, study conditions that promote meaningful processing of study words benefits S, so that S is better for words studied in a semantic than physical encoding condition.

Turning to the issue of consciousness, the retrieval process on a recognition test is usually characterized as an explicit retrieval process involving conscious recollection of the studied word. In comparison, conscious in S appears less transparent and more open to speculation. Should S be characterized as a consciously controlled process or an unconscious automatic process? The best we can do to address the question, at least for the present time, is to consider subjective reports (cf. Schacter, Bowers, & Booker, 1989). In research in our laboratory, subjects performing word fragment tests (with Completion, Cued recall and Exclusion instructions) were instructed to introspect about the nature of the mental processes that occurred during the test (Challis, Chiu, Cormier, & Tulving, 1993). For Completion, the general view was that a solution seemed to "pop into mind", which fits with the automatic, nonconscious nature of G. Subjects reported that after responding they would often recognize the word as studied. In Cued recall, subjects often verbalized the mental process as one in which a solution would "pop to mind" and they would respond if they recognized the solution as a studied word. For Exclusion, most subjects reported that they would withhold a solution if it was studied and try to come up with another solution. One of the more obvious interpretative difficulties is that consciousness thought to occur in S may actually occur after the response (as in Completion) and this consciousness may be misattributed to S.

The issue of consciousness in the G–S model harks back to observations made about the classic generate-recognize model, as evident in this remark by Tulving:

"There is uncertainty as to presence of a conscious state of remembering (recollective experience) in the sequence of hypothetical events according to the generation/recognition theories. Published accounts of the theories provide no guidance on this matter: we do not know whether, and if so, where, conscious awareness enters the picture. On an earlier occasion (Tulving, 1976) I thought both generation and decision stages of generation/recognition theories would run their course before the product is entered into consciousness. I did so because I could not quite imagine how the subject in a cued-recall experiment would explicitly think of and consciously reject all kinds of incorrect alternatives before encountering the correct one. Most people report that when they are "searching for" an item from a previously studied list, their "mind is blank" until suddenly the right item "pops into it". If my interpretation was wrong (cf. LeCocq & Tiberghein, 1981), and the decision-stage of the generation/recognition theory represents a conscious operation, the problem of the remembers mind being "blank" during "search" must be confronted." (Tulving, 1983; pp. 193–194).

Clearly, questions exist about the role of consciousness vis-à-vis the G–S model, but the same can be said of any model of memory. Notwithstanding, we will show that the G–S model provides a very satisfactory account of performance on word fragment tests.

2.   The G–S model and performance on word fragment tests

2.1 *Effects of study variables*

Study variables can be classified as perceptual or conceptual manipulations (e.g., Roediger & McDermott, 1993). A perceptual variable involves a manipulation of the physical form of the presented stimulus, as with modality of presentation (e.g., visual or auditory), symbolic format (e.g., word or picture) and language of presentation (English or Spanish). A conceptual variable involves a manipulation of conceptual processing across study conditions.

A perceptual study variable affects G because G is a data-driven process that benefits from the physical similarity of the stimulus at study and test. For instance, in the case of modality of presentation, a visual presentation of a target (as compared to an auditory presentation) represents a closer physical match to the visual word fragment, so G benefits more from a prior visual presentation of the target word. Since G is common to all word fragments regardless of instructions, a study variable such as modality of presentation has a similar effect on all word fragment tests (i.e., visual greater than auditory).

A conceptual variable affects S because S is a conceptually-driven process. Modality of presentation does not affect conceptual processing of the target word so the manipulation does not affect S. On the other hand, the familiar levels-of-processing (LOP) variable affects encoding of meaningful information (e.g., Craik & Lockhart, 1972) and therefore affects S. In the typical manipulation, subjects see a target word and perform a task that focuses on meaning (e.g., semantic-based judgment) or physical attributes of the word (e.g., counting letters). The semantic task promotes more meaningful processing of the target word which benefits S. Consequently, Cued recall and Exclusion, tests in which S plays a critical role, show a large LOP effect. Cued recall shows the traditional levels effect (semantic greater than physical) because semantically studied words are more likely to be selected and output on the test. Exclusion shows a "reversed" levels-of-process effect because semantically studied words are more likely to identified as studied words and therefore not output.

The effects of modality of presentation and LOP on word fragment tests were demonstrated in a single experiment by Chiu (1991, Experiment 1). Subjects saw or heard words and performed a semantic or physical study task. The test cues were word fragments with Completion, Cued recall and Exclusion instructions. The proportions of target word responses in the various study conditions are presented in Table 1. Modality of presentation had a similar effect on the three tests, whereas levels of processing had a different effect across the three tests. Completion was unaffected by levels, Cued recall showed the traditional levels effect, and Exclusion showed a reversed levels effect. Responses of nonstudied words were as expected: subjects in Cued recall withheld nonstudied words whereas subjects in Exclusion and Completion output all of the generated nonstudied words.

In the experiment by Chiu (1991, Experiment 1), subjects completed the word fragment test and then received a recognition test for the words presented at study. The results of recognition are presented in Table 2. Recognition showed a traditional LOP effect but no effect of modality of presentation, regardless of the type of prior fragment test. The pattern of findings in the Tables 1 and 2 illustrate the main points made in the previous several paragraphs.

The results reported by Chiu (1991) are rather compelling because the experiment directly compared the effects of a perceptual and conceptual study variable on several word fragment tests. Other researchers have reported experiments involving word fragment tests, but typically the tests have been Completion and Cued recall. For instance, Challis and Sidhu (1993, Experiment 1) showed that modality of presentation affected Completion and Cued recall whereas massed repetition benefited only Cued recall. (Various findings imply that massed repetition is a conceptual study variable.) In another study, Roediger et al. (1992) showed that Completion and Cued recall were greatly affected by

Table 1. *Effect of modality of presentation and level-of-processing on word fragment tests, from Chiu (1991, experiment 1)*

| Test instruc-tion | Study condition | | | | |
| | Visual | | Auditory | | |
	Physical	Semantic	Physical	Semantic	Nonstudied
Completion	.55	.54	.38	.36	.23
Cued recall	.25	.42	.13	.26	.02
Exclusion	.26	.04	.16	.06	.21

Table 2. *Effect of modality of presentation and level-of-processing on recognition, from Chiu (1991, experiment 1)*

| First test instruction | Study condition | | | | |
| | Visual | | Auditory | | |
	Physical	Semantic	Physical	Semantic	Nonstudied
Completion	.48	.81	.51	.78	.14
Cued recall	.37	.80	.26	.85	.04
Exclusion	.42	.88	.44	.89	.09

symbolic form of presentation (words versus pictures), whereas LOP affected only Cued recall. The presentation of words versus pictures is clearly a perceptual manipulation. A reading of Roediger and McDermott's (1993) comprehensive review of the relevant literature reveals a general pattern of findings consistent with the G–S model.

So far the discussion has focused on study variables that affect perceptual or conceptual processing. However, a variable can involve a manipulation of physical form and semantic processing. One such study variable entails reading a target word (cold) or producing a target word from a conceptual cue (hot ?). Reading invokes data-driven processing but little semantic processing of the target word, whereas producing a word from a cue promotes semantic processing but does not invoke data-driven processing of the target (e.g., Blaxton, 1989). This means better G of read words and better S for words produced from a conceptual cue. Completion depends on G so more read words are produced on the test. Cued recall and Exclusion depend on the relative contribution of G and S such that three patterns of findings may occur: (a) performance is the same in the two study conditions (better G of read words is offset by worse S of read words), (b) performance is better for read words (G makes a larger contribution) or (c) performance is worse for read words (S makes a larger contribution). Research that speaks to this issue is limited and more work is clearly warranted.

The effect of study variables on word fragment tests has focused extensively on the traditional LOP manipulation. Subjects see target words and perform different tasks designed to promote different levels of semantic processing. Consistent with the view that LOP is purely a conceptual variable, researchers have reported that LOP does not affect Completion (see Table 1). However, a survey of the literature reveals that Completion shows a small but rather consistent LOP effect, particularly with certain experimental designs (Challis & Brodbeck,

1992). There has been considerable debate as to why LOP effects Completion. However, recent work by Richardson-Klavehn and Gardiner (1998) provides strong evidence that small LOP effects in Completion can be attributed to differences in data-driven (or lexical) processing across study conditions.

Richardson-Klavehn and Gardiner (1998) examined the effects of LOP on word fragment tests. In Experiment 1, subjects studied words in graphemic, phonemic or semantic study conditions. At test, subjects were given word fragments with Completion, Cued recall, Inclusion or Exclusion instructions. The proportions of target word responses are presented in Table 3. In Completion, performance was lower in physical than phonemic and semantic conditions. In another experiment, subjects also made a lexical decision in the three conditions and Completion performance was the same across conditions. These and other findings strongly suggest that diminished lexical processing in the physical condition accounts for LOP effects on Completion. In turn, this conclusion implies that data-driven processes, including more lexical processes, contribute to G.

In the Richardson-Klavehn and Gardiner (1998) experiment, deeper conceptual processing occurred across the three study conditions (semantic > phonemic > physical) so cued recall improved across the three study conditions because of the contribution of S (i.e., deeper semantic processing benefits S). For a similar reason, Exclusion showed a reversed LOP effect. Inclusion showed a LOP effect like Cued recall because S contributes to performance on both tests.

Richardson-Klavehn and Gardiner (1998) also measured response times to produce a target. The response times were longest in Exclusion (6.1 s), intermediate for Cued recall (4.9 s) and Inclusion (4.8 s) and fastest in Completion (2.5 s). These results are compatible with the G–S model: In Completion subjects simply output generated words without regard to its presentation history, so responses are fastest. The other tests involve S so responses are longer. In Cued recall and Inclusion, generated words identified as studied are output. In Exclusion,

Table 3. *Effect of level-of-processing on word fragment tests, from Richardson-Klavehn and Gardiner (1998, experiment 1)*

Test instruction	Study condition			
	Physical	Phonemic	Semantic	Nonstudied
Completion	.41	.51	.50	.29
Cued recall	.10	.32	.57	.04
Exclusion	.20	.19	.04	.31
Inclusion	.48	.54	.66	.31

generated words identified as studied must be withheld by the S process and another word must be sought, so response times are longer.

In sum, the G–S model can account for the effects of various study variables on word fragment tests. Moreover, guided by the G–S model, a even better understanding of performance on word fragment tests is obtained by taking into account the number of solutions of a fragment.

2.2 *Single-solution versus multiple-solution fragments*

Word fragment cues can be constructed so they have single or multiple solutions; this is important for understanding performance on word fragment tests. First, consider single-solution fragments (e.g., -l-ph--t). In Completion, a generated item is output regardless of whether it was studied (elephant). In Cued recall, a generated word may be rejected because it was not studied, but no alternative word can be generated. Consequently, the number of studied words produced in Cued recall cannot exceed Completion. The generated word is always the target so if it is not identified and selected as a studied word, then the target is not output. Similarly, in Inclusion the number of target words produced will not exceed Completion, even though subjects were told to respond with target words. That is, the number of responses of target words in Completion will not be exceeded by responses on other word fragment tests, regardless of test instructions. This applies to studied and nonstudied target words.

The situation is different for multiple-solution fragments (--pp-r). In Completion, a generated item is output regardless of whether it was studied, and the word (pepper) may be a solution that is not the target. In Cued recall, a generated word may be rejected because it is not the studied word (pepper) and another solution may generated and output which is the target word (copper). Consequently, responses of studied words in Cued recall can exceed Completion, particularly for semantically studied words as these words have a higher probability of being identified and selected as studied words. Similarly, in Inclusion where subjects are told to try and respond with target words, responses of targets can exceed Completion.

These predictions about performance for single and multiple solution fragments provide an excellent test of the G–S model, and raise questions for the traditional view that two separate sources (implicit and explicit) contribute to word fragment tests. First, it is not clear how the two-source view explains the difference between single and multiple solution fragments. Second, the two-source view appears to predict better performance in Cued recall and Inclusion than in Completion, regardless of the number of solutions. Particularly in

Inclusion, subjects are instructed to retrieve targets from explicit and implicit memory so as to maximize the output of targets, therefore performance would be expected to exceed Completion.

We focus on single-solution fragments because the predicted result with multiple-solution fragments is less interesting in that the G–S model and the two-source view can accommodate the finding. A survey of the literature reveals many studies showing that responses of studied words in Cued recall and Inclusion exceeded Completion, particularly with semantic study conditions. For instance, see the results presented in Table 3 of this article (Richardson-Klavehn & Gardiner, 1998). Other studies showing a similar pattern include Graf and Mandler (1984), Greene (1986), Jacoby and Hollingshead (1990), and Reingold and Toth (1996).

The predicted result with single-solution fragments is well illustrated by an unpublished experiment (Challis, Chiu, Cormier, & Tulving, 1993). The experiment involved a LOP study manipulation and single-solution fragments with four test instructions (Completion, Inclusion, Cued recall, and Exclusion). The semantic study task was designed to promote very deep processing whereas the physical task promoted very shallow processing. The extreme LOP manipulation was evident on a conceptually driven test of free recall, which showed near perfect recall of semantically studied words and negligible recall of physically studied words. The proportion of target words produced on the four tests are presented in Table 4.

Performance for semantically studied items in Completion, Cued recall and Inclusion was similar because all generated items were output on these tests; all generated items were identified in Cued recall and Inclusion. For a similar reason, very few studied words were produced in Exclusion because generated words were identified and not output. In the physical condition, performance for Completion and Inclusion was similar because all generated items were output. Fewer targets were produced in Cued recall because many generated items were not identified as studied items. Compared to Cued recall, more studied words were produced in Exclusion because generated items were not identified as studied and output. The results show that responses of target words in Completion were not exceeded in the other tests.

We surveyed the literature for relevant studies and found numerous studies involving single solution fragments. In all cases, Completion performance was not exceeded by other word fragment tests (e.g., Challis et al., 1993; Challis & Sidhu, 1993; Challis et al., 1996; Hamann, 1992; Horton, Smith, Bargout, & Connolly, 1992; Roediger, Weldon, Stadler, & Riegler, 1992; Weldon, Roediger, & Challis, 1989).

Table 4. *Effect of level-of-processing on word fragment tests, from Challis, Chiu, Cormier, & Tulving (1993)*

Test instruction	Study condition		
	Physical	Semantic	Nonstudied
Completion	.41	.56	.28
Cued recall	.16	.54	.09
Exclusion	.31	.10	.22
Inclusion	.38	.57	.26

Table 5. *Performance on successive fragment tests as a function of levels-of-processing, from Challis, Chiu, & Cormier (1993)*

		Study condition			
		Physical		Semantic	
Test 1	Test 2	Test 1	Test 2	Test 1	Test 2
Completion	Completion	.45	.49	.64	.67
Cued recall	Completion	.23	.49	.60	.64
Exclusion	Completion	.39	.51	.01	.61

Consider another experiment with single-solution fragments using a LOP study manipulation (Challis, Chiu, Cormier, & Tulving, 1993). Subjects studied words in a physical or semantic condition and then received two successive fragment tests; the fragments were the same on the two tests. The first test was Completion, Cued recall or Exclusion; the second test was always Completion. The proportions of studied words are presented in Table 5. Performance on the first tests showed the expected pattern across tests (compare Tables 1, 3 and 4). Performance on the second test of Completion was unaffected by the prior test (cf. Challis & Roediger, 1993). The pattern of findings fits with the idea that Completion fully taps the one source of studied items so that Completion provides a measure of the maximum responses of studied words with single-solution fragment tests.

2.3 *Predicting Cued recall and Exclusion performance*

According to the G–S model, performance on Completion and a recognition test can be used to predict performance on Cued recall and Exclusion. Completion provides a measure of G and performance on a recognition test provides a measure of S (although the cognitive processes in both may not be identical). Cued recall and Exclusion reflect the contribution of G and S. Consider the following experiment: Subjects study a list of words. One group receives Completion and Recognition tests. Other groups receive only Cued recall or Exclusion. The proportion of target words produced on Completion (estimate of G) and subsequently identified on the recognition test (estimate of S) should predict Cued recall (G × S). The proportion of targets produced on Completion and not recognized should predict Exclusion (G × not S).

The aforementioned experiment was completed by Chiu (1991). The results of the word fragment tests and recognition were previously presented in Tables 1 and 2 of this article. The joint probabilities of responses in Completion and recognition for each subject x item was computed for the four study conditions (see Table 6). For Cued recall, predicted performance was computed as the joint probability of Completion and recognition for studied words (less the nonstudied baseline). For exclusion, predicted performance was the joint probability of Completion and failure of recognition for studied words. The predicted and observed scores for Cued recall and Exclusion are presented in Table 7. There is a very close match between observed and predicted performance in Cued recall and Exclusion.

Chiu (1991) predicted Cued recall and Exclusion using performance on successive tests of Completion and recognition. Another approach is to have subjects make a recognition judgment as they complete each fragment, what is referred to as generate-recognize instructions. Consider an experiment reported by Hamann (1992, Experiment 1; also see Jacoby & Hollingshead, 1990).

Table 6. *Joint probabilities of responses in completion and recognition as a function of study condition, from Chiu (1991)*

| | Study condition | | | | |
| | Visual | | Auditory | | |
Joint probability	Physical	Semantic	Physical	Semantic	Nonstudied
Rn, Fc	.31	.47	.23	.33	.06
Rn, nFc	.17	.35	.28	.43	.07
nRn, Fc	.22	.07	.15	.03	.17
nRn, nFc	.30	.12	.35	.20	.70

Note. Rn = "yes" response in recognition; nRn = "no" response in recognition; Fc = completion; nFc = noncompletion.

Table 7. *Predicted and observed performance in cued recall and exclusion as a function of study condition, from Chiu (1991)*

	Study condition			
	Visual		Auditory	
Performance	Physical	Semantic	Physical	Semantic
Cued recall				
Observed	.23	.40	.11	.24
Predicted	.25	.41	.17	.27
Exclusion				
Observed	.26	.04	.16	.06
Predicted	.22	.07	.15	.03

Table 8. *Performance on word fragment tests as a function of levels-of-processing, from Hamann (1992)*

	Study condition		
Test instruction	Physical	Semantic	Nonstudied
Completion	.79	.80	.60
Cued recall	.44	.80	.13
Generate-recognize (yes)	.27	.80	.03
Generate-recognize (total)	.73	.84	–

Subjects studied words in a physical or semantic condition and then received single-solution word fragments with Completion, Cued recall or Generate-recognize instructions. The main results are presented in Table 8. Generate-recognize (yes) are the proportions of targets generated and recognized. Generate-recognize (total) are the proportions of targets generated regardless of recognition.

In the semantic condition, performance was virtually the same across the three tests because recognition was optimal, so that all generated targets were output in the tests. As expected, in the physical condition performance was better in Completion than Cued recall because some generated items were not identified as studied. The difference in Cued recall and Generate-recognize(yes) can be attributed to a difference in the criterion for selecting a generated word as studied: Inspection of the nonstudied condition indicates lower false recognition of nonstudied items, which implies that the selection criterion was higher in Generate-recognize than Cued recall, resulting in lower output of generated items in the Generate-recognize(yes) condition. Another consideration is that S (in Cued recall) may not be identical to the process that occurs with generate-recognize instructions.

In both study conditions, Completion was virtually the same as Generate-recognize (total) because in both cases all of the generated items were output. This finding indicates that making a recognition judgment with the Generate-recognize instructions did not affect G. For similar kinds of findings to those presented above, and for additional discussion about generate-recognize conditions, see Jacoby and Hollingshead (1990) and Weldon and Colston (1995).

2.4 Amnesia and word fragment tests

Dense amnesic patients can show normal priming on word fragment completion but very impaired recall and recognition (e.g., Moscovitch, Vriezen, & Goshen-Gottstein, 1993). A few studies with amnesics have compared different word fragment tests, but the test instructions were not well described. One exception is a study by Graf, Squire, and Mandler (1984). Subjects studied words in a physical or semantic condition and received multiple-solution fragment cues. Subjects were told to complete the fragment with the first word that came to mind (Completion) or they were told to recall a word from the study list and failing that to guess a word that may have been presented (referred to as Cued recall but similar to Inclusion instructions).

The relevant results are presented in Table 9. For physically-studied words, amnesic and control subjects performed similarly because both groups output all generated items on both tests. For controls, recall instructions did not improve performance because generated items were not identified as studied items.

Table 9. *Performance of amnesic and control subjects on word fragment tests as a function of level-of-processing, from Graf et al. (1984)*

	Study condition			
	Physical		Semantic	
Test instruction	Control	Amnesic	Control	Amnesic
Completion	.38	.41	.54	.57
Cued recall	.40	.40	.69	.59

Table 10. *Performance on word fragment tests as a function of level-of-processing, from Horton et al. (1992)*

	Study condition	
Test instruction	Physical	Semantic
Completion	.74	.83
Simulate amnesia	.31	.10

Physical encoding resulted in very poor recognition by both groups (as evidenced by a separate recognition test) so that S did not impact performance. In contrast, with semantically studied words, recall instructions improved performance for controls because they better identified generated words. That is, controls selected studied words from those generated, whereas amnesics were unable to do this because of their impaired recognition.

On the issue of amnesia and word fragment tests, Horton et al. (1992) reported an interesting study with normal subjects. These authors used performance on fragment tests as a way of identifying people who are trying to simulate amnesia. In one experiment, normal university students studied words in physical or semantic conditions and received word fragment tests with Completion or Simulate Amnesia instructions (i.e., perform the completion test exactly like a person suffering from amnesia). The results with single-solution fragments (Experiment 3) are presented in Table 10. The instruction to simulate amnesia lead subjects to a adopt an exclusion strategy, in which they withheld generated items recognized as studied. The exclusion strategy produced a reversed LOP effect, as compared to the small levels effect in Completion (compare Tables 1, 3 and 4). Subjects in the simulate condition reported that they simply withheld solutions recognized as studied words.

2.5 Brain imagining with word fragment tests

Researchers have explored the brain pathways activated during completion of word fragment tests, particularly with positron emission tomography (PET). The imagining studies reveal some of the brain areas believed to be activated during three versions of word fragment tests. In the nonstudied baseline condition in which the target solution was not previously presented, subjects completed the fragment with the first word that comes to mind. The same task was performed in the primed completion situation, except the target word was previously presented. In the Cued recall variation, subjects were instructed to recall the study words. (For a current review and discussion of the relevant findings, see Roediger, Buckner, and McDermott, 1998; also see Blaxton et al., 1996).

Brain activations overlapped considerably over the three test variations, but there were some revealing differences. Compared to the nonstudied condition, Completion showed less activation of bilateral visual regions. This reduced neural activity on perceptual areas correlated with the greater tendency to respond with study words (and decreased voice latencies) in Completion. All of the areas activated during Completion were again present in Cued recall, with additional activation of areas including medial parietal cortex and right prefrontal cortex. Activation of these additional brain areas has been associated with performance on a recognition test. As well, voice onset latencies were longer in Cued recall.

The overall pattern of findings corresponds very well with the G–S model of word fragment tests. In Completion, the reduced neural activity on perceptual areas corresponds to the data-driven G process underlying production of study words. In Cued recall, the additional activation of brain areas associated with recognition corresponds to the additional S process in Cued recall. We expect additional studies of brain imaging with various techniques will provide additional support for the G–S model.

3.   The G–S model and other tests

The article focuses on word fragment tests but there has been research with other tests in which the physically degraded retrieval cue specifies the perceptual form of the studied target. For instance, in a masked word identification task, subjects try to identify words flashed briefly on a computer screen. We expect that the G–S model applies to all perceptually-cued tests because of the nature of the test cue and the cognitive system; when presented with a physically degraded word, the cognitive system automatically works to resolving the stimulus into a word. Considerable research shows that a variety of experimental and subject variables have the same effect on perceptually-cued tests (e.g., Moscovitch et al., 1993; Roediger & McDermott, 1993).

Research also suggests that the G–S model applies to some perceptual tests with cues that are not "perceptually degraded". Consider a graphemic cued test designed by Blaxton (1989), in which the test cue and target words have a similar physical form (purple for people). In a series of experiments, Blaxton showed that the test was affected by certain study variables (e.g., modality of presentation) in the same way as word fragment completion. Challis et al. (1996)

noted that Blaxton used study variables that have a large effect on G but not S, so graphemic cued recall and Completion would behave similarly. In turn, Challis et al. showed that LOP had a large effect on graphemic cued recall but a negligible effect on word fragment completion. LOP had a large effect on S, which contributes to graphemic cued recall but not Completion. In turn, Challis et al. designed a graphemic cued completion test in which subjects simply generated words with a physical shape similar to the test cue. Consistent with the G–S model, graphemic cued completion was unaffected by LOP.

Guided by the G–S model, Challis et al. (1996; also see the article by Velichkovsky in this book) designed an direct test that was not sensitive to LOP. The gist of their reasoning was this: The test must be designed so that retrieval of a studied word depends on the overlap in perceptual information in the test cue and the memory trace, which means the test cue must bear a physical resemblance. Second, the test must be designed to obviate the use of S to select studied words from those generated; if S contributes to performance then LOP would affect performance. They designed a "graphemically-similar recognition test" in which subjects were presented with test words (people) that were graphemically similar to studied target words (purple); subjects were instructed to identify words that had a similar shape to a studied word. Various findings (e.g., unaffected by LOP) were consistent with the G–S model.

4.   The G–S model and theoretical issues

The G–S model can explain and predict a range of performance on various word fragment cued tests, as illustrated in the present article. The range of findings poses a challenge for other contemporary accounts of performance on perceptual tests, although some of these theoretical accounts can incorporate the core ideas of the G–S model. For instance, proponents of the processing theory have used some of the ideas engendered in the G–S model as a way to explain performance on word fragment tests (e.g., Roediger et al., 1992). As well, the core ideas of the G–S model are quite compatible with a memory systems approach proposed by Tulving and colleagues (Schacter & Tulving, 1994; Tulving, 1983; Tulving & Schacter, 1990).

The memory systems view describes three systems (perceptual, semantic, and episodic) that interact in a monohierarchical arrangement. The perceptual representation system represents information of a presemantic nature and is involved in the redintegration of perceptual stimulus. A degraded stimulus (e.g., word fragment cue) must first be resolved by this system, perhaps in concert with the semantic system, before episodic memory comes into play. Episodic memory acts on a meaningful stimulus provided by the perceptual and semantic systems. The word fragment is not a viable cue for directly retrieving the word from episodic memory because there is insufficient overlap in the test cue information and the information in the episodic memory trace, in line with the encoding specificity principle (Tulving, 1983). Once the perceptual and semantic systems have resolved the word fragment into a meaningful stimulus, this information provides a cue for the retrieval of the studied word from episodic memory.

As to the issue of consciousness, questions arise. Implicit retrieval has been associated with the perceptual and semantic memory systems, which corresponds with the unconscious, automatic nature of G. However, the puzzling question concerns episodic memory, which is associated with the conscious recollection of past events. S is assumed to tap episodic memory but the selection process appears to occur largely unconsciously and automatically, without conscious recollection of the studied word (as discussed previously). One possible explanation relates to S and the retrieval situation. In a recognition test, subjects are presented with the target word and they can consciously deliberate as to whether the word was studied. In contrast, G provides a "unconscious mental representation" of the target word for S, and the absence of the physical stimulus during the S process may account for the unconscious nature of S (as compared to consciousness nature associated with a recognition test). In this vein, subjects report that selecting and outputting a studied word on a fragment test often seem to occur unconsciously and after they respond the word is often recognized as a studied word. Clearly, understanding the role and function of consciousness on perceptually-cued tests, indeed on all memory tests, is one of the great challenges of our time.

5. Concluding remarks

The article calls into question the popular view that implicit memory and explicit memory are two separate and independent sources of studied words on word fragment tests. The idea that a studied word can be retrieved directly from implicit memory or directly from explicit memory (with the contribution being determined by test instructions) may not be valid. Rather, we assert that studied items are retrieved from only one source, implicit memory. Explicit memory is not a source for studied words on fragment tests, but explicit memory may influence performance as it is involved in the selection of studied items from those provided by implicit memory. In this vein, implicit and explicit memory are stratified or hierarchical in the sense that implicit retrieval precedes explicit memory on with word fragment tests. These ideas are engendered in a G–S model of memory retrieval processes on perceptual tests.

Note

1. This article focuses on word fragment tests, but we later present evidence for the assertion that similar principles apply to other tests in which the physically-degraded retrieval cue specifies the perceptual form of the studied target.

References

Blaxton, T. A. (1989). Investigating dissociations among memory measures: Support for a transfer appropriate processing framework. *Journal of Experimental Psychology: Learning, Memory, and Cognition, 15,* 657–668.

Blaxton, T. A., Bookheimer, S. Y., Zeffiro, T. A., Figlozzi, C. M., Gaillard, W. D., & Theodore, W. H. (1996). Functional mapping of human memory using PET: Comparisons of conceptual and perceptual tests. *Canadian Journal of Experimental Psychology, 50,* 42–56.

Challis, B. H. & Brodbeck, D. R. (1992). Level of processing affects priming in word fragment completion. *Journal of Experimental Psychology: Learning, Memory, and Cognition, 18,* 595–607.

Challis, B. H., Chiu, C. Y., Cormier, H. C., & Tulving, E. (1993). Further support for a generation/recognition account of performance on word fragment cued tests. Unpublished manuscript.

Challis, B. H., Chiu, C. Y., Kerr, S. A., Law, J., Schneider, L., Yonelinas, A., & Tulving, E. (1993). Perceptual and conceptual cueing in implicit and explicit retrieval. *Memory, 1,* 127–151.

Challis, B. H. & Roediger, H. L. (1993). The effect of proportion overlap and repeated testing on primed word fragment completion. *Canadian Journal of Experimental Psychology, 47,* 113–123.

Challis, B. H. & Sidhu, R. (1993). The dissociative effect of massed repetition on implicit and explicit measures of memory. *Journal of Experimental Psychology: Learning, Memory, and Cognition, 19,* 115–127.

Challis, B. H., Velichkovsky, B. M., & Craik, F. I. M. (1996). Levels-of-processing effects on a variety of memory tasks: New findings and theoretical implications. *Consciousness and Cognition, 5,* 142–164.

Craik, F. I. M. & Lockhart, R. S. (1972). Levels of processing: A framework for memory research. *Journal of Verbal Learning and Verbal Behavior, 11,* 671–684.

Chiu, C. Y. (1991). A test of a modified generation/recognition model of recall. Unpublished master's thesis, University of Toronto, Ontario, Canada.

Graf, P. & Mandler, G. (1984). Activation makes words more accessible but not necessarily more retrievable. *Journal of Verbal Learning and Verbal Behavior, 23,* 553–568.

Graf, P., Squire, L. R., & Mandler, G. (1984). The information that amnesic patients do not forget. *Journal of Experimental Psychology: Learning, Memory, and Cognition, 10,* 164–178.

Greene, R. L. (1986). Word stems as cues in recall and completion tasks. *Quarterly Journal of Experimental Psychology, 38A,* 663–673.

Hamann, S. B. (1992). Comparing implicit and explicit performance in perceptual and conceptual tasks: Applicability of a generation/recognition model. Unpublished doctoral thesis, University of Toronto, Ontario, Canada.

Horton, K. D., Smith, S. A., Bargout, N. D., & Connolly, D. A. (1992). The use of indirect memory tests to assess malingered amnesia: A study of metamemory. *Journal of Experimental Psychology: General, 121,* 326–351.

Humphreys, M. S., Bains, J. D., & Pike, R. (1989). Different ways to cue a coherent memory system: A theory for episodic, semantic, and procedural tasks. *Psychological Review, 96,* 208–233.

Jacoby, L. L. (1991). A process dissociation framework: separating automatic and intentional uses of memory. *Journal of Memory and Language, 30,* 513–541.

Jacoby, L. L. & Hollingshead, A. (1990). Toward a generate/recognize model of performance on direct and indirect tests of memory. *Journal of Memory and Language, 29,* 433–454.

LeCocq, P. & Tiberghein, G. (1981). *Memoire et decision.* Presses Universitaires de Lille.

Moscovitch, M., Vriezen, E., & Goshen-Gottstein, Y. (1993). Implicit tests of memory in patients with focal lesions or degenerative brain disorders. In F. Boller & J. Grafman (eds.), *Handbook of neuropsychology* (pp. 131–173). Amsterdam: Elsevier.

Reingold, E. M. & Toth, J. P. (1996). Process dissociations versus tasks dissociations: a controversy in progress. In G. Underwood (ed.), *Implicit cognition.* Oxford: Oxford University Press.

Richardson-Klavehn, A. & Bjork, R. A. (1988). Measures of memory. *Annual Review of Psychology, 39,* 475–543.

Richardson-Klavehn, A. & Gardiner, J. M. (1998). Depth-of-processing effects on priming in stem completion: Tests of voluntary contamination, conceptual processing, and lexical processing hypotheses. *Journal of Experimental Psychology: Learning, Memory, and Cognition, 24,* 593–609.

Roediger, H. L., Buckner, R., & McDermott, K. B. (1998). Components of processing. In J. K. Foster and M. Jelic (eds.), *Memory: Systems, process, of function?* Oxford University Press.

Roediger, H. L. & McDermott, K. B. (1993). Implicit memory in normal human subjects. In F. Boller & J. Grafman (eds.), *Handbook of neuropsychology* (pp. 63–131). Amsterdam: Elsevier.

Roediger, H. L., Weldon, M. S., & Challis, B. H. (1989). Explaining dissociations between implicit and explicit measures of retention: A processing account. In H. L. Roediger

& F. I. M. Craik (eds.), *Varieties of memory and consciousness: Essays in honour of Endel Tulving* (pp. 3–41). Hillsdale, NJ: Erlbaum.

Roediger, H. L., Weldon, M. S., Stadler, M. A., & Riegler, G. H. (1992). Direct comparison of word stems and fragments in implicit and explicit retention tests. *Journal of Experimental Psychology: Learning, Memory, and Cognition, 18,* 1251–1269.

Schacter, D. L., Bowers, J., & Booker, J. (1989). Intention, awareness and implicit memory: The retrieval intentionality criterion. In S. Lewandowsky, J. C. Dunn, & K. Kirsner (eds.), *Implicit memory: Theoretical issues*. Hillsdale, NJ: Erlbaum.

Schacter, D. L. & Tulving, E. (eds.) (1994). *Memory systems 1994*. Cambridge, MA: MIT Press.

Tulving, E. (1976). Ecphoric processes in recall and recognition. In J. Brown (ed.), *Recall and recognition*. New York: Wiley.

Tulving, E. (1983). *Elements of episodic memory*. New York: Oxford University Press.

Tulving, E. & Schacter, D. L. (1990). Priming and human memory systems. *Science, 247,* 301–305.

Weldon, M. S. (1991). Mechanisms underlying priming on perceptual tests. *Journal of Experimental Psychology: Learning, Memory and Cognition, 17,* 526–541.

Weldon, M. S. & Colston, H. L. (1995). Dissociating the generation stage in implicit and explicit memory tests: Incidental production can differ from strategic access. *Memory & Cognition, 23,* 533–539.

Weldon, M. S., Roediger, H. L., & Challis, B. H. (1989). The properties of retrieval cues constrain the picture superiority effect. *Memory & Cognition, 17,* 95–105.

CHAPTER 5

Memory and awareness

Is memory information stratified
into conscious and unconscious components?

William P. Banks   Yung-Pin Chen   Matthew W. Prull

This article develops and tests two models of how conscious and unconscious sources of information influence memory decisions. Certainly, there is a rich mixture of conscious and unconscious processes in any performance of memory. Researchers (see, e.g., Banks & Atkinson, 1974; Jacoby & Dallas, 1981; Jacoby, 1991; Mandler, 1980; Yonelinas, 1994) have taken a number of different approaches toward identifying and measuring the separate conscious and unconscious components. In recent years the separation of memory performance into conscious and unconscious components has achieved central importance. This article examines one technique for this separation, process dissociation (Jacoby, 1991). We develop signal detection models of process dissociation in an attempt to generate an analysis of conscious and unconscious components free of the concerns raised by critics.

0.1 Plan for this article

This article has five sections. The first describes process dissociation and outlines some of its criticisms. The second shows how signal-detection theory (SDT) can address these criticisms. The third section offers what we call Model I, which gives a detection-theoretic treatment of a common intuitive model of decision processes in the memory tasks of process dissociation. As it turns out, when it is made explicit, the model makes predictions that are not confirmed. The disconfirmation causes us to consider other ways of understanding these memory tasks. The fourth section presents Model II, which is a multivariate detection model. It is in accord with the data and also makes predictions for source memory. In the fifth section an experiment is presented that tests these predictions.

The familiar form of SDT is the unidimensional case (Banks, 1970; Swets, Tanner, & Birdsall, 1961; Green & Swets, 1974; Macmillan & Creelman, 1991), but for the present analyses we have found that it is necessary to use a multidimensional representation, with separate axes for each source of information. Our multidimensional approach turns out to have parallels in other areas. One of these is General Recognition Theory (GRT), developed by Ashby and colleagues (Ashby, 1992; Ashby & Perrin, 1988; Ashby & Townsend, 1986; Ashby & Gott, 1988; Kadlec & Townsend, 1992). Another, related, area includes the multidimensional stimulus and decision spaces proposed by Thomas and Olzac (Thomas, 1985; Thomas & Olzac, 1992) and by Getty, Swets, and Swets (1981) for visual patterns. Our applications appear to be the first in which a multidimensional detection model is applied to recognition memory.

1.   Process dissociation and its critics

Process dissociation has had a remarkable impact on the literature in the brief time since it was introduced. It has been applied with success in many situations (Jacoby, 1991; Jacoby, Toth, & Yonelinas, 1993; Toth, Reingold, & Jacoby, 1994; Jennings & Jacoby, 1993). Its methods are designed to separate the conscious and unconscious components into parts that sum to make the whole. An elaboration of this technique in a multinomial analysis has been offered by Buchner and his colleagues (Buchner, Erdfelder, & Vaterrodt-Plünnecke, 1995; Buchner & Erdfelder, 1996; Buchner & Wippich, 1996a,b), and an alternative has been presented by Wainwright and Reingold (1996; see also Reingold & Wainwright, 1996).

These techniques share two different discrete assumptions about performance. The first is that old items (those from the to-be-remembered list) are either in a learned state or they are not. This is the assumption that underlies any linear correction-for-guessing formula (see Swets, 1986a). This assumption does not fare well when it is tested in memory experiments (see Banks, 1970; Snodgrass & Corwin, 1988; Yonelinas & Jacoby, 1996), or generally in any area of performance (Swets, 1986b), and in this article we adapt continuous signal-detection models to develop analyses that do not rely on this assumption.

The second discrete assumption is specific to process dissociation. This is that items are discretely located in conscious and unconscious memory stores. Some, or all, of the items may be in both stores, but items may not have graded degrees of conscious or unconscious strength. (The model of Yonelinas, 1994, is a hybrid variant of process dissociation, with discrete membership of items in the conscious store but continuous degrees of familiarity for unconscious information.) Here we offer a test of this assumption using our own data, and it fits to a first approximation. However, the models presented here do not need this latter assumption.

1.1 *Process dissociation procedure and analytic technique*

The following example illustrates how process dissociation might be used in recognition memory. First, the participants study two lists of words, one seen (the list is presented on a computer screen) and one heard (a tape recording of the list is played for the subjects). Participants are then given a recognition test in which they are presented with words from the heard list and the seen lists ("old" items), and words that were not presented ("new" items). According to the process dissociation procedure (PDP), the probability of correctly selecting an old word in recognition will be based on a combination of recollection of the source of the item (we term this the C, or conscious, component) and familiarity (termed here the U component). The C component is thought to reflect the deliberate, conscious, and intentional recollection of information, whereas U is thought to reflect automatic, unintentional influences of memory, reflected as a feeling of familiarity. In the original form (Jacoby, 1991) the two components were assumed to be independent, and thus they combine in normal recognition as follows:

$$P(\text{``Old''}) = C + U(1 - C). \tag{Eq. 1}$$

That is, the probability of calling an item "old" equals the probability of recollecting it (C) plus the probability of recognizing it on the basis of a feeling of familiarity (U). The probability U is multiplied by $(1 - C)$ because familiarity operates only on those trials when recollection has not already brought up the item, and the proportion of such trials is $(1 - C)$. Multiplying U by $(1 - C)$ here amounts to the assumption that U and C are stochastically independent (Joordens & Merikle, 1993).

In the PDP participants are given an *inclusion* test in which participants are to include both seen and heard items in making their judgments. Thus, the P("Old") in the above equation, applied to inclusion, would include both seen and heard items, and the conscious and unconscious sources for both sets of items would contribute to performance, as is assumed in Eq. 1.

The critical test in the PDP, introduced by Jacoby (1991), is termed the *exclusion* test. In this test the respondents are asked to make a conditional identification. They are to accept an item as positive if and only if it comes from a specific list. Thus, in an exclusion task with heard items as the positive set, they are to accept as positive only heard items, and to reject both new items and seen items. However, they will inadvertently violate the instructions from time to time by accepting items from the list they are supposed to reject, in this case the seen list. It is assumed that these violations (at least to the extent that they exceed the baseline of accepting New items) result from a sense of familiarity not associated with the list but from the unconscious strength of the items.

To estimate the quantity symbolized by the C and U, we assume that the unconscious effect has a chance to express itself in exclusion only when conscious recollection fails. That is, when facing the exclusion task, the subject can withhold an item if conscious information about it is available. Putting this assumption into algebraic form, we get

$$P(\text{``Old''}|\text{excluded item}) = U - UC = U(1-C), \tag{Eq. 2}$$

which is to say that exclusion contains unconscious items (U), but only those that do not also have representations in the conscious store (UC). To put this another way, the model of exclusion performance assumes that items are "tested" for C. Those that pass this test (by not having enough C to be excluded) are then accepted on the basis of the amount of U they have. This is what we make explicit in Model I and subject to test against available patterns of data.

With Equations 1 and 2 we can solve for the U and C components. First, the difference between inclusion and exclusion tests (trying to versus trying *not* to select the words that were seen), gives an estimate of conscious recollection,

$$C = P(\text{``Old''}) - P(\text{``Old''}|\text{excluded item}) = [C + U(1-C)] - [U(1-C)]. \tag{Eq. 3}$$

And, once C is obtained, the estimate of the automatic, unconscious component can be readily calculated by rearranging terms in Equation 2,

$$U = P(\text{``Old''}|\text{excluded item}) / (1-C). \tag{Eq. 4}$$

In the following we will frequently, for convenience, refer to P("Old"| excluded item) as exclusion, or the exclusion probability, and to P("Old") as inclusion, or the inclusion probability.

1.2 *Comments on the process dissociation approach*

We take note at this point of the ingenuity and appropriateness of Jacoby's (1991) use of the exclusion condition as a measure of unconscious influences.

First, it creates an "opposition" paradigm that pits two sources of information against each other. Thus, it reduces the concern raised by subliminal presentations or any form of unconscious influence that the influence was not unconscious but only nonreported (Holender, 1986; Reingold & Merikle, 1988). Making an unconsciously influenced incorrect response in such a circumstance represents a much higher standard of unconscious processing than inability to report a stimulus.

Second, exclusion shares with other techniques, such as stem completion (Graf, Mandler, & Haden, 1982) and the mere exposure effect (Kunst-Wilson & Zajonc, 1980), the property of being an incidental effect, but also one that has protection against conscious contamination. For example, in stem completion without exclusion instructions, subjects might actively use previously learned material in order to make the task easier. The appearance of old words as completions would then hardly be evidence for unconscious influences. Clearly, evidence for incidental effects is critically weak without exclusion instructions.

Third, exclusion shares with the Stroop (1992) "Gold standard" (MacLeod, 1992) the demonstration of an effect taking place against the subject's active intention. This parallel with Stroop and Stroop-like tasks (cf., Banks, Clark, & Lucy, 1975; Banks, 1977) brings up an important aspect of processes tapped by the exclusion task, and this is *control*. Likewise, in the sort of uncomfortable exclusion tasks studied under the rubric of "ironic control" (Wegner, Schneider, Carter, & White, 1987) the person attempting to exercise the control is all too painfully aware of the material to be excluded.

1.3 *Problems with the process dissociation approach*

While the process dissociation technique has had remarkable success (Jacoby, 1991; Jacoby, et al., 1993; Toth, et al., 1994; Jennings & Jacoby, 1993), it has also been the target of several important criticisms (Curran & Hintzman, 1995; Dodson & Johnson, 1996; Graf & Komatsu, 1994; Joordens & Merikle, 1993; Ratcliff, Van Zandt & McKoon, 1995; Roediger & McDermott, 1994). The approach we take in the present article is intended to avoid the problems raised by these criticisms. We can divide these criticisms into the following categories:

1.3.1 *Correction-for-guessing*
Several alternatives for correcting hit rates with linear transformations of FAs have been suggested (cf., for example, Roediger & McDermott, 1994). Multinomial models for process dissociation also use linear correction-for-guessing formulas (Buchner & Erdfelder, 1996; Buchner, Erdfelder, & Vaterrodt-

Plünnecke, 1995; Buchner & Wippich, 1996a,b; Reingold & Wainwright, 1996; Roediger & McDermott, 1994; Wainwright & Reingold, 1996). We term these *discrete* formulas because they all assume that an item is either in a learned or a non-learned state. They differ in the manner in which they use the observed FA rate to estimate the number of fortuitous guesses that inflate the hit rate.

The concern here is that the discrete assumption imbedded in correction-for-guessing techniques is overly restrictive and inconsistent with the data (as Yonelinas & Jacoby, 1996, and Yonelinas, Regehr, & Jacoby, 1995, also point out). However, it is clear that if no correction is made, performance will not be comparable across conditions unless false alarms are constant.

1.3.2 *Discrete storage in C and U*
A second and entirely different discrete assumption of the process dissociation equations is that items are in either the C or the U state, or both, but never have any partial C or U information. This can be seen in Eq. 3, in which C = Inclusion – Exclusion. This equation amounts to a "correction" by which the inclusion performance has subtracted from it the exclusion performance to leave the C component. This correction assumes that there is a specific number of items from the total set in the C store. Inclusion performance includes these plus some U items. Subtracting out the exclusion performance leaves the C component. Joordens and Merikle (1993) showed that the relation of Eq. 3 is quite general across models of the correlation between C and U storage and is not specific to the independence model.

The poor fit of discrete models in correction-for-guessing does not imply that the discrete assumption about C and U is a bad one. The two discrete assumptions are quite different. We can test this assumption by plotting C as a function of U, just as we can test the discrete family of correction-for-guessing functions by plotting Hits as a function of False Alarms.

1.3.3 *Recognition criterion in inclusion and exclusion*
A third issue is whether the criterion for choice of items is the same in inclusion and exclusion performance (Curran & Hinzman, 1995; Dodson & Johnson, 1996; Graf & Komatsu, 1994). If there are different criteria, measures of inclusion and exclusion are not comparable, and the estimates of U and C must be in error. The detection measures we propose allow this question to be tested directly because they give measures of criterion as well as memory strength. In addition, they allow us to compute strength measures that do not vary with criterion and thus are protected from this criticism.

1.3.4 *Exclusion and source memory*

Another concern about process dissociation is that it may be merely a fancy measure of source discrimination rather than a measure of unconscious or automatic components of memory (F. Craik, as cited in a footnote in Roediger & McDermott, 1994). The argument is that exclusion performance is simply an effect of forgetting of the source of information and is not a measure of unconscious influences in memory. As we find (see Table 1), exclusion performance is not identical to source judgment when they are compared directly. Model II, presented at the end of this chapter, gives an exact prediction of the relationship between source and exclusion judgments.

1.3.5 *Effects of ROC slopes below 1.0*

As will be explained more fully at the end of the next section, performance at a very strict criterion can be misleading. When the hit and false alarm rates are both below 0.50, and the variance of old items is greater than the variance of new items, chance performance can be mistaken for weak but above-chance performance. Neither a correction-for-guessing formula nor the popular detection-theory measure d′ is immune to this problem. We find that this problem has affected every exclusion condition in the process dissociation literature, with the exception of one (Yonelinas, 1994, Experiment 3). We will explain this problem more fully below and present one measure that is not subject to this problem.

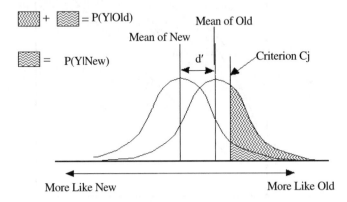

Figure 1. *Hypothetical distribution of old and new items on a familiarity continuum, as assumed by a Gaussian model of Signal Detection Theory.*

2.   Signal detection theory analysis of process dissociation

Signal detection theory describes performance as the effect of criterial placement along a decision axis, with signal and noise distributions located on this axis. The observer is assumed to accept any event above the criterion as a signal. Correct acceptance of a signal is termed a Hit, and incorrect acceptance of a noise event as a signal is termed a False Alarm.

The equal-variance Gaussian version of SDT is represented in Figure 1. Strengths are continuous, and new as well as old items are assumed to have some strength. The strengths of both are distributed as normal curves with (in this case) equal variance. The means of the old and new distributions are displaced on the strength axis, with d′ measuring the distance between them. To make a response, a subject chooses a criterial cutoff and accepts as targets all items that fall above the criterion. The two distributions determine what False Alarm, or P(Y|New), and Hit rates, or P(Y|Old), will result from this cutoff. The figure shows a hypothetical criterion C_j, and the False Alarm and Hit rates that result from adopting it. This C_j is relatively strict. As C_j is made more lenient (is moved to the left), more Hits and False Alarms will be accepted.

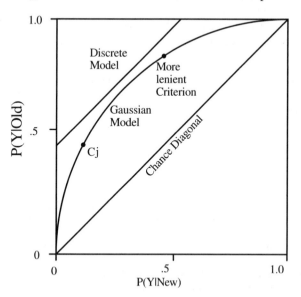

Figure 2. *Receiver (or Relative) Operating Characteristic based on Gaussian model (Figure 1) and a discrete model described in the text. This is the model that corrects for guessing by subtracting False Alarms from Hits. Plotting here is in linear probability coordinates.*

A useful way to look at results with differing false alarm rates is the Relative (or Receiver) Operating Characteristic (ROC). This is a plot of the Hit rate as a function of the False Alarm rate. A ROC is traced out as Hits and False Alarms vary with changes in the criterion.

Two ROCs are shown in Figure 2. The Gaussian ROC is the curved one, and the result of operating at criterion C_j in Figure 1 is plotted as point C_j. If the criterion were moved to more lenient cutoffs (to the left in Figure 1), the operating point would move to the right along the Gaussian operating characteristic in Figure 2. An important difference between the Gaussian and the discrete models is in the shape of the operating characteristics they generate. The ROC for the discrete model plotted here has the formula, where P(Y|Old) is the observed "percent correct," $P(Y|Old) = P*(Y|Old) + P(Y|New)$. This equation embodies the correction-for-guessing assumption that a person knows a certain number of items, the "true" correct or $P*(Y|Old)$, and increases the score from there to the observed P(Y|Old) by guessing. The number of guessed items equals P(Y|New), by the assumption that one New item is selected for every Old correctly guessed. Consequently, we can "correct" the hit rate to $P*(Y|Old)$ by applying the formula, $P*(Y|Old) = P(Y|Old) - P(Y|New)$, in effect just subtracting out the assumed proportion of lucky guesses that inflated the observed P(Y|Old) to get the "true" $P*(Y|Old)$ the subject would have had with no guesses at all.

Because the distributions of Figure 1 are Gaussian, the relation swept out between Hits and False Alarms is linear in probability coordinates, as shown in Figure 3, where the x- and y-axes are the z-scores of the False Alarm and Hit probabilities. This is sometimes termed a *z-ROC*. The slope of the Gaussian z-ROC is equal to the standard deviation of the new distribution divided by the standard deviation of the old distribution. The simplest Gaussian case of equal standard deviations is shown in the figure, with a d′ of 1.0. Also shown in Figure 3 is the operating characteristic traced out for the discrete model that was a straight line in linear coordinates (Figure 2). Here it is bowed.

An important *caveat* that applies to nearly every published article using SDT to analyze recognition memory is that the underlying distribution of the type presented in Figure 1 very rarely has equal variance for signal and noise. Typically the signal distribution has a larger variance (Ratcliff, McKoon, & Tindall, 1994). This conclusion comes from the fact that the slopes of the z-ROCs are less than 1.0. Generally they fall in the range 0.50 to .80, indicating Gaussian distributions in which the old item standard deviation is from 1.25 to 2.00 times the standard deviation of the new items. The dashed z-ROC in Figure 3 corresponds to targets having 2.0 times the standard deviation of the distracters.

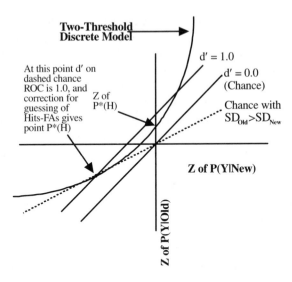

Figure 3. *Same plot as in Figure 2, but a z-ROC in which plotting is linear with the Z-score of the probability rather than with probability. The discrete model in this plot has the same assumptions as that in Figure 2, but a slightly lower discriminability.*

In item 5 of the previous section we noted that low-slope z-ROCs present some problems that are illustrated in Figure 3. We can now show how this works. Consider the ROC plotted with dashed lines passing through the point (0,0). This ROC represents chance performance because the means of old and new distributions are coincident. However, because of the slope, every point to the left of the (0,0) point will yield a $d' > 0$ if the d' is computed on the basis of the Hit and False Alarm rates on the function. The intersection with the $d' = 1.0$ ROC is marked. The ROC assumed by the discrete correction function $P^*(Y|Old)$ $= P(Y|Old) - P(Y|New)$ is also shown. This function intersects the dashed line at a Hit rate of about 0.16 and a False Alarm rate of 0.022. If that correction had been applied, the corrected Hit rate, $P^*(Y|Old)$, would have been 0.138 (0.16-.022), in other words, it would have been concluded that the "true" corrected performance was nonzero. However, both the d' and the corrected Hit rate would have been artifactual. Unfortunately, the exclusion data of every process dissociation experiment but one that we have considered fall in this region, in which Hit Rate and False Alarm Rate are both less than 0.50.

What would be the consequence of this artifact? In the case shown in Figure 3, the proper measure for exclusion performance should be exactly zero.

That would mean that a d′ of zero or a corrected Hit rate of zero is the correct measure. We can consider the effect of instead taking the observed exclusion Hit rate of .16 shown in the figure. Suppose, for the sake of example, that the Hit rate in inclusion is .80. By the process dissociation equations (Eqs. 2 and 3), the calculations would yield .64 for the C component and .44 for the U component. Even if the inclusion Hit rate were corrected for guessing to .138, the U would still be a substantial .41 (with a C of .66). However, if the lack of discrimination in exclusion were properly reflected in the measure, with a corrected Hit rate of zero, the C component would be .80, and the U component would be 0.0, a far cry from .44 or .41.

A measure that properly represents the discriminability represented by this ROC could be something like d_s, d_a, or D(Δm, s) (see Green & Swets, 1974, pp. 96–98; Macmillan & Creelman, 1991, pp. 65–71; Swets & Pickett, 1982, pp. 30–33) Each of these measures requires two components, one for the distance between the means and another for the slope. For example, the measure of discriminability, Δm, would be zero, and the slope measure, s, would be 0.50.

We offer instead the single-component measures Az or Ag. These measures correspond to the area under the entire ROC, computed in two different ways. Area is a proper measure of performance because of the demonstration by Green and Swets (1974) that area under the ROC corresponds to the proportion correct in two-alternative forced-choice. The measure Az is the area under the best-fitting Gaussian ROC and is a two-parameter measure that assumes a linear z-ROC with slope and intercept in z-coordinates as parameters. The measure Ag is the area calculated by "connecting the dots" (Banks, 1970; Macmillan & Creelman, 1991). It does not assume any shape for the ROC and is properly a nonparametric detection measure. Because they summarize the entire ROC, they are not subject to distortions that apply only to parts of the ROC.

In this article we computed most of the areas as Az, using the program of Metz (1991). In some cases we had to use Ag because there were not enough points for the two-parameter fit required by Az. In practice we find that Az and Ag are quite close to one another. In the rare case in which a ROC is very poorly fit by a two-parameter Gaussian, the two will differ, and Ag would be the better choice.

2.1 *How can we use Signal Detection Theory to measure C and U?*

As Macmillan and Creelman (1991) pointed out, there is no threshold in the Gaussian SDT models and thus no concept of a subthreshold or unconscious stimulus. Given the truth of this statement, and at the same time the evidence that there can be strong influences on our behavior that are independent of conscious control, it seems reasonable to treat conscious and unconscious effects as separate, and to have a separate d′ for conscious and unconscious components of memory performance. These sources of performance are defined in Equations 5 and 6.

$$C = d'_C \qquad\qquad\qquad\qquad\qquad\qquad\qquad\qquad\text{(Eq. 5)}$$

$$U = d'_U, \qquad\qquad\qquad\qquad\qquad\qquad\qquad\qquad\text{(Eq. 6)}$$

We need not, of course, stop with two, and in fact Bower's (1996) associative model of implicit memory would allow any number of Type 1 associations (those whose strength we would measure with $\mathbf{d'_C}$) within the conscious domain and any number of Type 2 (measured by $\mathbf{d'_U}$) within the unconscious domain.

Having made this distinction we need a model of how these two sources of information combine to produce the overall d′ for the task. There are two general ways in which multiple sources of information can be combined, and SDT has methods of analysis for both of these (see Green & Swets, 1974; Swets, 1984). The first is that decisions are made separately on the basis of the two sources of information, and the decisions are then combined in some manner. This is termed the *Decision-Combination* model (Swets, 1984, p. 205). The second is to assume that the information is combined before decisions are made, and the decision is then made on the basis of the combined information. This is termed the *Information Combination* model (see Green & Swets, 1974, pp. 271–275).

A simple analogy for these two types of rule can be drawn in contrasting styles of executive decision. An information-combination executive would ask each subordinate officer to provide information, which the executive would then combine and weigh in making a decision. This would be like forming a single d′ for a task on the basis of component values of $\mathbf{d'_C}$ and $\mathbf{d'_U}$. Model II, presented in a later section, represents one approach to combining information from different sources to come up with a single d′.

By contrast, the executive following the decision combination model would ask each officer to weigh the evidence in his or her area of expertise and then to vote for one alternative or another. The executive would tally the votes but would not have access to the information each subordinate used. The decision would be based on some weighted sum of the votes. In a regular election for a political candidate, each vote normally has an equal weight ("one man, one vote," as the saying goes), but this need not be the only way to combine votes. The executive in this example could have some subordinates with more credibility than others and give their votes more weight than those of the others in computing a decision.

3.   Model I: A hybrid of information integration and decisional combination

Sorkin and Dai (1994) derived an expression for the sum of information from several sources. Equation 7 below gives their equation for the combination of information from two sources.

$$d'_{1+2} = \sqrt{\frac{d'^2_1 + d'^2_2 - 2r_{12}d'_1d'_2}{(1-r^2_{12})}} \qquad \text{(Eq. 7)}$$

where the d'_{1+2} is the resulting distance between signal and noise when information from d'_1 and d'_2 is combined, and r_{12} is the correlation between variations in the two distributions.

This equation lends itself quite naturally to process dissociation, with r_{12} expressing the degree of correlation between the two sources of information. Here $r_{12} = 1.0$ for the case in which conscious and unconscious information is redundant, $r_{12} = 0.0$ for the independent case, and $r_{12} = -1.0$ for the case in which the two sources of information are disjunctive or exclusive (see Joordens & Merikle, 1993). The equation is indeterminate for the exclusive and redundant cases, and we will not develop alternative approaches here.

The independent case, however, reduces to the following familiar equation (Green & Swets, 1974, pp. 271–275; Swets, 1984; Kadlec & Townsend, 1992; Tanner, 1956):

$$d'_{1+2} = \sqrt{d'^2_1 + d'^2_1} \qquad \text{(Eq. 8)}$$

The inclusion d' is assumed to include the information from both the U and C stores. Given independence, we can use Eq. 8 to express the d' for performance on the inclusion task as

$$d'_I = d'_{U+C} = \sqrt{d'^2_U + d'^2_C} \qquad \text{(Eq. 9)}$$

to predict overall performance (measured by d') on the inclusion task.

It is not necessary to assume separate dimensions for U and C in order to derive Eq. 9, only independence of the variability of the distributions. Furthermore, multiple independent components can sum in this manner, as Green and Swets (1974, p. 275, Eq. 9A.18) show. The general equation is

$$d_I' = \left[\sum_{i=1}^{n} (d_i')^2 \right]^{1/2} .$$

(Eq. 10)

If d_U' or d_C' were themselves composed of components, as in Bower's (1996) Type-1 and Type-2 associations, and these were independent, then the total memory strength, d_I', for an inclusion test would sum over these associations in this manner.

Equation 10 thus gives an information-combination model for inclusion, or simply recognition performance in general. The exclusion condition is a more difficult case. One does not add components to model exclusion performance but rather opposes them. The process involved in exclusion is to accept targets on the basis of U but reject them on the basis of C. Thus, the larger d_U' , the more likely will be *acceptance* of to-be-rejected targets in exclusion, but the larger d_C', the more likely will be *rejection* of these items in exclusion. There is no simple way to add d_U' and subtract d_C' in the form of equations like Eq. 9 or 10 to compute the resulting d' when it is composed of opposing components. However, the verbal model of exclusion suggests an analogy and a two-dimensional model.

3.1 *Model I's approach to exclusion*

Here is the analogy: Consider that the respondent performing in the exclusion condition is behaving much like the Royal Taster sampling the King's food for poison. Any hint of the bitter taste of strychnine, say, or the metallic taste of arsenic, and the food is rejected. By analogy, this is like inspecting candidate items for membership in the excluded list; if one finds any hint of the conscious trace of the origin of the item to be excluded, it is rejected. On the other hand, if the food has an appealing flavor it is more likely to be passed on to the King than if it is unappetizing. This sort of general quality of flavor of the food is like the unconscious component. The more of this it has, the better the chance of its being passed, assuming of course that there is not a trace of a conscious component.

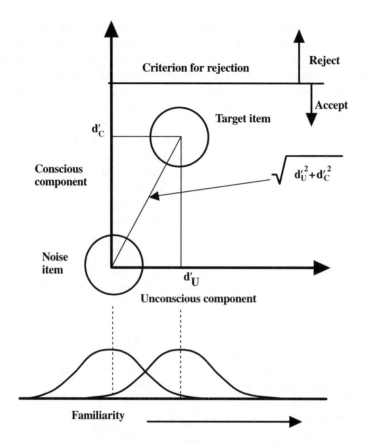

Figure 4. *Illustration of Model I. Target (old) items have separate conscious and unconscious components of strength, which is the d' distance between means of new and old distributions. This distance is equal to the square root of the sum of the squares of the separate d' strengths of the old item distributions on the conscious and unconscious axes. The new distribution is assumed to have a mean of zero on both axes, with some variance on both as well. The distance between these means is assumed to predict performance in inclusion, otherwise simply termed recognition memory. Exclusion performance is predicted by assuming first that the subject rejects items above some criterion on the conscious axis, then accepts items on the basis of unconscious information. The criterion shown here has a very lenient, and unrealistic, criterion for rejection. Items with a rather high level of conscious strength would be admitted with this criterion.*

The model in Figure 4 illustrates how this process might work. First, a geometrical interpretation of Eq. 9 is shown, by which the discriminability of a target from the noise is the distance in Euclidean space predicted by the orthogonal combination of the conscious and unconscious components. The distance between the means in this figure is the d′ for inclusion, as predicted from the d'_U and d'_C, given that they are independent components. (As we will see, however, the d′ for recognition also depends on the criterial bounds employed in this 2-dimensional space. This is discussed in the Appendix. For the moment we will consider only the simplest case, in which this is the prediction.)

The exclusion model illustrated in Figure 4 assumes a two-part decision process. The conscious axis is submitted to a criterial test: items above a criterial value of C are excluded, just as foods are rejected if the degree of poison detected is above a certain level. The criterial level shown in Figure 4 is very high (this Royal Taster's King would not last long, nor would the Taster). Items below this cutoff are then accepted on the basis of the degree of U they exhibit (or on how good they taste to the Royal Taster), and a ROC can be plotted as different criterial values of U are employed. This two-step model thus has a first step in which C is used to reject items, and a second step in which U is the basis on which to accept items.

This scheme could be understood as a continuous version of Eq. 2, in which exclusion equals $U - U \cdot C$; that is, the proportion of items accepted in exclusion equals the total of the unconscious store, minus those in the store that also have conscious representation. Here, however, instead of having discrete representations in U or C, we allow a continuous distribution of the two components, and a criterion to eliminate the equivalent of $U \cdot C$ items that have more than a certain level of C.

A convenient way of visualizing the selection on the U axis after selection of items falling below a criterion on C is to plot the distribution of old and new items after the selection. Below the U axis a decision axis shows hypothetical distributions of target and noise remaining after selection. The assumption that selection in the exclusion condition is based on U (while rejection is based on C) dictates that the decision axis be parallel to the U axis, and be a projection of the distributions onto this axis. The subject would then base selections on criterial values of U along this axis. Note that these projected distributions are now conditional probability distribution functions, and their area will be less than 1.0.

An operating characteristic is traced out as criteria are varied along this projection on the U axis, creating the Hit and False Alarm proportions. Under these assumptions, with a very high criterion on the C axis, the d′ for exclusion will be close to d'_U.

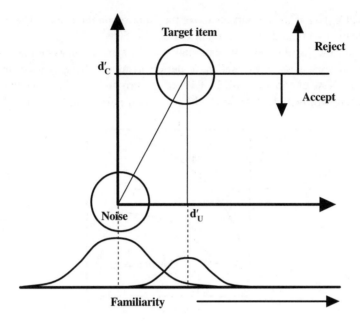

Figure 5. *Same as Figure 4, except that the criterion for rejecting on the basis of conscious information is a bit more strict, being at the mean of the target distribution.*

However, if the criterion on the C axis is lower (and this seems more realistic than the very high criterion in Figure 4) as seen in Figure 5, very unusual ROC's result and the predicted d' for exclusion is smaller than d'_U. To see this, consider the hypothetical selection process in Figure 5. Here the criterion on C for rejecting candidates falls at the middle of the target distribution. The projections shown at the bottom of Figure 5 show what would happen with this criterion on the C axis and a relatively large d'_U. The remaining Old items will have a normal distribution on U with the same mean but with 50% of the original area. While the decisions are made along this U axis, only the portion of the target distribution that is below the criterion on C will be subject to this decision process; the remaining .50 of the target distribution will already have been rejected. Therefore, the maximum Hit Rate will be .50. Thus as criteria sweep from the right to the left along the decision axis for acceptance on the basis of unconscious information, the proportion of Hits will equal

$$P(Y|Old) = P(X_U > c, Y_C < d'_C) \le P(Y_C < d'_C) = 0.50, \tag{Eq. 11}$$

where $P(X_U) > c$ is the proportion above the criterion on the U axis. The denominator sums to 1.0, and the maximum Hit rate is .50.

The New distribution will be normal with the same mean as before, but with a reduced area. If $d'_C = 1.0$ and the criterion assumed above is used, the area under the New distribution will be 84% of the original and the maximum False Alarm rate will be .84; if $d'_C = 1.5$, the maximum False Alarm rate will be .93.

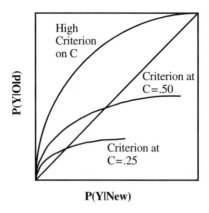

Figure 6. *Relative operating characteristics (ROCs) for exclusion predicted by Model I with a very lenient criterion for excluding on the basis of conscious information (High C), and a criterion set at the .50 and the .25 points of the distribution on the basis of the conscious trace. Note that the maximum P(Y|New) is limited by these criteria, and the ROC stops at that point rather than continuing to the right-hand end of the unit square. According to Model I the d'_U can be recovered by rescaling the ROC so that the asymptotic values of P(Y|Old) and P(Y|New) equal 1.0. This rescaled ROC would be a normal ROC that goes from (0,0) to (1,1), and its d' would be d'_U.*

Figure 6 shows hypothetical ROCs resulting from various placements of C. If the criterion on C is high enough (as in Figure 4), a relatively ordinary ROC is obtained and the d' obtained from this ROC will be close to the d'_U. If the criterion on C is at the 50% point on the target axis, as is shown in Figure 5, the ROC will terminate not at the upper right corner, but at the point 0, .50, given that .50 is the largest Hit rate possible in this situation. The middle ROC in the figure shows this case, and the lower ROC shows the case when the C criterion allows only 25% of the target distribution to be considered.

The original d'_U can be recovered by reconstructing the original distribution, if the proportion by which the target distribution is below the criterion on the C axis can be determined. Fortunately, this proportion has a simple interpretation in terms of the ROC. It is the horizontal asymptote of the ROC. Estimating this boundary will allow the target distribution to be renormalized and d'_U to be estimated. If the criterion on C is low enough to reduce the noise distribution appreciably, the proportion by which the noise distribution is reduced can be reconstructed in a similar manner.

3.2 How well does this model work?

What we have here is an interpretation of the intuitive model of the process of exclusion that is explicit enough to make quantitative predictions. As it turns out, the model of exclusion does not work very well at all. The problem is that this model simply does not predict the form of ROCs obtained in exclusion. Figure 7 plots several ROCs for exclusion. These include ones obtained in our laboratory and others replotted from Yonelinas (1994), Experiments 1 and 2.

The top panel is a replication of Jacoby (1991), Experiment 3. We attempted to replicate the target experiment as closely as possible, with one change. On the response sheet for both inclusion and exclusion, subjects checked "Yes" or "No," in the manner in which they responded in the Jacoby experiment, but then following that judgment they rated their confidence in the judgment on a 1–4 scale. The resulting confidence categories allowed construction of an 8-point scale from which an ROC could be plotted. As can be clearly seen, the plot is nothing at all like the predictions in Figure 6. Instead of curving over to terminate at some middle level of Hits when False Alarms equal zero, it snakes around the chance diagonal and aims to the {1.0,1.0} point. Fit by the Metz (1991) program the Az is .498, essentially at chance (chance is 0.50).

The lower panel shows four exclusion conditions from Yonelinas (1994). These are from his Experiments 1 and 2, in which subjects had either long or short lists to learn and then exclusion and inclusion tasks on these lists, with a 6-category confidence rating scale. (There is also an Experiment 3 that had an exclusion condition, but it is not plotted.) These are plotted without lines for clarity. The S-shape seen in the top panel is apparent, though not as pronounced. The mean Az for these four conditions is 0.51.

Figure 8 plots the same data as Figure 7, but in normal-normal coordinates. The prediction of Model I, illustrated in Figures 4 and 5, is a distinctly curved z-ROC. The linearity of the z-ROC functions obtained for the exclusion data suggest an altogether different model, which we will describe in the next section.

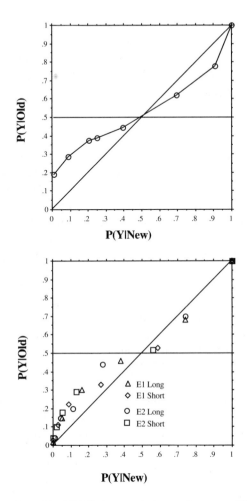

Figure 7. *Two plots of empirical ROCs from exclusion performance. The top figure is from a replication of Jacoby (1991, Experiment 3) and the bottom figure is replotted from Yonelinas (1994), Experiments 1 and 2.*

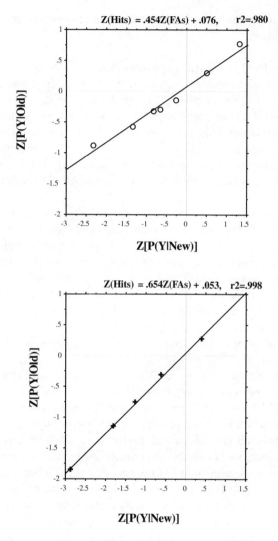

Figure 8. *Top figure is the top of Figure 7, plotted as a z-ROC; bottom is the average of values from the bottom of Figure 7, plotted as a z-ROC.*

4.   Model II: Combination of information in a multidimensional representation

Above we considered an explicit implementation of the assumptions of the PDP, using continuous distributions. As was seen, these assumptions do not work. Here we will try a different model. This model may be most easily understood by showing how the basic representation would be set up. Assume first that a subject has studied two lists, one seen on a computer screen (Seen list), and another heard from a tape recording (Heard list). Then in recognition testing the subject gets an inclusion test in which both Seen and Heard items are to be accepted as Old. Confidence ratings are taken, and ROCs for Seen and Heard targets are plotted.

Let us assume that the d' for the discrimination between Seen and New is 1.5, and the d' for discriminating between Heard and New is 1.25. The first step is to conceive of these d''s as distances in a spatial representation. We begin with a unidimensional decision axis. On this axis we could place the mean of the New distribution at a point we could arbitrarily call 0.0, the mean of Seen as a point 1.50 units to the right of New, and Heard as 1.25 units to the right of New. This picture would look much like Figure 1, except that there would be two target distributions rather than one. This would all be all that is needed if — and this is the crucial point — the means of the Seen and Heard distributions are .25 units apart (i.e., 1.50–1.25). Are they?

To answer this question we need to measure the discriminability between these populations of items. In the present case we did this with a source discrimination test in which subjects are presented only Seen and Heard items and were asked to decide which is the list of origin for each item on the test. Assume that subjects are presented items from both lists and are asked to respond "Seen" or "Not Seen" to each one. From this experiment we would plot a ROC in which the vertical axis is the probability of responding "Seen" when a Seen item was presented (analogous to Hits) and the horizontal axis is the probability of saying "Seen" when the item in question is actually a Heard item (analogous to a False Alarm). The d' derived from this ROC is the discriminability of the sources. Interpreted as a distance, it allows us to place the means of Seen and Heard relative to each other. If this distance is considerably greater than .25, a two-dimensional representation is needed.

Let us assume this distance is 1.0, that is that there is a value of $d' = 1.0$ for the discrimination between Seen and Heard. This distance necessitates use of a two-dimensional representation because of the triangle inequality. The representation is a set of bivariate normal distributions, in which means are points in the space and the spread of the distributions is indicated by contour boundaries. The means are plotted as points in Figure 9. The density for each of the distributions could be represented as the height of a hill emerging from the page with its center and highest point over the mean in each case. For convenience we assume that the variance of these distributions is equal in all directions. The representation in Figure 9, and the method for generating it, which is essentially to get d″'s for each pairwise combination of categories, essentially the same as proposed by Thomas and Olzac (1992), and plotted in their Figure 10.2. A similar translation from confusion (discriminability) to distance is presented by Getty et al. (1981).

In this bivariate case, the dispersions of the distributions cover two dimensions. Nevertheless, the decision of "yes" versus "no" is unidimensional, and to make a decision we must collapse the two dimensions of the space to one dimension in some manner. We conceptualize this collapsing process as a projection of the distributions to a single decision axis, much as in Figures 4 and 5 the distributions were collapsed onto an axis parallel to the U dimension. In the present

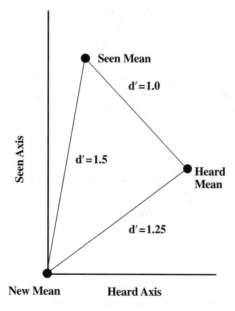

Figure 9. *Illustration of how the triangle inequality forces data into a two-dimensional representation. Here it is assumed that the d' for discriminating whether an item was seen or heard is 1.0, and the recognition d''s (discrimination between targets and new items) are 1.5 for seen items and 1.25 for heard items.*

case, the decision axis can take any direction in the space, and the angle the axis takes is a free parameter in using models like Figure 9 to fit experimental data.

Figure 10 shows a hypothetical decision axis drawn through the bivariate representation. The decision axis entails two concepts. First, the axis itself represents the dimension along which the decisions are made; that is, this is the axis on which the distributions are projected for the sake of making a decision. The detection decision is always the unidimensional decision "yes" or "no." No matter how many dimensions the original space has, the information must be

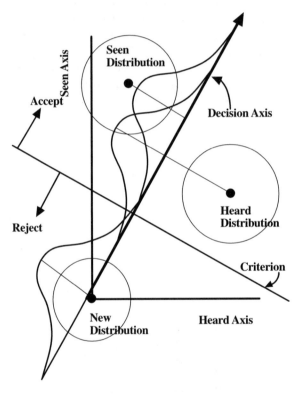

Figure 10. *Use of hypothetical representation of Figure 9 to create a decision model for recognition. The means are placed as in Figure 9, and the circles have been added to indicate the spread of the distributions, which have equal variance on the two dimensions and no correlation term. Here the appropriate decision axis is radial, passing from the mean of the new distribution through the space. The three distributions are projected onto this axis, and the resulting normal distributions are the basis for acceptance and rejection of candidate items as previously presented.*

projected to a single dimension for this decision. Once the distributions are projected to this axis they are treated exactly as the unidimensional case. We are using the orientation of the decision axis in the multivariate space as a way of describing the decision process. In Figure 10 the axis is oriented for the discrimination between list items and new items. Note how different discriminations in subsequent figures define different orientations of the decision axis.

The second matter we must consider is the form of the decision criteria. Between each criterion the observations are cumulated and projected to the decision axis. Linear criterial bounds drawn across the bivariate normal space will generate normal curves as projections on the decision axis. For the sake of decision, each criterial bound divides the space into two regions, accept and reject, as shown in Figure 10. Any observation falling in the region above the criterial bound is accepted as a "Yes" or a "Seen or Heard" item. Any observation falling below the criterion is judged a "No" or "New" item. As criterial bounds are moved along the decision axis, different probabilities of Hits and False Alarms are obtained, and an ROC is traced out.

While we have assumed linear criterial boundaries in this figure, there are cases in which the criteria must be curvilinear. The optimal boundary is linear when the variances of the two distributions are equal, and they are quadratic when the variances are unequal (Ashby, 1992b). In either case the decision axis is an important organizing concept. With linear bounds, the decision axis is normal to them and defines the direction of the decision. With quadratic bounds, the decision axis is the axis of symmetry, and it also defines the direction of the decision. Frequently a decision will be between one class of item and two other classes, with unequal variance. Linear boundaries will be optimal for one set of decisions and quadratic for the other; however, the same decision axis can be assumed in both cases. In general, the simplest way to explain the decision process is to refer to the direction of the decision axis in the space, and we use the direction of the decision axis to explain our predictions, and the angle the axis has with respect to an arbitrary axis as a free parameter in the fitting.

We need to consider how d' for the discrimination between two distributions is affected by the angle ϕ by which the decision axis deviates from the line connecting their midpoints. Appendix A shows how d'_E, which is the effective d', varies with ϕ and d'_I, which is the maximum d' possible for the discrimination between the two sets of items. The conclusion is that $d'_E = d'_I(\cos\phi)$. This means, in general terms, that d'_E is at a maximum when $\phi = 0$, that is, when the decision axis is coincident with or parallel to the line connecting the midpoints between the two means, and it declines to zero as ϕ approaches 90°. This finding can be applied to any number of means in the space. The d' for the discrimination between any two means in the space is multiplied by the factor $\cos\phi$ to obtain the d' for the discrimination defined by that particular decision axis.

In Appendix A only linear criterial bounds are treated. However, the same qualitative conclusions, and quantitative ones to a first approximation, hold for quadratic criterial bounds. This can be seen intuitively because the quadratic bounds are symmetrical about the decision axis, and thus the tangent to these bounds is normal to the decision axis where it crosses it. Because the data are densest in the region along the line connecting the means of the distributions, a large proportion of the data fall in the region where the quadratic is approximated by a line normal to the decision axis. Banks and Chen (in preparation) have shown that where quadratic criterial bounds are appropriate, linear ones yield linear z-ROC's and d''s only slightly smaller than those obtained with quadratic bounds.

Figure 11 shows a decision axis drawn for source memory discriminations. Here the response instructions are to discriminate seen and heard items. Note that for this decision the axis is roughly parallel to the line connecting the means of the two target distributions. Criterial boundaries are normal to this axis. The decision is "heard" for observations to the right of a criterial bound and "seen" for observations to the left.

Figure 12 shows the decision axes for recognition (inclusion) and source discrimination as in Figures 10 and 11. Added to this are hypothetical decision axes for exclusion. The decision axis nearly parallel to the "Heard" axis represents the decision axis for accepting "Heard" (i.e., exclude "Seen") in exclusion, with Heard items positive and New and Seen items as negative items. That is, the subject in this task is asked to say "Yes" to Heard items and "No" to Seen and New items. This axis provides a good prediction for many aspects of exclusion behavior. The projections on the axis give a d' for the positive items in exclusion that is slightly lower than the d' in inclusion (Dodson & Johnson, 1995, noted that this is frequently reported). The d' for excluded items is close to zero; that is, Seen is approximately as far from Heard in the projection on the decision axis as is New.

We are also now in a position to explain the ROCs we found for the excluded items. Figure 13 shows a decision space for an exclusion task in which Heard items are targets and New and Seen are to be excluded. First, as noted, the variance of the New distribution is less than the variance of the Seen distribution. Second, the decision axis has been put through the space in such a way that New and Seen means fall on the same point on the axis.

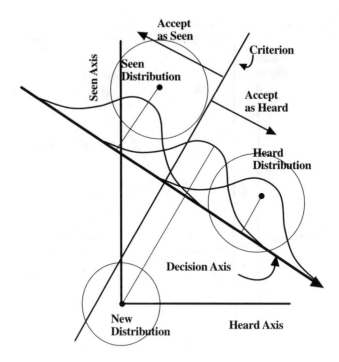

Figure 11. *Here the representation of Figure 9 is used to predict source memory judgments. The decision axis for source memory is approximately perpendicular to the recognition memory decision axis shown in Figure 9. For the largest d' in source discriminations, this decision axis should parallel the line connecting the centers of the seen and heard distributions (see Appendix A). However, it is an empirical question whether in any given situation the decision axis subjects use is optimal in this sense.*

The most important point about the projection of New and Seen is that while the means are identical, the variance of the Seen distribution is greater than the variance of the New distribution. This last relation results in the tails of the Seen distribution being higher than the tails of the New distribution. Thus, as the criterion moves from the conservative end of the decision axis (from the right in this figure), P(Y|Seen) > P(Y|New) until the criterion reaches the common mean of the distributions, where P(Y|Seen) = P(Y|New). For the more liberal regions on the left of the axis, P(Y|Seen) < P(Y|New). The ROC generated by sweeping criteria across these distributions will be above the chance diagonal in the lower left quadrant, it will cross the diagonal at the point (0.50, 0.50), and it will be below the diagonal for the upper right quadrant. It will, in short, look like the

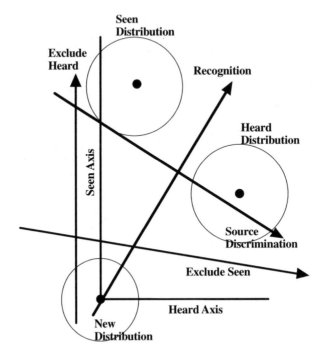

Figure 12. *The representation of Figure 9 is here shown with hypothetical decision axes for item recognition, source discrimination, exclusion of seen items, and exclusion of heard items. These are not orthogonal, but each can produce a different pattern of data.*

ROCs in Figure 7. Because these are normal distributions, the z-ROC will be linear: the slope will equal the ratio of the standard deviations, and the plot will be like those in Figure 8.

In sum, and this is a very important conclusion, it appears that *a single representation of the kind in Figure 9 can predict recognition, source memory, and exclusion performance.* The trick is to choose the correct decision axes for each decision, and then to get ROCs for the decisions among the distributions that are projected on the appropriate decision axis. Clearly, this approach is superior to the first model we considered, in which candidate items were first tested for a conscious component, then accepted on the basis of unconscious familiarity. In the next section we determine how well this scheme can apply to experimental data.

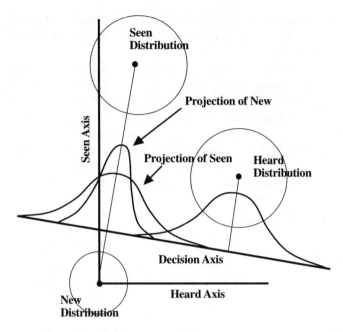

Figure 13. *Hypothetical projection of the Figure 9 distributions onto a decision axis set up for exclusion of seen items. Here the target sets are shown as having a larger standard deviation (SD) than the new set. The distribution at the right end of the axis is that of the correctly accepted heard items in exclusion. The seen distribution, on the other hand, is shown as having the same mean as the new distribution, and therefore as being not discriminable from it. However, because of the difference in variance a criterion at C_j will yield a P(Y|Old) for seen items that is larger than the P(Y|New). The z-ROCs for both seen and heard items with this decision axis will have a slope less than 1.0.*

5. Integration of recognition, source memory, and exclusion: An experimental test

This experiment was designed to test whether inclusion (that is, simple recognition memory), exclusion, and source memory can be subsumed under the same representation. Twenty-four Pomona students participated in the 15-minute experiment. They were presented two lists of 40 words each, one Seen and one Heard, in a classroom setting. The Seen list was presented with a slide projector, at a rate of 5 sec per word. After presentation subjects were given a brief break and then presented the Heard list, which was read at a slow rate (about 3 sec per word) by the experimenter. To reduce the effects of primacy and recency on the data, the first and last three words in each list were fillers drawn from the same pool as the targets but not tested.

Each list contained two types of word. Half of each list was drawn from a pool of one- and two-syllable words with a word frequency mean of 57.1 occurrences per million in the Francis and Kuçera (1982) norms. The other half of each list was composed of common male surnames, such as Bill, Jim, Dan, Harry, etc. The motivation for this design was to create within the same experiment one pair of lists that was more easily discriminated than the other. It was expected that the two types of item, names and common words, would have approximately the same memory strength for recognition, but very different degrees of source discrimination.

After subjects had been presented the Heard words they were given a pair of test sheets. The first sheet tested inclusion for all subjects. It had inclusion instructions and 80 items in random order. The 80 contained 40 common words and 40 male names. Of the words, 20 were New words drawn from the same pool as the targets, 10 words were from the Seen list, and 10 words were from the Heard list. The 40 names consisted of 20 New names from the same pool as the targets, 10 male names from the Seen list, and 10 male names from the Heard list. After each word was an 8-point scale for their judgments of memory, with 1 = "certain it was not presented" and 8 = "certain it was presented." The instructions explained that they were to use intermediate numbers for intermediate degrees of confidence.

After completing the first sheet, subjects were asked to turn to the second one. For 12 of the subjects this second sheet had exclusion instructions and for the other 12 it had source memory instructions. In the data reported here all 12 of the subjects in the source memory condition gave usable data, but 4 of the 12 in the exclusion condition returned incomplete response sheets. The exclusion sheet had a total of 80 words in random order. The 80 words consisted of the 10 common words from the Seen and Heard lists that had not been used in the inclusion condition, the 10 male names from the two lists that were not used in the inclusion condition, and 20 new male names as foils, and 20 new words as foils. The source memory testing sheet had only 40 words. They were the same as the list words on the exclusion sheet but they lacked the foils. Exclusion instructions asked subjects to respond with 8 if they were certain they had seen the item and 1 if it was heard or not presented. Source memory instructions asked subjects to respond with 8 for items they were sure they saw and 1 for items they were sure they heard. As in inclusion, the instructions stressed that they were to use intermediate numbers for intermediate degrees of confidence.

We have two sets of results, the traditional ones based on percents at the "yes-no" decision cutoff or, in the case of source memory, the mean source discrimination scores, and the "distance" between the items based on the signal detection measures. Percent of acceptance was based on the proportion of items given a rating of 5–8. Thus, it was assumed that a rating of 1–4 was a "no" and 5–8 was a "yes."

Table 1 shows the mean proportion "yes" in inclusion for the two subsets of subjects, the source discrimination performance for the discrimination subjects, the exclusion performance (false acceptances), and the C and U components for the Heard Words and the Heard Names for the exclusion subset of the data.

Table 1. *Results for each category of word tested. Shown under inclusion probability, P("Yes"), are separate columns for the group that had source discrimination (SD) as their second test and the group that had exclusion as their second test. Source discrimination is given with the first column reporting the mean rating, in which 1 = certain it was heard and 8 = certain it was seen; the second column reports the probability of a rating of 5 or greater. Exclusion proportion is the proportion of items in each category given a rating of 5 or greater. The PDP measures are the conscious (C) and unconscious (U) components according to the process dissociation decomposition.*

Category	Inclusion P("Yes")		Source Discrimination		Exclusion Proportion	PDP Measures	
	SD Group	Exclusion Group	Rating	P(Seen)		C	U
Heard Word	.583	.567	3.13	.29	.117	.45	.21
Heard Name	.667	.667	3.95	.44	.192	.47	.36
Seen Word	.717	.708	4.96	.62	.550		
Seen Name	.517	.450	4.93	.65	.492		
Word Foil	.246	.125			.071		
Name Foil	.300	.167			.133		

There are several patterns in all three measures that show an effect of the names being more confusable than the words. First, the source discrimination data show that the names are more similar than the words in ratings of Seen vs. Heard (mean difference of .98 vs. 1.83 on an 8-point scale), as well as in the difference between the proportions accepted as Seen (.44 vs. .65 for names and .29 vs. .62 for words). If one conceives of a continuum between "seen" and "heard" on which an item can be placed, the placement of a seen word with perfect discrimination would be 8.0, and placement of a heard word with perfect discrimination would be 1.0, according to the scale we used. An item whose list identity was unknown, or for which memory of list of origin had been completely forgotten, should fall at 4.5 on this scale. In our study the mean placement of the names was closer to the middle of the scale than the mean placement of the words. This can be interpreted to mean that the names were more confusable than the words, or had weaker source memory than the words.

Second, the name foils had a higher probability of leading to a False Alarm (.233 for mean of the two groups) than the word foils (.186). This difference leads to a difference between word and name targets in the discriminability measure used in Table 2 (see below). For words the discriminability between targets and foils is .80 for Seen and .74 for Heard, while for names it is .74 for Seen and .69 for Heard. This difference suggests that the higher probability of Hits for names than words in the heard condition (.667 vs. .575) is criterial, and not the effect of greater memory strength for names. Again, the names are more difficult to discriminate than the words.

Third, the exclusion results (in which the instructions were to accept seen items and reject both new and heard) show that correct rejection was less likely for name foils than word foils (.133 vs. .071 False Alarm probability), that rejection of heard names was less likely than rejection of heard words (.192 vs. .117 incorrect acceptances), and that acceptance of seen names was less likely than acceptance of seen words (.492 vs. .550 Hit probability). Once again, this could be interpreted as less discrimination between the names than the words. Also note that these results show that exclusion is not exactly the same as source discrimination. If it were the probabilities of acceptance in the exclusion condition should be quite close to the probabilities of judging an item as seen in source discrimination.

The PDP analysis in the far right column gives a different interpretation to the pattern of acceptances in the source memory condition. By this account the names and words had about the same C component, but the names had a considerably larger U component. The greater confusion between names than the unrelated words would therefore result from the U component the names have in common, which is weaker for the unrelated words. Thus, when a subject sees a name, a general familiarity associated with names in general is aroused because they were so frequently presented in this experiment. This general familiarity increases the acceptance of the names without source identification. It remains to be seen which is the better interpretation, worse source memory for names than words, or greater U for names than words. It could be argued that the apparent increase in U results simply and trivially from less discriminative cues to source for names than words. On the other hand, it could be argued that the greater confusions in source memory between lists for the names is an expectable result from a greater U component for the names, that is, from a greater generalized sense of familiarity for them. The following section shows how item discriminability can predict exclusion performance. This does not show whether U or source confusion is central.

5.1 Prediction of exclusion from source memory

In this section we use the pattern of discrimination between new and old items and between items from the two lists to predict exclusion performance. The prediction works by setting up a representation like that in Figure 9 and taking the projection appropriate for predicting exclusion performance, as described in Figures 10–13. The representation is created by applying a multidimensional scaling program to the inter-item discriminabilities, as measured in recognition and source discrimination testing. The distances between each item and the new distribution are taken from recognition performance, and the distances between the target items are based on source discriminations between them. It is important that the predicted distances between items in exclusion performance are not used to create this spatial representation.

Table 2 is a table of inter-mean discriminability distances measured in terms of d_a (Swets & Pickett, 1982). These distances were computed in the following manner. First, the Az or Ag measure of area was taken from the ROC for each

Table 2. Measures of d_a for discrimination between all categories of item. Discrimination between sources is marked **SD**; unmarked d_a's are for discrimination between old and new categories of item. These measures were taken in separate tests in which respondants confidence-rated the list membership of items or else rated whether they were old or new.

	Heard Word	Seen Word	Word Foil	Heard Name	Seen Name	Name Foil
Heard Word	0					
Seen Word	.76 SD	0				
Word Foil	.74	.80	0			
Heard Name	.61 SD	.68 SD	.79	0		
Seen Name	.73 SD	.54 SD	.81	.64 SD	0	
Name Foil	.65	.73	.60	.69	.74	0

case. Thus, for example, a ROC was set up with Seen Word as the target category and Word Foil as the distractor category to calculate the entry in the cell that is the intersection between the two (and contains the value 0.80). The area under this ROC was computed. This area was then treated as if it were percent correct in two-alternative forced choice (2AFC), and the d' that would be associated with this level of accuracy in 2AFC was found in Elliott's tables (1964). This value of d' is more properly termed d_a because it is the discriminability measure for the entire family of ROCs that would have that area (see Swets & Pickett, 1982, p. 32). The measure d' refers only to the one member of that family that has equal old and new variance. In this case the area was 0.71; such a percentage of accuracy in 2AFC requires a d_a of 0.80. All the other discriminations between target words and foils were computed in this manner.

Some discriminations were not between targets and foils but between two categories of targets. These were obtained from the source discrimination subjects and are marked **SD** in the table. For these, ROC's were set up as discussed in the previous section, with one category arbitrarily designated as targets and the other as foils. If "Heard" was chosen as the target category, then the ROC was set up with a response of "1" to a heard word as a Hit and a response of "1" to a seen word as a False Alarm. The area under this ROC would predict the probability with which a subject could select the heard item when presented with a seen and a heard item to choose between in 2AFC judgment. This proportion was then converted to a d_a in the same manner as applied to the target-noise discriminations.

The d_a's in Table 2 were submitted to Alscal, which is a multidimensional scaling program provided by the SPSSx 6.1 package. This program generates a spatial representation to fit the interpoint distances. The data of Table 2 were entered as distances. The variables were entered in the order in which they are listed along the margin of Table 2, with Heard Word first and Name Foil last. A Euclidean model was specified, with a maximum of two dimensions, and with ordinal measurement assumed for the distances. After 15 iterations, the stress measure was .022, with $r^2 = .997$ for the correlation between the original distances (i.e., the numbers in Table 2) and those in the two-dimensional fit (the interpoint distances taken from Figure 14).

Figure 14 plots the configuration generated by Alscal. The labels "Seen Axis" and "Heard Axis" are added for convenience. The representation captures some of the intuitive aspects of the data, as well as quantitative relations. We can compare the distances in this figure with the data in Tables 1 and 2. First, consider the inclusion results, which presumably use a radial decision axis, that is that they are measured in terms of their distance from the origin, where Word Foils is placed.

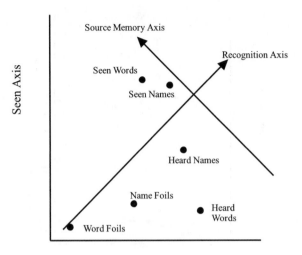

Figure 14. *Bivariate distribution of the classes of item used in this experiment. This is the spatial representation derived by ALSCAL from the values of d_a in Table 2, which were in turn based on list discrimination and item recognition. Decision axes for recognition and source discrimination are shown.*

Seen words are further from the origin than Heard words, and consequently Seen have a higher Hit rate and a larger d′ than Heard. Also, the Heard Names are further from the origin than the Heard Words. Likewise, Seen Names are accepted at a higher rate than the Heard Names, and the means for Seen Names are further from the mean for either set of foils than the Heard Words.

The source memory results are also well predicted by this spatial representation. A decision axis running through this space with a slope of approximately negative 1, as in Figure 11, has projections of the means of Seen Words, Seen Names, Heard Names, and Heard Words in exactly the order that predicts their relative rates of confusion. As was planned when the stimulus set was constructed, the names are more confusable between lists than the words.

The critical prediction here is for exclusion. None of the distances in the matrix (Table 2) used to generate the spatial representation of Figure 14 was derived from the exclusion data. The object is to take the spatial configuration derived only from distances measured by source discrimination and inclusion (recognition) performance and predict exclusion performance.

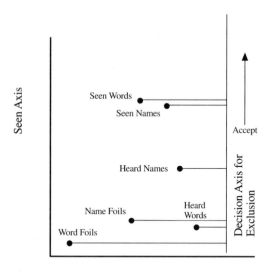

Figure 15. *Same as Figure 14 with a hypothetical decision axis for exclusion, with Seen as the correct target category and exclusion for Heard. The orthogonal projections of the means are shown, giving the relative placements of these items.*

In Figure 15 we have drawn a hypothetical decision axis for exclusion performance with seen items as the positive category, and heard and new items as those to be rejected. Projections from the means are shown dropped to this axis. For the prediction of exclusion performance we measured the distance of the means from the center of the Foil distribution (arbitrary units). This distance was then used to predict the exclusion data seen in Table 1. The prediction is shown in Figure 16.

The prediction is of the mean placements of the distributions of the various categories of item on the axis, as determined by the exclusion probabilities. We assume that the distributions have a common standard deviation and that there is a single criterion determining P("Yes") probabilities. That is, the P("Yes") probabilities are assumed to be equal to the proportion of the respective distributions falling above a common criterion. The mean placements of the distributions are dictated by the P("Yes") observed in exclusion. As can be seen, this decision axis in this representation can account for exclusion performance well, with $r^2 = .984$ for the relation between predicted and observed placements of exclusion means.

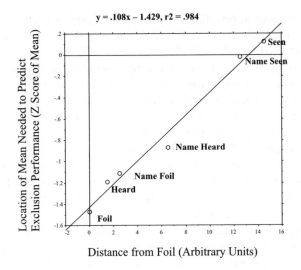

$$y = .108x - 1.429, r2 = .984$$

Distance from Foil (Arbitrary Units)

Figure 16. *The x-axis is the projection of the distributions on a best-fitting decision axis for exclusion, with Seen as the positive category and Heard excluded. The y-axis is a z-transform of the probability of saying "yes" to an item. These values give the distance, in z-score units, of the mean of the hypothetical distributions from the criterion for "yes" in exclusion. The "yes" proportions are seen in the exclusion column of Table 1.*

6. Conclusions

1. A common underlying multidimensional representation can predict recognition (inclusion), source discrimination, and exclusion performance. In this article distances in d_a units derived from recognition and source discrimination were used to generate the spatial representation. Decision axes appropriately constructed in this space yield the predictions when criteria are drawn through the space. In the experiment reported here, exclusion performance was predicted very well from a representation that was constructed only from recognition and source discrimination data.

2. The generally accepted model of exclusion performance was shown to be wrong when made explicit in terms of a 2-dimensional decision model. According to this model, subjects accept items in exclusion according to their degree of familiarity (denoted U here), but reject them if they have some detectable trace of their origin from the to-be-excluded list. The rejection criterion is variously stated as a conscious component (termed C

here), or source information, or recollective identification by retrieval. Each one of these approaches predicts ROC functions that are quite different from those obtained for exclusion. Clearly, subjects do not "test" exclusion items for conscious source of origin and then reject them if they detect some conscious trace. Rather, they combine source and strength in a multidimensional representation. Then they choose an appropriate combination of these two, captured by the decision axis, to use in selecting items for source judgments, recognition memory, or the exclusion task.

3. Exclusion performance invariably falls in a region of the ROC in which it may represent chance performance. The present approach gives an account of exclusion performance that can explain the low slope of the exclusion ROC and can explain the apparently zero discrimination of exclusion items even though they can be discriminated in other contexts.

4. The multivariate representation proposed here resolves the problem posed by apparent lack of discrimination in exclusion, but at the same time it presents a representation in which there is no obvious interpretation for Familiarity or Conscious vs. Unconscious components. It may be possible to use nonconscious familiarity processes to explain the patterns of confusion among items in a representation like that of Figure 14, but the representation itself does not have anything analogous to a conscious or unconscious axis.

5. Stratification of memory into conscious and unconscious realms is not a simple matter according to this analysis. The rejection of Model I removes support for the idea that memory information comes with conscious and unconscious information as separate components that can be used strategically. This does not reject separate conscious and unconscious traces in memory. However, subjects do not use these types of information as discrete pieces of information but combine them continuously. Model II, which fits the data quite well, suggests that these two sorts of information are best conceived of as being maintained in a single multidimensional representation. Subjects make various decisions about items by giving these sources of information different weights, and making decisions along a unidimensional derived axis, which we plot as the decision axis in summarizing the behavior.

6. We believe that the general methodology used here may have great utility in many other applications. For example, this representation and the associated decision process may help resolve questions about the relation between source and item memory. Further, the device of a decision axis as proposed here may have uses in predicting performance in many other situations in which the psychological structure of the domain has more than one dimension.

Note

1. This research was supported by Sontag Research Grants and an Irvine Foundation Grant to WPB. The authors thank Edwin Wong and Alex Huang for their assistance in this research.

Appendix

Appendix A

This Appendix explains how the d' for discrimination between two normal bivariate distributions is affected by rotating from the decision axis that gives the maximum d' to one at an angle ϕ relative to this axis. In this case we are dealing with two distributions presented for memory testing, one of which is the noise (or New) distribution centered with its mean at the origin (0,0). The other is the target (Old) distribution, plotted with its mean at (U,C) in the first quadrant. Here we assume that the two dimensions (which are here labeled U and C, as in Model I, but could have any designation) are independent for both distributions.

We show, first, that a decision axis at angle ϕ to the axis connecting the means of the two distributions results in a d'_E that equals $d'_I[\cos\phi]$, where d'_I is the d' for the decisions along the axis that connects the two means. We then show that d'_I is the maximum d' obtainable by any decision axis in this space. We are assuming that the projections onto the decision axis are based on linear criterial bounds in the space and that these bounds are normal to the decision axis in question. Linear decision criteria in this bivariate space are appropriate, given the independence and equal variance of the two distributions (Ashby, 1992b). We also assume uniformity on U and C, that is, that the two variances for both distributions are equal on U and C. The uniformity assumption, combined with the assumption of no correlation between U and C for either distribution, results in completely symmetrical bivariate distributions. We have indicated this by representing the distributions with a circle centered at the mean.

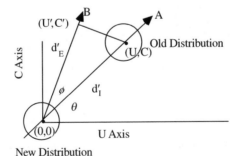

Figure A1. *Bivariate normal distributions representing Old and New sets of items in memory testing, plotted with hypothetical U (unconscious) and C (conscious) components of performance. The decision axes A and B are drawn with d' for each projection.*

Consider first the decision axis, marked A, that passes through the means of the two distributions in Figure A1. The bivariate distributions are projected onto this axis with means (0,0) and

(U,C), and for convenience, with a unit standard deviation, SD = 1.0. The equals the distance [(U,C)–(0,0)] divided by the SD, which is simply [(U,C)–(0,0)] because of the assumption of unit variance.

The projection of these distributions on decision axis B still has the same SD because of the uniformity assumption and the lack of correlation between the distributions. The projection of the point (U,C) is (U′,C′), and, by a simple trigonometric relation, the length [(0,0),(U,C)] is multiplied by $\sin\phi$ to equal [(0,0),(U′,C′)]. The size of d'_E equals this projected length divided by the SD. Since the SD is 1.0 here,

$$d'_E = d'_I[\cos(\theta)].$$ Equation A1

The decision axis B need not pass through (0,0) for Eq. A1 to hold. The same value of d'_E will be attained by a projection of these distributions on any decision axis that is parallel to B.

The value of d'_E attains its maximum when $\phi = 0.0$. Thus represents the maximum d′ because at $\phi = 0.0$, $d'_E = d'_I$. Therefore, a decision axis that passes through the means of the distributions yields the maximum value of d′.

If the SDs of the distributions are not equal on both dimensions, and/or if the dimensions are correlated, Eq. A1 will need a term representing the projected SD, and the d′ will depend on the projected SD as well as the projected distance. Likewise, the axis that yields the maximum d′ may not pass through the means of the two distributions if the uniformity and independence assumptions are violated.

We can give a more general expression to Eq. A1 by considering the angle θ that decision axis A makes with the abscissa. If we represent axis B by the linear equation C = mU, where m is the slope and label the angle of decision axis A θ, then we have $m = \tan(\theta + \phi)$, $\frac{m}{\sqrt{1+m^2}} = \sin(f+q)$, and $\frac{1}{\sqrt{1+m^2}} = \cos(f+q)$. We define d'_U as the U component of d'_I, that is, as the projection of the line [(0,0),(U,C)] onto the U axis, and d'_C as the C component of d'_I. We can now derive an expression for d'_E as a function of the components, d'_U and d'_C. First, we can rewrite Eq. A1 as

$$d'_E = d'_I[\cos(\theta + \phi - \theta)].$$ Equation A2

This becomes, by trigonometric identity:

$$= d'_I[\cos(\theta + \phi)\cos(\theta) + \sin(\theta + \phi)\sin(\theta)], \text{ and}$$ Equation A3

$$= d'_I\left[\left(\frac{1}{\sqrt{1+m^2}}\frac{d'_U}{d'_I}\right) + \left(\frac{m}{\sqrt{1+m^2}}\frac{d'_C}{d'_I}\right)\right];$$ Equation A4

$$= \frac{d'_U + m\,d'_C}{\sqrt{1+m^2}}$$ Equation A5

References

Ashby, F. G. (1992a). *Multidimensional models of perception and cognition*. Hillsdale, NJ: Erlbaum.

Ashby, F. G. (1992b). Multidimensional Models of Categorization. In F. G. Ashby (ed.) (1992a), *Multidimensional models of perception and cognition* (pp. 449–483). Hillsdale, NJ: Erlbaum.

Ashby, F. G. & Gott, R. E. (1988). Decision rules in the perception and categorization of multidimensional stimuli. *Journal of Experimental Psychology: Learning, Memory, and Cognition, 14,* 33–53.

Ashby, F. G. & Perrin, N. A. (1988). Toward a unified theory of similarity and recognition. *Psychological Review, 95,* 124–150.

Ashby, F. G. & Townsend, J. T. (1986). Varieties of perceptual independence. *Psychological Review, 93,* 154–179.

Banks, W. P. (1970). Signal detection theory and human memory. *Psychological Bulletin, 74,* 81–99.

Banks, W. P. (1977). Encoding and processing of symbolic information in comparative judgments. In G. H. Bower (ed.) *The Psychology of Learning and Motivation,* Vol. 11. NY: Academic Press.

Banks, W. P. & Atkinson, R. C. (1974). Accuracy and speed strategies in scanning active memory. *Memory & Cognition, 2,* 629–636.

Banks, W. P. & Chen, Y-P. (in preparation). Detection analysis of conscious and unconscious memory components.

Banks, W. P. Clark, H. H. Lucy, P. (1975). The locus of the semantic congruity effect in comparative judgments. *Journal of Experimental Psychology: Human Perception & Performance, 104,* 35–47.

Bower, G. (1996). Reactivating and activation theory of implicit memory. *Consciousness and Cognition, 5,* 27–72.

Buchner, A., Erdfelder, E., & Vaterrodt-Plünnecke, B. (1995). Toward unbiased measurement of conscious and unconscious memory processes within the process dissociation framework. *Journal of Experimental Psychology: General, 124,* 137–160.

Buchner, A. & Erdfelder, E. (1996). On assumptions of, relations between, and evaluations of some process dissociation measurement models *Consciousness and Cognition, 5,* 581–594.

Buchner, A. & Wippich, W. (1996a). Unconscious gender bias in fame judgments? *Consciousness and Cognition, 5,* 197–220.

Buchner, A. & Wippich, W. (1996b). Investigating fame judgments: On the generality of hypotheses, conclusions, and measurement models. *Consciousness and Cognition, 5,* 226–231.

Curran, T. & Hintzman, D. L. (1995). Violations of the independence assumption in process dissociation. *Journal of Experimental Psychology: Learning, Memory & Cognition, 21,* 531–547.

Dodson, C. S. & Johnson, M. K. (1996). Some problems with the process-dissociation approach to memory. *Journal of Experimental Psychology: General, 125,* 181–194.

Elliott, P. B. (1964). Tables of d'. In Swets, J. A. (ed.), *Signal Detection and Recognition by Human Observers.* New York: Wiley.

Francis, W. N. & Kuçera, H. (1982). *Frequency analysis of English usage: Lexicon and grammar.* Boston, MA: Houghton Mifflin.

Getty, D. J., Swets, J. B., & Swets, J. A. (1981). The observer's use of perceptual dimensions in signal identification. In D. J. Getty & J. H. Howard, Jr. (eds.), *Auditory and visual pattern recognition* (pp. 361–380). Hillsdale, NJ: Lawrence Erlbaum Associates.

Graf, P. & Komatsu, S. (1994). Process dissociation procedure: Handle with caution! *European Journal of Cognitive Psychology, 6,* 113–129.

Graf, P., Mandler, G., & Haden, P. E. (1982). Simulating amnesic symptoms in normal subjects. *Science, 218(4578),* 1243–1244.

Green, D. M. & Swets, J. A. (1974). *Signal detection theory and psychophysics.* Huntington, NY: Krieger.

Holender, D. (1986). Semantic activation without conscious identification in dichotic listening, parafoveal vision, and visual masking: A survey and appraisal. *Behavioral & Brain Sciences, 9(1),* 1–66.

Jacoby, L. L. (1991). A process dissociation framework: Separating automatic from intentional uses of memory. *Journal of Memory and Language, 30,* 513–541.

Jacoby, L. L. & Dallas, M. (1981). On the relationship between autobiographical memory and perceptual learning. *Journal of Experimental Psychology: General, 110,* 306–340.

Jacoby, L. L., Toth, J. P., & Yonelinas, A. P. (1993). Separating conscious and unconscious influences of memory: Measuring recollection. *Journal of Experimental Psychology: General, 122,* 139–154.

Jacoby, L. L., Yonelinas, A. P., & Jennings, J. M. (1997). The relation between conscious and unconscious (automatic) influences: A declaration of independence. In J. Cohen & J. W. Schooler (eds.), *Scientific approaches to the question of consciousness.* Hillsdale, NJ: Lawrence Erlbaum Associates.

Jennings, J. M. & Jacoby, L. L. (1993). Automatic versus intentional uses of memory: Aging, attention, and control. *Psychology and Aging, 8,* 283–293.

Jones, G. V. (1987). Independence and exclusivity among psychological processes: Implications for the structure of recall. *Psychological Review, 94,* 229–235.

Joordens, S. & Merikle, P. M. (1993). Independence or redundancy? Two models of conscious and unconscious influences. *Journal of Experimental Psychology: General, 122,* 462–467.

Kadlec, H. & Townsend, J. T. (1992). Implications of marginal and conditional detection parameters for the separabilities and independence of perceptual dimensions. *Journal of Mathematical Psychology, 36,* 325–374.

Kunst-Wilson, W. R. & Zajonc, R. B. (1980). Affective discrimination of stimuli that cannot be recognized. *Science, 207,* 557–558.

MacLeod, Colin M. (1992). The Stroop task: The "gold standard" of attentional measures. *Journal of Experimental Psychology: General, 121,* 12–14.

Macmillan, N. A. & Creelman, C. D. (1991). *Detection theory: A user's guide.* New York: Cambridge University Press.

Mandler, G. (1980). Recognizing: The judgment of previous occurrence. *Psychological Review, 87,* 252–271.

Metz, C. E. (1991). ROCFIT, Apple Macintosh version. Department of Radiology, University of Chicago, Chicago, IL.

Ratcliff, R. McKoon, G., & Tindall, M. H. (1994). Empirical generality of data from recognition memory receiver-operating characteristic functions and implications for the global memory models. *Journal of Experimental Psychology: Learning, Memory, and Cognition, 20,* 763–785.

Ratcliff, R., Van Zandt, T., & McKoon, G. (1995). Process dissociation, single-process theories, and recognition memory. *Journal of Experimental Psychology: General, 124,* 352–374.

Reingold, E. M. & Merikle, P. M. (1988). Using direct and indirect measures to study perception without awareness. *Perception & Psychophysics, 44(6),* 563–575.

Reingold, E. M. & Wainwright, M. J. (1996). Response bias correction in the process dissociation procedure: A reevaluation? *Consciousness and Cognition, 5,* 595–603.

Roediger, H. L. & McDermott, K. B. (1994). The problem of differing false-alarm rates for the process dissociation procedure: Comment on Verfaellie and Treadwell (1993). *Neuropsychology, 8,* 284–288.

Snodgrass, J. G. & Corwin, J. (1988). Pragmatics of measuring recognition memory: Applications to dementia and amnesia. *Journal of Experimental Psychology: General, 117,* 34–50.

Sorkin, R. D. & Dai, H. (1994). Signal detection and the ideal group. *Organizational Behavior and Human Decision Processes, 60,* 1–13.

Stroop, J. R. (1992). Studies of interference in serial verbal reactions. *Journal of Experimental Psychology: General, 121,* 15–23.

Swets, J. A. (1984). Mathematical models of attention. In R. Parasuraman & D. R. Davies (eds.) *Varieties of attention.* New York: Academic Press.

Swets, J. A. (1986a). Indices of discrimination or diagnostic accuracy: Their ROCs and implied models. *Psychological Bulletin, 99,* 100–117.

Swets, J. A. (1986b). Form of empirical ROCs in discrimination and diagnostic tasks: Implications for theory and measurement of performance. *Psychological Bulletin, 99,* 181–198.

Swets, J. A. & Pickett, R. M. (1982). *Evaluation of diagnostic systems.* NY: Academic Press.

Swets, J. A., Tanner, W. P., & Birdsall, T. G. (1961). Decision processes in perception. *Psychological Review, 68,* 301–340.

Tanner, W. P. (1956). Theory of recognition. *The Journal of the Acoustical Society of America, 28,* 882–888.

Thomas, J. P. (1985). Detection and identification: How are they related? *Journal of the Optical Society of America, A, 2,* 1457–1467.

Thomas, J. P. & Olzak, L. A. (1992). Simultaneous Detection and Identification In Ashby, F. G. (ed.), *Multidimensional models of perception and cognition.* Hillsdale, NJ: Erlbaum.

Toth, J. P., Reingold, E. M., & Jacoby, L. L. (1994). Toward a redefinition of implicit memory: Process dissociations following elaborative processing and self-generation. *Journal of Experimental Psychology: Learning, Memory, and Cognition, 20,* 290–303.

Wainwright, M. J. & Reingold, E. M. (1996). Response bias correction in the process dissociation procedure: Approaches, assumptions, and evaluations. *Consciousness and Cognition, 5,* 232–254.

Wegner, D. M., Schneider, D. J., Carter, S. R., & White, T. L. (1987). Paradoxical effects of thought suppression. *Journal of Personality & Social Psychology, 53,* 5–13.

Yonelinas, A. P. (1994). Receiver-operating characteristics in recognition memory: Evidence for a dual-process model. *Journal of Experimental Psychology: Learning, Memory, and Cognition, 20,* 1341–1354.

Yonelinas, A. P., Dobbins, I., Szymanski, M. D., Dhaliwal, H. S., & King, L. (1996). Signal-detection, threshold, and dual-process models of recognition memory: ROC's and conscious recollection. *Consciousness and Cognition, 5,* 418–441.

Yonelinas, A. P., Regehr, G., & Jacoby, L. L. (1995). Incorporating response bias in a dual-process theory of memory. *Journal of Memory and Language, 34,* 821–835.

Yonelinas, A. P. & Jacoby, L. L. (1994). Dissociations of processes in recognition memory: Effects of interference and of response speed. *Canadian Journal of Experimental Psychology, 48,* 516–534.

Yonelinas, A. P. & Jacoby, L. (1996). Response bias and the process-dissociation procedure. *Journal of Experimental Psychology: General, 125,* 422–434.

CHAPTER 6

Conscious and automatic uses of memory in cued recall and recognition

Douglas L. Nelson   Vanesa M. McKinney   David J. Bennett

Every day we are faced with questions, from others or ourselves, and we must use a fallible memory system to provide the answers. Such questions often concern answers that consist of a blend of new information with information acquired long ago. Moreover, such questions can take different forms, sometimes requiring the recall of related information and sometimes requiring recognition of what is implied in the question itself. In either case, our phenomenological experience is that questions sometimes prompt answers as a result of a conscious intention to remember and sometimes prompt answers readily and automatically regardless of our intent. The purpose of this chapter is to describe our attempts to disentangle the relative contributions of conscious and automatic uses of memory for remembering a mix of known and new information. As will become clear, we assume that these uses of memory rely on different representations.

We focus on memory for a mix of known and novel information because everyday life involves a stream of experience with known information in novel contexts. Most everyday memory tasks require us to process familiar information in new situations. For example, as we drive through a new neighborhood we see a stop sign ahead and, even though our attention may be partially diverted, perceptual and memorial processes automatically prompt the appropriate action when the sign is reached. We see a billboard encouraging us to save money, think about the implications, and stop at the sight of our bank to revise our savings plan. In these examples it should be clear that information about signs and money is not being newly acquired, nor is it simply being retrieved from memory as knowledge such as when answering a question such as "What do people put in a bank?" Instead, known information is being encoded in a new context, and both known and novel aspects of the experience have the potential of being retrieved in the presence of some cue presented sometime later, e.g., sight of the bank. The thesis of the present chapter is that known and novel information contribute independently to remembering with the relative contribution of each source of information determined by how the retrieval cues are used.

1.   Modeling memory for the mix of known and new

We attempt to model memory for the mix of known and new information by using extralist cuing and recognition procedures. In extralist cuing, subjects study a list of to-be-remembered target words, and are then given cues that were absent during study to prompt the recall of these targets (e.g., Nelson, Schreiber, & McEvoy, 1992). The cues can be of various types, and subjects can be oriented toward using these cues in various ways by manipulating the test instructions. For example, subjects might study the words CAKE and SKI as part of a longer list, and the test cues for these targets could be WEDDING and LODGE, respectively. The purpose or use of the cues is defined by the test instructions. Subjects might be asked to use these cues to recall related words from the study list, to recall related words with studied words excluded, or to produce the first related words that come to mind (e.g., Jacoby, 1991; Nelson, Schreiber, & Holley, 1992; Nelson, Bennett, & Xu, 1997; Roediger & McDermott, 1993). In recognition testing, subjects study a list of words but the test cues consist of the targets instead of related words. Both tasks are amenable to manipulations of the use of the cues during testing and are well-suited for investigating the recovery of known information recently experienced in a novel context.

Previous work shows that what is known about a word beforehand plays a central role in determining whether the word will be recalled. For example, research using the extralist cuing procedure has shown that the probability of recalling a recently studied word varies with the number of associates linked to it in memory as a result of past experience, what we call set size (Nelson, Schreiber, & McEvoy, 1992). Probability of recall also varies with the number of connections among these associates, what we call connectivity (Nelson, Bennett, Gee, Schreiber, & McKinney, 1993). Both set size and connectivity are measured through the use of free association norms. With other characteristics of the test cues and the target words controlled, targets with smaller sets of associates and targets with more connections among their associates are more likely to be recalled. Target set size effects are found for concrete and abstract words, low and high frequency words, homographic and non-homographic words, fast and slow presentation rates, and non-semantic and semantic levels of processing (Gee, 1997; Nelson & Schreiber, 1992; Nelson, Schreiber, &

McEvoy, 1992; Nelson & Xu, 1995). Set size effects are not due to guessing because the magnitude of these effects is uninfluenced by whether the test instructions require, encourage, or forbid guessing (Nelson, Schreiber, & McEvoy, 1992).

Target set size effects are obtained in the extralist cuing procedure despite the fact that the associates of the target are not presented, nor is any attention drawn to them during the task. Related observations also suggest that subjects are unaware of this activation and its influence. First, such effects are found when subjects study the targets under intentional or under incidental conditions and even when they study them in the presence of rhymes (e.g., Nelson, Schreiber, & McEvoy, 1992). Second, when asked to estimate set size on a seven-point scale, estimates of associative set size are poorly correlated with counts of set size obtained in free association. In contrast, similar estimates are moderately correlated for rhyme and for taxonomic categories (Schreiber, 1993). Perhaps more importantly, although the associates of a word can be brought to consciousness as when free associating, we have never seen anyone attempt to learn a list of words by this procedure unless explicitly asked to learn in this manner (Nelson, Bajo, & Casanueva, 1985). Given a request to remember the words in the list or to rate their concreteness or count their vowels, free association would seem like an odd learning strategy and so it comes as no surprise that subjects do not do it. We assume that the existence of knowledge or even the automatic activation of such knowledge is not equivalent to conscious processing. In our view, conscious processing is more reasonably defined as occurring when knowledge is being used and the user is aware of its use (e.g., Dienes & Barry, 1997). For example, if people are asked to count the vowels in a word, they use their knowledge of vowels to select them and they can can report on what they are doing if asked. In contrast, if it can be shown that the associates of a word influence the probability of its recall in the absence of knowledge of these associates, then we assume that such associates exert their influence automatically and unconsciously.

All of our results point to the conclusion that the associates of a studied word are activated automatically and that they influence recall without awareness. Other findings indicate that a requirement to switch attention to a multiplication task for several minutes prior to testing can substantially reduce the influence of these associates. Interestingly, studying lists of words during the interim has little or no influence on the magnitude of these effects (Nelson, McEvoy, Janczura, & Xu, 1993). So long as subjects maintain their attention on the memory task the magnitude of these effects remains unmodified, but when they switch attention to a different task these effects wither away, with words having smaller associative sets essentially losing their advantage. In general,

target set size and connectivity effects show the hallmarks of a priming phenomenon that can be maintained through sustained attention to the task at hand
(Nelson, McKinney, Gee, & Janczura, 1998).

2.   Test instructions and retrieval intention

Of particular relevance to this chapter, target set size affects cued recall automatically and regardless of the subjects' intent during testing. This conclusion is
supported by the results found with *indirect test* and *process-dissociation*
procedures. In indirect test procedures, all subjects are given similar learning
experiences with orientation toward the test cues being the critical manipulation
(see Roediger & McDermott, 1993 for a review). Direct test subjects are told to
use each cue to recover a related word from the study list, whereas indirect test
subjects are asked to recover a word that is related to the test cue with no
reference made by the experimenter to the recent study episode. The underlying
rationale of using the indirect test procedure assumes that direct tests tap into
processes associated with conscious recollection whereas indirect tests tap into
processes associated with the automatic aspects of retrieval.

In the process-dissociation procedure subjects also recover words under
different instructional sets but in this case estimates of conscious and automatic
components are based on opposition logic (e.g., Jacoby, 1991; Jacoby, Begg, &
Toth, 1997). Under inclusion instructions, subjects are asked to use test cues to
recover related study words and to guess when unsure. They can be successful
because they consciously recollect the studied word, with a probability C, or
because the studied word comes to mind automatically, with probability A. These
two bases for responding are assumed to be independent so the probability of
recalling a studied word under inclusion instructions can be estimated by:

$$\text{Inclusion} = C + A(1 - C) \tag{1}$$

Under exclusion instructions, subjects are asked to exclude study words and to
report only new words that are related to the test cue. According to the opposition logic, a studied word should be reported only when it comes automatically
to mind without remembering that the item was recently studied. Thus, the
probability of recalling a studied word under exclusion instructions is:

$$\text{Exclusion} = A(1 - C) \tag{2}$$

Under this rationale, the difference in the recovery of studied words for these two
instructions provides an estimate of conscious processing: C = Inclusion – Exclusion.

Given this estimate of C, the probability of a studied word coming to mind automatically is: A = Exclusion/(1 − C).

Regardless of whether indirect tests or the process-dissociation procedures are used, target set size appears to influence both conscious and automatic uses of memory. Target set size effects are as apparent under direct test instructions as they are under indirect test instructions (e.g., Nelson, Schreiber, & Holley, 1992). Similarly, with the process-dissociation procedure, set size affects the estimates of both conscious and automatic uses (Nelson, Bennett, & Xu, 1997). Words with smaller sets of associates are more likely to be recovered when subjects are engaged in conscious attempts to use test cues to recover specific list words and when they use the cues automatically to bring any related word to mind. What is most interesting is that at least one variable that appears to influence target recovery automatically exerts its effects in the same way regardless of how the test cue is ostensibly being used.

The effects of target set size contrast with the effects of manipulations of levels of processing during the study trial. Compared to non-semantic processing, semantically oriented processing of the target has a sizable influence on direct tests and on the conscious component of the process-dissociation procedure. However, the advantage of semantic processing during study is diminished on indirect tests and has little apparent influence on automatic processing as estimated by the process-dissociation procedure. This interaction is robust and is apparent for different types of cues (e.g., Challis & Brodbeck, 1992; Nelson, Schreiber, & Holley, 1992; Richardson-Klavehn & Gardiner, 1998; Toth, Reingold, & Jacoby, 1994). This contrast between set size and levels of processing effects is interesting because both effects are related to the influence of meaning on recall. Meaning linked to manipulations of level of processing is related to the novel aspects of processing. Such encoding exerts its influence as a result of consciously controlled processing activities carried out during the study trial, and it seems to have a differentially larger effect on the consciously driven aspects of the target recovery process. In contrast, meaning related to set size effects is linked to the known aspects of the processing and it appears to exert its influence automatically during encoding and retrieval, regardless of how subjects are using the test cue.

3. PIER: A theory about memory representations and retrieval intentions

The contrasting effects of levels of processing and set size manipulations pose a difficult problem for theory because they suggest that parsimonious explanations for performance on direct and indirect tests cannot be explained by frameworks that rely solely on conceptually-driven and data-driven processes (e.g., Roediger, 1990). Both set size and levels of processing effects are related to conceptually-driven processing, but they have dissociated influences on tests that foster conscious and unconscious uses of memory. We have attempted to explain the contrast by relying on our model of cued recall, called PIER[1], which was initially designed to explain why set size affects cued recall (Nelson, Schreiber, & McEvoy, 1992) and which has been updated to incorporate the influence of connectivity and other variables (Nelson et al., 1998).

PIER assumes that studying a familiar word creates two sources of information about the experience. One source results from processing the novel aspects of the experience and consists of an explicit representation determined by conscious processing activities carried out while processing the target, such as reading it aloud, rehearsing it with other words, rating its concreteness, naming its vowels, and so on. The explicit representation constitutes a record of what people do consciously and can remember doing during the learning episode. Levels of processing exerts its influence on the explicit representation. The other source of information is related to the known aspects of the experience that reflects the results of activating the target and its associates in long-term working memory (LTWM), e.g., the word CAKE presumably activates ICE CREAM, BIRTH-DAY, CHOCOLATE, and so forth. Such activation is required for comprehension (e.g., Kintsch, 1988), and it produces an implicit trace in LTWM that we call the implicit representation. Theoretically, variables such as set size and connectivity affect the probability of sampling the target as an implicit representation in LTWM.

What is particularly important, PIER also assumes that the relative contributions of explicit and implicit sources of information about the studied word are influenced by the intention of retrieval. If the goal set by the test instructions is to recall recently encoded information, e.g., a word from a recently studied list, then the model assumes that target recovery is based on success with the explicit representation, the implicit representation, or both. Theoretically, each source of information contributes independently to target recovery during intentional uses of memory. The problem for the subject is to use the test cue to recover recently encoded information and such information can be recovered from traces produced as a result of conscious processing activities during study or as a result of what the test cue automatically activates. In contrast, in automatic uses of memory target recovery is based primarily on success with the implicit representation, with what the test cue automatically activates in LTWM during testing. In PIER 2, the updated model, related information that has recently been primed in LTWM comes to mind automatically, whereas memories produced as a result of recent conscious processing activities come to mind when people intend to bring them to mind (Nelson et al., 1998).

Given these assumptions about encoding and intention, levels of processing effects should be more apparent when subjects are engaged in intentional retrieval that is directed toward a specific target. The explicit representation embodies the results of consciously applied encoding activities. In contrast to levels effects, target set size effects should be apparent in both consciously controlled and automatic uses of memory during testing because the implicit representation produced during the study trial contributes to target recovery regardless of the intention of the retrieval effort. In PIER 2, target set size effects arise as a result of searching through what has been activated by the test cue and the target in LTWM, with the success of this search determined by a formal sampling rule (Nelson et al., 1998). The gist of this rule is that the probability of sampling the target is higher when the set is smaller than when it is larger because fewer associates compete with sampling the target. What is presently more important, the sampling rule determines the effectiveness of the implicit representation for both intentional and automatic uses of memory. Words with smaller associative sets have a sampling advantage that will be apparent whenever the implicit representation is utilized.

The specific purpose of this chapter is to present the results of two experiments that determine whether connectivity among the associates of a studied word, like its set size, affect consciously controlled as well as automatic influences of memory as predicted by PIER 2. Connectivity is determined by measuring the mean number of connections among the associates of a word, as illustrated in Figure 1 for two hypothetical targets. Targets A and B each have six associates, two of which are back connected to the target, and the only difference is that Target A has many more connections among its associates than Target B. Measuring connectivity requires norming a word to determine its associates and then norming each of its associates with independent groups of subjects so that an $n \times n$ associative matrix can be created (Nelson, Bennett, Gee, Schreiber, & McKinney, 1993 for details). Such matrices can then be examined to determine the number of connections among the associates and, at this time, such matrices have been created for 3,500+ words for the purpose of classifying words on the basis of mean connectivity. Although research on the effects of connectivity is relatively new, current findings indicate that words with more connections among their associates are more likely to be recalled than words with fewer connections (Nelson, Bennett, Gee, Schreiber, & McKinney, 1993). This finding has been consistently obtained when other variables have been carefully controlled, such as set size, concreteness, frequency, cue-to-target strength, and so on.

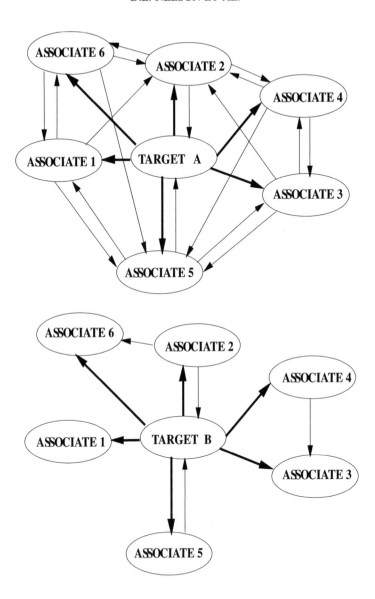

Figure 1. *An illustration of associative connectivity. Target A is representative of a high connectivity word because each of its associates is connected to an average of 2.67 (16/6) other associates in the set, and Target B is representative of a low connectivity word because each of the associates is connected to an average of .33 (2/6) words in the set.*

Whereas set size provides an index of how many relatively strong associates are linked to a given word, connectivity provides an index of the complexity of its organizational structure. Rather than involving immediate links from the target, connectivity measures connections among its more remote links. We thought that it was important to evaluate PIER 2 using a variable other than set size, and associative connectivity seemed like an ideal choice. Like set size, connectivity theoretically exerts its influence on sampling the implicit representation of the target, but it responds differently to the conditions of encoding and it is differentially affected by the nature of the retention test. Unlike target set size effects, connectivity effects depend on semantic processing during the study trial. The presence of many connections among the associates of the target facilitates recall when subjects have been asked to remember the target words and, under incidental conditions, when they have been asked to rate them for concreteness. However, such effects are reduced under incidental conditions when subjects have been encouraged to process the words non-semantically (Nelson, Bennett, Gee, Schreiber, & McKinney, 1993). Furthermore, unlike target set size effects (Nelson, Canas, & Bajo, 1987), high levels of connectivity among the associates of the target increase the probability of its recognition (Nelson, et al., 1998).

PIER 2 attributes connectivity effects to the spread of activation among the associates that returns to the target and increases the strength of its implicit representation in LTWM. Connectivity among the associates of a word theoretically affect its encoding strength as an activation in LTWM, with higher levels of strength attained when attention to meaning has been maintained during encoding. Given these assumptions, PIER 2 predicts that words with higher levels of connectivity among their associates will be recalled and recognized with a greater likelihood when attention to meaning has been maintained during the study trial. Experiment 1 tested this prediction in an extralist cuing test by manipulating target connectivity as well as level of processing. Experiment 2 tested this prediction in a recognition test by varying target connectivity in an intentional learning task. The process dissociation procedure was used in both experiments. Because connectivity affects the strength of the implicit representation thought to be involved in both consciously controlled and automatic uses of memory, the manipulation of connectivity was expected to influence estimates of both C and A. These influences, however, were expected to be more apparent after semantic than after non-semantic processing in Experiment 1. Finally, level of processing was expected to affect recollective more than automatic uses of memory.

4. Experiments

4.1 *Experiment 1*

4.1.1 *Method*

Design and subjects. The experimental design formed a $2 \times 2 \times 2$ mixed-model factorial. Study instructions (rate concreteness, name vowels) were manipulated between subjects, and test instructions (inclusion, exclusion) and target connectivity (high, low) were manipulated within subjects. Forty-eight subjects participated, with 24 assigned in order of appearance to the concreteness condition and 24 to the vowel condition. Within each of these conditions, half of the subjects were assigned to one list and the remaining half were assigned to another.

Procedure. Subjects participated in individual sessions and received a single study-test trial. Target words appeared in upper case letters and were presented by a Macintosh computer at a 3-s rate. Subjects given instructions to rate concreteness were told that we were interested in what words mean to people and that, as part of our research, we needed to obtain information about the sensory referents of words. They were asked to pronounce each word aloud and rate it on a 5-point scale, with a 1 indicating that the word was abstract and did not have a ready sensory referent and a 5 indicating that the word referred to an object, person, or thing that could be experienced through the senses. The scale was available throughout the experiment. Subjects given vowel naming instructions were asked to read each word aloud and then name its vowels as rapidly as possible. Both groups were given a short practice run on people's names to familiarize them with the task and presentation rate and neither group was told about the upcoming memory test.

As soon as the last word was presented, the experimenter read the test instructions. Subjects were told that a list of cue words would be presented one at a time on the screen and that they were to read each cue aloud when shown. They were also told that there would be an instruction below each cue indicating how the cue was to be used. If the instruction read "in the list," then they were asked to recall a word from the study list that was meaningfully related to the test cue. These instructions defined the inclusion condition. Alternatively, if the instruction read "not in the list" then they were asked to produce the first word that came to mind that was meaningfully related to the test cue but that was not in the study list. These instructions defined the exclusion condition. Examples were provided to further clarify the instructions, and subjects were encouraged to guess when unsure. None of the subjects seemed to have any difficulty in following these instructions. Finally, the test trial was paced by the subject and the orders of the test cues and targets were unsystematically randomized for each subject. For each list one-half of the items within each set size type were tested under inclusion instructions and the remaining one-half were tested under exclusion instructions. Items were counterbalanced over instructions and subjects.

Materials. The values for target connectivity and other word characteristics were taken from a normative database in which an average of 150 subjects were asked to provide the first word to come to mind for each cue word provided (Nelson, McEvoy, & Schreiber, 1998). These values were used in constructing two lists that are presented in Appendix A. Thirty-six words served as targets in each list, with half having highly connected sets of associates and half having sparsely connected sets. The associates of high connectivity targets averaged 2.97 (SD = .40) connections to other associates in the set, and the associates of low connectivity targets averaged only .50 (SD = .25) connections to other associates.

Other target characteristics were controlled. At each level of connectivity, the targets consisted of relatively frequent, concrete words with moderately sized sets. The averages for target set size, concreteness, and Kuçera and Francis (1967) frequency were, respectively, 12.65 associates, 5.55 in rated concreteness, and 32 occurrences per million words. The test cues used to prompt the recall of these targets were also taken from the association norms such as cue set size which averaged 14.10 associates per cue. More importantly, cue-to-target strength averaged .10 according to the norms. That is, about 10% of the 150 subjects in the normative sample produced each target word in free association. We assume that this figure provides the best estimate of the baseline probability of producing the targets in the absence of a recent study trail and that this estimate applies both when subjects are operating under inclusion instructions and when they are operating under exclusion conditions. Finally, by using the normative database, care was taken to ensure that each test cue was related only to its target and not to any other targets appearing in the list.

4.1.2 *Results*

The probabilities of target recall and the estimates of conscious and automatic uses of memory computed according to the process dissociation procedure are shown in Table 1. As can be seen, both level of processing and connectivity affected estimates of conscious uses of memory. Conscious uses were more effective after concreteness ratings than after vowel naming, $F(1,46) = 22.34$, $MSe = .052$. They also tended to be more effective when target words were high in connectivity than when they were low in connectivity, but this difference was not significant, $F(1,46) = 2.69$, $MSe = .030$, $p < .11$. More importantly and as expected, the effects of connectivity on conscious uses were manifested primarily after subjects had engaged in semantic processing during the study trial. The interaction between the two variables was significant, $F(1,46) = 4.67$, and a Fisher's two-tailed LSD of .10 indicated that the effects of connectivity were significant after subjects had performed the concreteness rating task but not after they performed the vowel naming task. These results replicate previous findings obtained in the extralist cuing task in showing that words with many connections among their associates are more likely to be remembered particularly after the targets have undergone semantic processing during the study trial. More importantly, the present findings show that both level of processing and connectivity affect conscious uses of memory.

Table 1. *Probabilities of target recovery as a function of level of processing, test instructions, and connectivity, with estimates of conscious (C) and automatic (A) uses of memory*

Level of Processing	Connectivity	Test Instructions		C	A
		Inclusion	Exclusion		
Rate Concreteness	High	.52	.07	.44	.27
	Low	.35	.04	.31	.11
Name Vowels	High	.25	.10	.15	.13
	Low	.26	.09	.17	.13

Because the presence of zero scores under exclusion instructions underestimates the contribution of automatic influences of memory, several subjects with such scores were eliminated from the analysis (Jacoby, Begg, & Toth, 1997). As can be seen in Table 1, connectivity affected automatic influences of memory but, once again, this influence was more apparent after concreteness ratings than after vowel naming. The interaction between level of processing and connectivity was significant, $F (1,29) = 7.13$, $MSe = .013$, Fisher's $LSD = .08$. This interaction was especially interesting because it can be examined from two different theoretical perspectives. From the perspective of PIER 2, high levels of target connectivity among the associates of the target affected automatic influences of memory only when subjects had engaged in semantic processing during the study trial. From the perspective of someone interested in levels of processing effects, this interaction indicated that semantic processing during study significantly affected the estimate of automatic processing but only when the target words had many connections among their associates. From this perspective, it is possible that the effects of levels on automatic processing that are sometimes obtained (e.g., Brown & Mitchell, 1994; Challis & Brodbeck, 1992; Richardson-Klavehn

& Gardiner, 1998), may have been related to the presence of high connectivity words in the study list.

Finally, of the four A means shown in Table 1, only one was significantly different from the baseline provided by the normative data. Only high connectivity words whose concreteness had been rated during study were recovered significantly above baseline under automatic uses of memory, (.27 vs. .10, t(29) = 6.21). This finding echoes results obtained with manipulations of target set size which show that words with small but not those with large sets differ significantly from baseline in terms of automatic uses (Nelson, Bennett, & Xu, 1997).

4.2 Experiment 2

The purpose of Experiment 2 was to determine whether connectivity would also affect both conscious and unconscious uses of memory in recognition where the test cues consist of the targets rather than related words. The procedure followed the 2-list task developed by Jacoby and his colleagues (e.g., Jacoby, 1991; Jacoby, Toth, & Yonelinas, 1993; Jacoby, Woloshyn, & Kelley, 1989). Subjects first *saw* a list of words that they were asked to read aloud and then they *heard* a list that they were asked to remember for a recognition test. At test, subjects were presented with words from both lists, along with an equal number of new words. Under inclusion instructions they were told to classify a word as "old" if the test word was presented in either study list whereas, under exclusion instructions, they were asked to classify a word as "old" only if it was heard. Under exclusion instructions, the rationale was that consciously recollecting that an item was seen will cause the subject to reject it and call it "new." Conscious identification of an item as seen means that the item should be excluded from the set defined by the instructions as "old." Hence, any increase in the probability of miss-classifying seen items as "old" presumably reflects an automatic influence of memory because conscious recollection of a seen word as seen would have the opposite effect. Such recollection would lead to its correct rejection. The logic of opposition suggests that a seen word would be mistakenly classified as "old" only if it came automatically to mind and the subject failed to recollect a specific experience with it as a seen item.

Given this rationale, the specific purpose of Experiment 2 was to determine whether words with more connected sets of associates would benefit conscious, automatic or both influences of memory. High levels of connectivity facilitate recognition, suggesting that recognition can be influenced by the recent activation of conceptually related information in LTWM (Nelson et al., 1998). Furthermore, levels of processing manipulations indicate that, compared to non-semantic processing, semantic processing during the study episode enhances recognition (e.g., Craik & Tulving, 1975). Given such findings, it is reasonable to assume that implicit and explicit representations each contribute to recognition. In addition, PIER 2 predicts that connectivity among the associates will affect both consciously controlled and automatic uses. This prediction follows from the assumption that conscious uses of memory rely on both explicit and implicit representations whereas automatic influences are affected by only the implicit representation.

4.2.1 Method

Design and subjects. The experimental design formed a $2 \times 2 \times 2$ mixed-model factorial. The order of instructions (inclusion first, exclusion first) was counter-balanced over subjects so that one-half of the subjects received the block of inclusion trials first and the block of exclusion instructions second and the remaining subjects received the blocks in the reverse order. Order of instructions was manipulated between subjects, and test instructions (inclusion, exclusion) and target connectivity (high, low) were manipulated within subjects. Forty-eight subjects participated, with 24 assigned in order of appearance to inclusion first and 24 to exclusion first conditions.

Procedure. The first list was presented visually under the conditions used in Experiment 1, e.g., upper case letters, 3-s rate. Subjects were told that they were going to see a long list of words on the computer screen, that they were to read aloud the items as fast as possible, and that their reading times were being recorded (not true). The second list was presented by the computer out of sight of the subject with the experimenter reading each word aloud on its appearance. Subjects were asked to repeat the words aloud after the experimenter and were told that they would be given a recognition test on these items. Before each list a short practice list of first names was presented to acquaint them with the procedure.

The test list was presented immediately after the heard list, and it consisted of the seen and heard words and an equal number of new words randomly intermixed. Each item was shown on the monitor and remained on until the subject made the response whereupon the experimenter recorded the decision and then struck a key that presented the next test item. As each item was presented subjects had to read it aloud and follow one of the two instructions. As noted, exclusion instructions asked subjects to respond "old" to any word from the list just heard, and that seen words and new words were to be designated as "new." They were specifically told that if they remembered reading the word, then it should be designated as "new." Inclusion instructions asked subjects to designate a word as "old" if it appeared in either the seen or the heard list and to respond "new" only when they thought that the word was not from either list. All subjects were told to expect new words along with words from the presented lists. The appearance of all study and test items was unsystematically randomized for each subject.

Materials. Three lists of 48 words were constructed and they are presented in Appendix B. Each list contained 24 high connectivity words averaging 3.28 (SD = .56) connections per associate and 24 low connectivity words that averaged .53 (SD = .22) connections per associate. These lists were used equally often as seen, heard, and new items, and they appeared equally often under inclusion and exclusion instructions. With this completely counterbalanced design, separate estimates of false alarms on high and low connectivity words could be obtained. The words tended to have average set sizes (11.99 associates), they tended to be concrete (5.44), and they tended to be mostly low to moderate in frequency (21 times per million). Finally, as determined by the norms, there were no direct connections among any of the words within a given list and every attempt was made to minimize connections between words in the different lists.

4.2.2 Results

The results showing the probabilities of classifying seen items as "old" under each instructional condition are presented in Table 2, along with the estimates for conscious and automatic processing and the false alarms. These data are pooled over instruction order, and as can be seen, connectivity among the associates of the target appeared to influence both components of processing, although the influence on the automatic component was small.

Table 2. *The probabilities of classifying seen items as "old" under inclusion and exclusion instructions as a function of connectivity, with estimates of conscious (C) and automatic (A) uses of memory, and false alarms.*

	Test instructions, false alarms and estimates of C and A				
Connectivity	Inclusion Instructions	Exclusion Instructions	False Alarms	C	A
High	.74	.34	.13	.40	.57
Low	.67	.37	.13	.30	.53

The false alarm rate was equivalent for high and low connectivity items (.13). An analysis of variance of the false alarms indicated that neither order, nor instructions, nor connectivity, nor any of the interactions among these variables were significant, with all Fs near unity. These findings suggest that the criterion for automatic influences of memory were the same in the two instructional conditions and for each level of connectivity (Jacoby, 1991). Given the equivalence of false alarm rates, all analyses were confined to "hits" on seen items. The emphasis on the word hits is intentional because this response under exclusion instructions is really an error. Under exclusion instructions seen items were supposed to have been rejected and classified as "new."

The analysis of the conscious component indicated that connectivity had a significant effect on conscious uses of memory, $F(1,46) = 10.24$, MSe = .022. Instruction order and the interaction between order and connectivity were not reliable, both Fs < 1. The estimate of conscious uses was significantly greater when connectivity was high than when it was low. The analysis of the automatic component was carried out on all of the data because only two scores of zero were obtained in the exclusion condition in the entire experiment. Unfortunately, the analysis of the automatic component indicated that the apparent effect of connectivity was not reliable, $F(1,46) = 1.23$, MSe = .024. Although high connectivity words showed a 4% advantage over low connectivity words, this difference was not significant. Furthermore, although the estimate of the automatic component was higher when inclusion instructions were presented first (7%) than when exclusion instructions were presented first (1%), neither order nor the interaction of connectivity and order were reliable, $F = 3.22$ and $F < 1$, respectively.

4.3   Discussion of results of Experiments 1 and 2

The results of the extralist cuing study (Experiment 1) are consistent with previous findings in showing that level of processing manipulations affect the success of conscious uses of memory and have a small but non-significant effect on the automatic influences of memory. These results replicate the findings of many previous studies of levels effects (e.g., Brown & Mitchell, 1994; Challis & Brodbeck, 1992). The results also show that, as with set size, connectivity among the associates of the target appears to have small effects on both uses of memory. However, unlike set size effects, these influences were more apparent after the concreteness rating task than after the vowel naming task. Words with smaller associative sets and words whose associates are more highly connected influence both recollective as well as automatic uses of memory, but the effect of connectivity was more apparent after semantic processing.

The results of the recognition study (Experiment 2) indicated that connectivity has a reliable effect on conscious uses of memory and a small but non-significant effect on automatic influences of memory. However, we have reason to believe that the potential influence on automatic influences may have been underestimated. The target words tended to occur relatively infrequently in the language, and the study instructions for the Heard list indicated that memory would be evaluated by a recognition test. The results of recognition experiments conducted after Experiment 2 indicate that connectivity effects are reduced under each of these conditions (Nelson et al., 1998). First, connectivity effects are less apparent when subjects know that memory will be tested by a recognition test than when they do not know how they will be tested. Second, connectivity effects are less apparent for words that are lower in frequency of occurrence than for those that are higher in frequency of occurrence. Although only direct test instructions were used in the more recent experiments, our speculation is that connectivity among the associates would have had significant effects on automatic uses as well as conscious uses of memory if the items had been higher in frequency and if the subjects had not known how they would be tested. We believe that both of these conditions tend to foster more sustained semantic processing which appears to be essential for producing connectivity effects.

5.   Explanations of the findings

5.1   *PIER 2*

The present findings are consistent with predictions derived from PIER 2. According to this model, processing a familiar word generates an explicit representation that encodes novel information associated with conscious processing activities and an implicit representation consisting of the activation of it and its associates. The strength of the explicit representation is influenced by rehearsal time, level of processing, divided attention, encoding strategies, presentation frequency, and, in short, by a multitude of variables that influence conscious processing during encoding. In PIER 2, levels of processing effects in recall and recognition are attributed to the influence of encoding strength on the explicit representation using the sampling rule provided by SAM (Nelson et al., 1998; Gillund & Shiffrin, 1984).

The implicit representation reflects the parallel activation of the lexical representation of the word and its strongest associates in LTWM. In PIER, one of the main functions of LTWM is to provide ready access to known information stored as general knowledge about stimulus. To the extent that activation returns to the target via connections among its associates, it increases the encoding strength of the implicit representation of the target (Nelson et al., 1998). PIER 2 assumes that the amount of resonant activation is a direct function of the number of connections among the associates and to the target from these associates, but the model assumes that the size of the associative set has no effect on such resonance. The initial activation of the associates by the target is automatic and unconscious as is the resonant activation from the associates to the target. However, the influence of resonant activation is susceptible to switches of attention, so continued attention to meaning during the study trial increases the effects of connectivity relative to when attention is switched to vowel naming. Switches of attention during the study trial as well as switches of attention after the study trial can significantly disrupt the influence of the implicit representation (Nelson et al., 1998).

Given these assumptions, PIER 2 predicts that connectivity among the associates will have greater facilitating effects on the cued recall and recognition of the target when subjects focus encoding on the semantic features of that target than when they focus on non-semantic features. In contrast, the influence of the number of associates in the set should be unaffected by the level of processing adopted during study because the associates are activated in parallel and theoretically have no influence on resonant activation. In PIER 2 connectivity effects arise from activation coming back to the target from its associates whereas set size effects arise from competition arising from unique associates of the target (or the cue) activated at the time of testing. In either case, the recovery of the target from the implicit representation is determined by sampling processes operating during retrieval. Although the influence of each variable is handled by the same sampling rule, the source of influence is thought to be different. This difference allows the model to explain why level of processing influences the magnitude of connectivity effects without influencing the magnitude of set size effects. Furthermore, this difference allows the model to explain why connectivity among the associates facilitates cued recall and recognition whereas the influence of target set size is limited to cued recall. Finally, because the model assumes that both connectivity and set size effects arise from activation in LTWM, the model can explain why both of these effects can be substantially reduced when attention has been diverted to another task for a few minutes prior to testing.

What is more pertinent for understanding the effects of test instructions, PIER 2 assumes that explicit and implicit representations of the target contribute independently to memory performance in both extralist cuing and recognition tasks. Targets can be recovered from either or both representations, with the relative contribution of each representation determined by how the test cues are used. By manipulating test instructions subjects can be asked to use the cues to recall recently studied list words (direct test instructions) or they can be asked to use the cues to recover related words that are compatible with the test cues (indirect test instructions). When test cues are used intentionally to recall recently studied targets, both representations contribute independently to target recovery and, when the cues are used more passively to gain access to related knowledge, recovery depends primarily on the implicit representation as a recent activation in LTWM.

For meaningfully related test cues, the explicit representation appears to contribute little to the probability of target recovery when subjects rely on passive automatic uses of memory regardless of whether such uses are fostered by using the process dissociation procedure (Nelson, Bennett, & Xu, 1997) or by using indirect test instructions (e.g., Nelson, Schreiber, & Holley, 1992). The explicit representation also appears to contribute little to target recovery for amnesics regardless of what instructions they are given (see Squire, Shimamura, & Graf, 1985). In contrast, the implicit representation contributes to the recovery of the target when subjects direct their retrieval efforts to the recent study episode and when they direct it to any past information that is related to the test cue. Connectivity effects, like set size effects, appear to affect the estimates of both C and A. PIER 2 assumes that many of the research findings on indirect versus direct memory can be attributed to the relative influence of the two representations engendered by the test instructions. Different test instructions effectively change the goal of the retrieval process by asking subjects to implement different uses of memory for words that are related to the test cues (Anderson, 1990). Hence, the implicit representation plays a role in retrieving related information regardless of whether subjects recover the target as a result of a conscious use of memory or as a result of an automatic influence of memory produced by the test cue. In contrast, the explicit representation plays a role primarily when search processes are specifically directed to the relevance of a recent study episode.

5.2 Comparison of PIER 2 to dual process theory

Several characteristics of PIER 2 in relation to Jacoby's views should be noted. Jacoby and his colleagues (e.g., Jacoby, 1991; Jacoby, Toth, & Yonelinas, 1993) appear to treat *uses/processes* of memory as synonymous, emphasizing conscious and automatic uses of memory when referring to fragment completion and emphasizing conscious and automatic processes when referring to recognition. They suggest that, in contrast to direct/indirect test procedures, the process dissociation procedure furnishes "process pure" estimates of conscious and unconscious processes. In contrast, PIER 2 distinguishes between uses and processes. The process dissociation procedure, like manipulations of direct/indirect test instructions, is treated as an effective alternative method for assessing conscious and automatic uses of memory during retrieval. However, uses of memory are not regarded as being synonymous with processes. The model assumes that conscious uses of memory during testing influence the recovery of consciously encoded information and, more importantly, that conscious uses of memory can be influenced by automatic processes. Automatic processes initiated by the presentation of the test cue can supplement target recovery even when the subject is operating in a conscious processing mode of retrieval. According to PIER 2, C represents a particular *use* of memory that provides an estimate of the combined influence of both conscious and automatic processes, and in this sense, the model assumes that process dissociation procedure does not provide process pure estimates of processes.

Our main reason for doubting the process pure assumption is related to our interpretation of the causes of set size and connectivity effects. For example, if C provides a pure estimate of conscious processes, then why do target set size and target connectivity affect C in cued recall and why does connectivity affect C in recognition? One answer to this question that preserves the process pure assumption is that set size and connectivity manipulations affect conscious as well as automatic processes. Within the context of Jacoby's dual process theory, variables can influence both types of processes so set size and connectivity could be considered as examples of such variables. It might be argued that the decision to terminate the sampling process in the extralist cuing task is a conscious process and that, because sampling can be terminated more efficiently when set size is small or when connectivity is high, these variables influence conscious processes (Nelson, Bennett, & Xu, 1997). In this argument, these variables affect both an automatic process (sampling) and a conscious process (decision). Hence, the decision to accept or to reject an item as the target can be treated as a single conscious process that can be applied in both tasks. This solution preserves the process pure assumption, but it fails to explain how set size and connectivity influence the conscious decision process. If another process is required to achieve this influence, then processes in addition to sampling and decision need to be proposed and their status with regard to consciousness would need to be determined. More importantly, this solution assumes that cued recall and recognition involve an automatic generative process that is followed by a conscious decision process. Unfortunately, this solution violates the independence assumption that serves as the basis for the process dissociation procedure because it assumes that the automatic process is redundant to the conscious process and, in this situation, the procedure cannot be applied (Jacoby, Begg, & Toth, 1997).

Another answer to this question that preserves the process pure assumption is based on a wholly different explanation than that offered by PIER 2, one that is grounded in the supposition that set size and connectivity strengthen the explicit representation directly. We might assume that an episodic representation is produced during study and that this representation is stronger or more multi-faceted after semantic processing or after undivided attention as well as when set size is small and connectivity among the associates is great. This episodic view is appealing because it would explain why these variables affect C without assuming the existence of a separate implicit representation.

Although an episodic account is pleasing in its simplicity, even to us, it fails to explain a host of other findings. For example, if targets with smaller associative sets produced stronger episodic encodings, then words with smaller sets should be easier to free recall and recognize as well as being more accessible in cued recall. However, set size effects are reversed in free recall (Nelson, McEvoy, & Schreiber, 1990) and are not found in recognition (Nelson et al., 1987). Many years ago we were convinced that set size had to affect recognition and that we just had to do the experiment correctly to show the result, but 25 experiments failed to show such effects and the effort was abandoned when students politely and sensibly refused to continue. Other problems with the episodic account arise as well. For example, even though recall levels remain relatively high, why do set size and connectivity effects disappear after attention is diverted to a multiplication task for several minutes? What is even more germane, how would the episodic account explain why set size and connectivity also affect automatic uses of memory? A reasonable response to this question might be to argue that set size and connectivity affect the strength of the episodic encoding of the target and they exert their respective influences automatically. Unfortunately, this explanation backfires because it undermines the claim that the process dissociation procedure provides process pure estimates. If process pure estimates are being obtained and if these variables exert their respective influences automatically, then they should affect the magnitude of A but not the magnitude of C. The findings suggest that set size and connectivity affect estimates of both A and C and any explanation that attributes their influence to only a single process defeats the process pure claim.

Based on these and other findings we concluded several years ago that we could not create an effective episodic explanation for set size effects (Nelson, Schreiber, & McEvoy, 1992), and such an account also appears to flounder when applied to the explanation of set size and connectivity effects obtained in the process dissociation procedure. The problem to put it simply is that this procedure appears to be contaminated so long as it is regarded as a means for providing pure estimates of conscious and unconscious processes (see Gruppuso, Lindsay, & Kelley, 1997 for a similar view). However, abandoning the claim that the process dissociation procedure estimates conscious and automatic *processes* renders the process pure problem irrelevant. If the procedure is regarded as another effective means for estimating conscious and automatic *uses* of memory, then it provides an effective alternative method for exploring the influences of intention during retrieval. Accordingly, people can be engaged in a conscious use of memory that is directed toward recovering a recently studied word and in this effort it seems perfectly reasonable to presume that all sources of information about the target experience are likely to play a role, including sources of information that tie the target experience to specific explicit experiences and sources that tie it to priming in LTWM. Similarly, when influenced by an automatic use of memory, it seems reasonable to assume priming plays the major role. Hence, along with direct/indirect test methods (e.g., Roediger & McDermott, 1993) and the remember/know procedure (e.g., Gardiner & Java, 1990), the process dissociation procedure should add to our ability to disentangle the relative contributions of conscious and automatic *uses* of memory.

In our view, the adjudication of the processes involved in various memory tasks is best left to task analyses and the development of models as traditionally has been the case. Once a specific single process has been identified, the process dissociation procedure could presumably be used to determine whether the process operates consciously or unconsciously. However, even this approach is problematic because the method requires the isolation of a single process and it hard to imagine the day when memory researchers will succeed in reducing tasks such as recognition and recall to a single process that can be detached from all other processes and investigated effectively to determine whether it operates consciously or unconsciously.

Finally, two additional points about PIER 2 in relation to Jacoby's treatment of recognition are relevant (Jacoby, 1991). He holds a dual-process theory in which the conscious process (recollection) enables the recovery of episodic memories associated with studying an item and the automatic process (familiarity) gives rise to undifferentiated feelings of "oldness" that is unaccompanied by the recovery of detail. In this theory, familiarity is based on fluent processing resulting from the prior presentation of an item. In contrast, PIER 2 does not attribute set size and connectivity effects to greater fluency of processing. Target set size and connectivity effects are built into the sampling equations for both cued recall and recognition (Nelson et al., 1998). The sampling equation attributes these effects to processes occurring during the encoding and retrieval of the implicit representation regardless of whether someone is engaged in a conscious or an automatic use of memory. The same sampling rule is used, for example, whenever the target is recognized as a result of priming in LTWM.

The second point about PIER 2 in relation to Jacoby's (1991) views is related to his assumption that familiarity, the automatic process, represents an attribution based on the episodic experience rather than the priming of an abstract representation of a familiar word. We differ on this point because we assume that priming is essential for our effects and find it impossible to explain such effects without assuming that priming the target and its associates is somehow involved in conscious and automatic uses of memory. However, the difference here is not as great as it seems. We assume that preexisting representations of the target and its associates are abstract only in the sense that context can no longer be recovered after an item has been experienced in hundreds of contexts. Such information simply represents past episodes. We also assume that the implicit representation produced as a result of activating the target and its associates *can be* influenced by what happens during the episodic experience. Explicit and implicit representations are independent and the formation of one may or may not be influenced by the other. For example, connectivity but not set size effects are affected by whether attention is switched to non-semantic features of the target during study, and both set size and connectivity effects are influenced by whether attention to the memory task is sustained through testing or diverted just prior to testing. In PIER 2 priming effects are affected by the details of the study experience and in this sense we see priming effects as being context specific. Such effects are so context specific that studying targets in the presence of meaningfully related words nearly eliminates both set size and connectivity effects, presumably because associates that are unrelated to the meaning produced by the conjunction of the word pairing are inhibited (Nelson et al., 1992; Nelson, Gee, & Schreiber, 1992). These considerations should make it clear that PIER 2 does not assume that priming effects involve abstract representations that are somehow isolated from the episode.

6.   Consciousness and stratification

The findings of our experiments on set size and connectivity and the model that has been driven by these findings imply that conscious and unconscious uses of memory can contribute independently to performance. The *encoding assumptions* of PIER 2 assume that a word acts as a cue for activating related knowledge in LTWM and, simultaneously, for initiating consciously controlled processing activities dictated by the situation. The activation of related knowledge is driven by the need for comprehension. A word is understood by activating related words and, although complex, its comprehension is a highly learned skill acquired in using language (e.g., Ericsson & Kintsch, 1995; Gernsbacher & Faust, 1991). According to PIER 2, the presentation of a word acts as a cue with comprehension serving as the goal of processing it and, because this goal is highly learned, its related associates are retrieved implicitly, automatically and presumably without conscious awareness. The presentation of a word also serves as a cue to initiate consciously directed mental activities to meet goals that are self-initiated or that are imposed by instructions. Hence, PIER 2 assumes that the target to be encoded serves as a cue to initiate two kinds of processing, one that occurs automatically in order to meet the goal of comprehension and one that occurs intentionally in order the meet the goal defined by the novel aspects of the task demands. Each of these processing activities theoretically produces independent memory traces that, in the terms of the model, are identified with implicit and explicit representations.

The *retrieval assumptions* of PIER 2 also presuppose important roles for automatic and conscious processing activities. All retention tests entail the presentation of cues of some sort and all memory tests define some goal that is to be achieved as a result of using these cues. PIER 2 assumes that the presentation of a test cue, like the presentation of a target, automatically activates related information and that the goal of such activation is comprehension. In addition, the presentation of the test cue initiates consciously controlled processing activities dictated by goals defined by the test instructions. Such instructions define the purpose of the effort to remember and, at least in memory experiments, all tests of remembering require the engagement of conscious processing that is directed toward the achievement of some goal however defined. PIER 2 assumes that, in cued recall, retrieval goals that direct subjects to a recent study experience cause them to use the cue to search through their memory of the list learning experience to find a list word that matches. In recognition, subjects use the cue, the target itself, to decide whether the word is a member of the study list. PIER 2 relies on SAM to describe these processes (cf., Gillund & Shiffrin, 1984). However, the model assumes that in order for these efforts to succeed, subjects must comprehend the cue and that such comprehension is automatic. Comprehension requires activating the associates of the test cue, and the activation of one of its associates, the target, presumably activates its implicit representation in LTWM. This activation is automatic and the model assumes that the target can be recovered from such activation, though such recovery will be a function of its set size, the connectivity of its associates, as well as other factors and other conditions of the experiment. The important point is to note that this activation operates automatically while the subject is engaged in a act of retrieval regardless of whether that act is directed toward a specific list word or toward recovering a word that is simply related to the cue.

PIER 2 implies that the automatic and conscious processing of a known word can go on simultaneously. Such processing is stratified during encoding in the sense that each type of processing can serve different purposes, e.g., automatic uses of memory serve to encode what is known and conscious uses serve to encode what is new. It is stratified during retrieval in the sense that each type of processing relies on different retrieval structures. Both encoding and retrieval processes are stratified in terms of different levels of control operating on different kinds of information. PIER 2 clearly implies that conscious and automatic processing rely on different cognitive structures and, given that many if not most everyday memory tasks require the processing of known information in new contexts, it seems reasonable to assume that the memory system has created specialized structures for dealing with both the repetitive and the novel aspects of experience. Presumably, different neural structures underlie different forms of cognition, as some have suggested (e.g., Tulving, 1985; Tulving & Schacter, 1990). We have avoided speculations about the nature of the underlying neural structures not because of any aversion to linking brain and cognition but because our work has been limited solely to the cognitive aspects of experience.

Acknowledgments

This research was supported by grant MH 16360 to Douglas L. Nelson from the National Institute of Mental Health. The authors are indebted to Cathy McEvoy for her extremely helpful comments on earlier drafts of the paper.

Note

1. PIER stands for Processing Implicit and Explicit Representations.

Appendix A: Materials used in Experiment 1

List 1		List 2	
Test Cue	Target	Test Cue	Target
ASTEROID	PLANET	TRUMPET	PLAYER
ROB	THIEF	RAG	TOWEL
MONK	RELIGION	TUNE	RADIO
BOXER	SHORTS	SWEATER	SHIRT
ARTIST	PAINTING	PAINT	COLOR
AUTHORITY	TEACHER	MOVIE	THEATER
REFEREE	SOCCER	NECKLACE	BRACELET
TWIN	BROTHER	CHIEF	BOSS
UNDERSTANDING	COMPASSION	MOLECULE	CHEMISTRY
SEAT	CUSHION	WEDDING	CAKE
BANJO	INSTRUMENT	BUTTERFLY	INSECT
DRUGS	ALCOHOL	TORNADO	DESTRUCTION
BUBBLE	BATH	WICKER	FURNITURE
PENNY	COPPER	BOWLING	LANE
MUSHROOM	FUNGUS	READER	WRITER
NEURON	ATOM	AEROBICS	WORKOUT
TERMITE	PEST	PLASTIC	CUP
DRAWER	DESK	RESERVATION	DINNER
PEACH	PIT	CABBAGE	PATCH
PASTE	TOOTH	IVORY	TUSK
CUB	SCOUT	BLUEJAY	ROBIN
WASTE	BASKET	WEIGH	SCALES
CYLINDER	TUBE	VESSEL	BLOOD
ADDRESS	PHONE	FINGER	TOE
SLUG	SNAIL	CASHEW	PEANUT
LIBERTY	BELL	LODGE	SKI
ERASER	CHALK	TAIL	CAT
GOURMET	CHEF	PAD	PENCIL
SENTENCE	STRUCTURE	FOAM	SHAVE
SOLVE	PUZZLE	VIRTUE	PATIENCE
CLIPPERS	NAILS	NAVIGATOR	PILOT
FILM	CAMERA	PICKLES	DILL
ROOST	NEST	POTENTIAL	POSSIBILITY
GAUGE	METER	WINDOW	PANE
BONE	MARROW	SMELL	NOSE
BOOTS	COWBOY	FUNGUS	MUSHROOM

Note. The first 18 targets shown in each list have high connectivity associates and the last 18 in each list have low connectivity targets.

Appendix B: Materials used in Experiment 2

List 1		List 2		List 3	
High Connectivity	Low Connectivity	High Connectivity	Low Connectivity	High Connectivity	Low Connectivity
BROTHER	ALPHABET	APE	ANTIQUE	CAKE	ATTENTION
BRUISE	BALLOT	AUTUMN	ARROW	CLARINET	BASKET
CHILL	CAMERA	BISHOP	CARDBOARD	DELIGHT	BOXER
COIN	CAT	BRANDY	CHOWDER	EDUCATION	COLUMN
COMMENT	CHALK	CLINIC	CLOCK	FLASK	CRIB
COUCH	COLT	DIME	FLAG	GEM	CROW
DINNER	CONDITION	EMPLOYEE	FOUNTAIN	INFERNO	ERASER
GRIEF	DISCOVERY	GRAMMAR	HAIR	INSECT	HOSE
INTELLECT	DREAM	HARBOR	INDIAN	MICROPHONE	LEGION
MORTGAGE	GLOVES	MYTH	JUGGLER	ORCHARD	MUMMY
NECKLACE	GLUE	NOTEBOOK	LIGHTNING	PLAYER	MUSTARD
OREGANO	HAMMER	PAINTING	LILY	PROTON	PARROT
PRAYER	IVORY	PAVEMENT	OWL	PUB	PATCH
PURPLE	KITE	PLANET	PEANUT	RAFT	POISON
RIFLE	LOSER	PLATE	PICKLE	SEAM	POSSIBILITY
SCUBA	PENDULUM	PUDDING	PILOT	SHRUB	PUZZLE
SEASHORE	PHONE	RECTANGLE	PORCH	SOCCER	SHEPHERD
SHERIFF	RAISIN	REEF	PUMPKIN	SPHERE	SKI
SURGERY	SCOUT	SAPPHIRE	SCALES	SPONGE	SNAIL
SWEATER	SEATBELT	SAUSAGE	SKELETON	SPOUSE	STALLION
TORNADO	SHOE	TEMPERATURE	STRATEGY	SUFFOCATE	STONE
TROMBONE	TEA	TERROR	TOOTH	THEATER	TOES
VERB	TITLE	THIEF	TRACTOR	VERDICT	TUNA
WHISKEY	WIRE	VOLLEYBALL	TRIBUTE	VEST	WEB

References

Anderson, J. R. (1990). *The adaptive character of thought*. Hillsdale, NJ: Erlbaum.

Anderson, J. R. & Pirolli, P. L. (1984). Spread of activation. *Journal of Experimental Psychology: Learning, Memory and Cognition, 10,* 791–798.

Brown, A. S. & Mitchell, D. B. (1994). A reevaluation of semantic versus nonsemantic processing in implicit memory. *Memory & Cognition, 22,* 533–541.

Challis, B. H. & Brodbeck, D. R. (1992). Levels of processing affects priming in word fragment completion. *Journal of Experimental Psychology: Learning, Memory, and Cognition, 18,* 595–607.

Craik, F. I. M. & Tulving, E. (1975). Depth of processing and the retention of words in episodic memory. *Journal of Experimental Psychology: General, 104,* 268–294.

Dienes, Z. & Berry, D. (1997). Implicit learning: Below the subjective threshold. *Psychonomic Bulletin & Review, 4,* 3–23.

Ericsson, K. A. & Kintsch, W. (1995). Long-term working memory. *Psychological Review, 102,* 211–245.

Gardiner, J. M. & Java, R. I. (1990). Recollective experiences in word and nonword recognition. *Memory & Cognition, 18,* 23–30.

Gee, N. R. (1997). Implicit memory and word ambiguity. *Journal of Memory and Language, 36,* 253–275.

Gernsbacher, M. A. & Faust, M. E. (1991). The mechanisms of suppression: A component of general comprehension skill. *Journal of Experimental Psychology: Learning, Memory and Cognition, 17,* 245–262.

Gillund, G. & Shiffrin, R. M. (1984). A retrieval model for both recognition and recall. *Psychological Review, 91,* 1–67.

Grupusso, V., Lindsay, D. S., & Kelley, C. M. (1997). The process dissociation and similarity: Defining and estimating recollection and familiarity in recognition memory. *Journal of Experimental Psychology: Learning, Memory, and Cognition, 23,* 259–278.

Jacoby, L. L. (1991). A process dissociation framework: Separating automatic from intentional uses of memory. *Journal of Memory and Language, 30,* 513–541.

Jacoby, L. L., Begg, I. M., & Toth, J. P. (1997). In defense of independence: Violations of assumptions underlying the process-dissociation procedure? *Journal of Experimental Psychology: Learning, Memory, and Cognition, 23,* 484–495.

Jacoby, L. L., Toth, J. P., Yonelinas, A. P. (1993). Separating conscious and unconscious influences of memory: Measuring recollection. *Journal of Experimental Psychology: General, 122,* 139–154.

Jacoby, L. L., Woloshyn, V., & Kelley, C. M. (1989). Becoming famous without being recognized: Unconscious influences of memory produced by dividing attention. *Journal of Experimental Psychology: General, 118,* 115–125.

Kintsch, W. (1988). The role of knowledge in discourse comprehension: A construction-integration model. *Psychological Review, 95,* 163–182.

Kuçera, H. & Francis, W. N. (1967). *Computational analysis of present-day American English.* Providence, RI: Brown University Press.

Nelson, D. L., Bajo, M. T., & Casanueva, D. (1985). Prior knowledge and memory: The influence of natural category size as a function of intention and distraction. *Journal of Experimental Psychology: Learning, Memory, and Cognition, 11,* 94–105.

Nelson, D. L., Bennett, D. J., Gee, N. R., Schreiber, T. A., & McKinney, V. M. (1993). Implicit memory: Effects of network size and interconnectivity on cued recall. *Journal of Experimental Psychology: Learning, Memory, and Cognition, 19,* 747–764.

Nelson, D. L., Bennett, D. J., & Xu, J. (1997). Recollective and automatic uses of memory. *Journal of Experimental Psychology: Learning, Memory, and Cognition, 23,* 872–885.

Nelson, D. L., Canas, J., & Bajo, M. T. (1987). The effects of natural category size on memory for episodic encodings. *Memory & Cognition, 15,* 133–140.

Nelson, D. L., Gee, N. R., & Schreiber, T. A. (1992). Sentence encoding and implicitly activated memories. *Memory & Cognition, 20,* 643–654.

Nelson, D. L., McEvoy, C. L., Janczura, G. A., & Xu, J. (1993). Implicit memory and inhibition. *Journal of Memory and Language, 32,* 667–691.

Nelson, D. L., McEvoy, C. L., & Schreiber, T. A. (1990). Encoding context and retrieval conditions as determinants of the effects of natural category size. *Journal of Experimental Psychology: Learning, Memory, and Cognition, 16,* 31–41.

Nelson, D. L., McEvoy, C. L., & Schreiber, T. A. (1998). The University of South Florida word association, rhyme, and word fragment norms. http://www.usf.edu/FreeAssociation.

Nelson, D. L., McKinney, V. M., Gee, N. R., & Janczura, G. A. (1998). Interpreting the influence of implicitly activated memories on recall and recognition. *Psychological Review, 105,* 411–433.

Nelson, D. L. & Schreiber, T. A. (1992). Word concreteness and word structure as independent determinants of recall. *Journal of Memory and Language, 31,* 237–260.

Nelson, D. L., Schreiber, T. A., & Holley, P. E. (1992). The retrieval of controlled and automatic aspects of meaning on direct and indirect tests. *Memory & Cognition, 20,* 671–684.

Nelson, D. L., Schreiber, T. A., & McEvoy, C. L. (1992). Processing implicit and explicit representations. *Psychological Review, 99,* 322–348.

Nelson, D. L. & J. Xu (1995). Effects of implicit memory on explicit recall: Set size and word frequency effects. *Psychological Research, 57,* 203–214.

Richardson-Klavehn, A. & Gardiner, J. M. (1998). Depth-of-processing effects on priming in stem completion: Tests of voluntary contamination, conceptual processing, and lexical processing hypotheses. *Journal of Experimental Psychology: Learning, Memory, and Cognition, 24,* 593–609.

Roediger, H. L., III. (1990). Implicit memory: Retention without remembering. *American Psychologist, 45,* 1043–1056.

Roediger, H. L., III., McDermott, K. B. (1993). Implicit memory in normal human subjects. In F. Boller and J. Grafman (eds.), *Handbook of Neuropsychology. Vol. 8.* Amsterdam: Elsevier.

Schreiber, T. A. (1993). Feelings of knowing are based upon implicitly activated knowledge about the test cue and the target. (Dissertation submitted to the University of South Florida).

Squire, L. R., Shimamura, A. P., & Graf, P. (1985). Independence of recognition memory and priming effects: A neuropsychological analysis. *Journal of Experimental Psychology: Learning, Memory, and Cognition, 11,* 37–44.

Toth, J. P., Reingold, E. M., & Jacoby, L. L. (1994). Toward a redefinition of implicit memory: Process dissociations following elaborative processing and self-generation. *Journal of Experimental Psychology: Learning, Memory, and Cognition, 20,* 290–303.

Tulving, E. (1985). How many memory systems are there? *American Psychologist, 40,* 385–398.

Tulving, E. & Schacter, D. L. (1990). Priming and human memory systems. *Science, 247,* 301–306.

CHAPTER 7

From levels of processing to stratification of cognition

Converging evidence from three domains of research

Boris M. Velichkovsky

The theme of this volume is the possibility that cognitive mechanisms are stratified on several hierarchically related levels. An issue which is directly relevant to this goal is the levels-of-processing approach introduced in (modern) memory research by Craik and Lockhart (Craik & Lockhart, 1972; see also Lockhart & Craik, 1990)[1]. The first publication of these authors became one of the most influential papers in contemporary cognitive psychology. Craik and Lockhart proposed a new methodological approach to the study of memory and, in addition, formulated two theoretical postulates. Their method consisted of a variation of encoding of the material in the situation of incidental learning. In almost all cases, this variation is either encoding under perceptual instruction emphasizing attention to the physical features of material or semantic encoding aiming at categorization of the same input. The first theoretical postulate predicted the whole continuum of the depths of processing whereby a deeper (i.e., semantic) encoding of material would lead to better memory performance than a shallow (i.e., perceptual or physical) encoding. The better memory performance after a deep, semantic encoding became known as the levels-of-processing (LOP) effect. According to their second thesis, memory performance is a byproduct of such perceptual-cognitive processing which evolves from shallow to deep representation of the input.

The cumulative citation index of the levels-of-processing approach reached the mark of 2000 by the beginning of the 90s (Roediger, 1995). However, by far not all of these references were positive. In particular, theoretical objections concentrated on circularity in the definition of depth: One took memory performance as the criterion of depth of processing and, later on, found the confirmation of this criterion in the data about memory performance (e.g. Baddeley, 1978). Another important set of ideas was related to the concepts of transfer-appropriate processing and domain specificity. Accordingly, there is no inherent continuum of higher versus lower levels, but several, perhaps many, qualitatively different forms of processing that are parallel and, in a sense, equivalent. With respect to memory performance the prediction was that even "shallow" encodings could demonstrate a better memorization than "deep" ones if the specific memory test initiates retrieval processes similar ("appropriate") to that at encoding stage. Indeed, there have been several demonstrations in this direction (e.g. Morris, Bransford, & Franks, 1977), though even with an appropriate "shallow" test the amount of memory performance seemed to be lower than after an appropriate "deep" test like free recall or recognition (Fisher & Craik, 1977).

Empirical data deviating from the expectations of the levels-of-processing approach in its initial form have been found particularly often with the introduction of implicit, or indirect tests of memory. As a rule, these tests demonstrate few if any influence of encoding manipulations on the corresponding priming measures (e.g. Roediger, Weldon, Stadler, & Riegler, 1992). Even when post-hoc meta-analytic studies (Challis & Brodbeck, 1992) were able to show a tendency to stronger priming with semantic encoding, these effects of the level of processing were indeed rather weak and less systematic than in direct memory measures. The most parsimonious explanation would be that of explicit awareness of some subjects in some experiments about the proper goal of implicit tests. This differential influence of the level-of-processing manipulation on explicit and implicit tests has to be considered a challenge for the further research: The same pattern of results can be found not only with English or German words but also with Japanese Kanji (Cabeza & Ohta, 1993), as well as with nonverbal material such as faces or landscapes (Loftus, Green, & Smith, 1980).

In this chapter, we want to discuss the reasons why such a vague notion as "depth of processing" works. Our method will be a comparison of several recent investigations that seem to demonstrate new evidence for levels effects in three different domains: multivariate memory research, brain imaging and eye-movement studies. While these results are related in the first line to the issue of stratification of cognitive processing they also shed some light on the possible variety in forms of awareness of situation and on the role of conscious intention in the reformatting cognitive mechanisms involved in the solution of a task.

1.   Memory experiments with a better design

We start with memory research, where an increasing number of authors are becoming aware of one methodical drawback of most contemporary studies. This drawback is the 2x2 experimental design. Besides the traditional psychological preference for dichotomies, it has its grounds in the intensive search for double dissociations and recently in the conception of modularity of mind (Fodor, 1983; Cosmides, Tooby, & Velichkovsky, 1997). This latter has evolved in the last 15 years to be the dominant theoretical framework of cognitive science. The main problem with such local experiments is that their results cannot be directly compared with one another. Thus, although in some studies of levels of processing one used manipulations other than perceptual and semantic, the results are hardly comparable with data of previous experiments — despite the impression that, for example, self-referential (and also other-referential: see Bower & Gilligan, 1979) encoding demonstrate a better performance in explicit memory tests than semantic processing of the material (Miall, 1986). Generally, meta-analysis of data is a possible but also rather crude way to compare such experiments, which are in many respects completely different (Nyberg & Tulving, 1996).

It was Teresa Blaxton (1989) who for the first time investigated a large group of memory tests under the same experimental conditions. In that investigation, she discovered, for instance, that there are no essential differences between explicit and implicit tests if one other dimension is taken into account, namely, the emphasis on perceptual versus conceptual (semantic) processing. This difference in behavior of perceptual implicit tests and conceptual implicit tests has been confirmed in several later studies (Cabeza & Ohta, 1993; Hamann, 1990; Tulving & Schacter, 1990). Though these results seem to be of direct relevance for LOP studies, Blaxton, unfortunately, did not manipulate encoding conditions in a systematic way as is prescribed by levels-of-processing approach. If it is possible in one and the same experiment to vary — systematically and in a broad range — both encoding conditions and memory tests, then one could decide among different models of modular or hierarchical organization of cognitive processes with much greater certainty than before.

With this goal in mind, we performed several experiments in recent years (see Velichkovsky, Challis, & Pomplun, 1995; Challis, Velichkovsky, & Craik, 1996). An influence of as many as 5 different encoding conditions (plus one control condition) of visually presented lists of words on altogether 13 memory tests was been analyzed. Memory tests were selected according to the major theoretical points of view, such as perceptual versus conceptual and implicit versus explicit. With the large matrix of encoding and retrieval conditions, several predictions are possible. All of them presuppose a kind of affinity between specific encoding and retrieval conditions, known as transfer appropriate processing. In other respects, the predictions based on different conceptions also differ. From the strong modular view, one would expect that there will be several more-or-less equivalent clusters of interaction between encoding and retrieval in memory performance. For instance, one could expect at least, that perceptual encoding interacts with perceptual tests and that semantic encoding interacts with conceptual memory tests. Some other interactions are conceivable but always without inherent relationships between them. From a hierarchical point of view, one could expect that the clusters of interaction will be more asymmetric by building something like a gradient from weak to strong and perhaps even stronger memory effects.

Our data were quite compelling on these predictions. As it is shown in Figure 1, if the encoding conditions are re-ordered in the sequence of perceptual

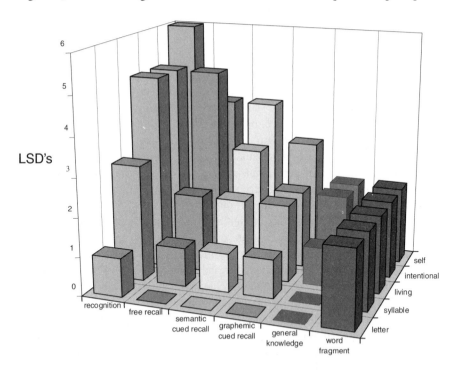

Figure 1. *The number of statistically significant deviations from baseline in 6 memory tasks in dependence on 5 encoding conditions (after Challis, Velichkovsky, & Craik, 1996).*

(counting of letters deviating in form), phonological (counting of syllables), semantic (categorizing as living thing), and meta-cognitive (evaluation of personal importance) encoding, the resulting interactions — LOP effects — grow in a systematic, gradiental way across at least explicit memory tests. The more traditional case of intentional encoding finds its place between semantic and meta-cognitive encodings with only one deviation in the free-recall task where intentional learning demonstrates a stronger effect than meta-cognitive encoding. At first sight, LOP functions in the sub-group of implicit memory tests (which were word fragment completion and general knowledge tests) look different: they are much flatter or there seems to be no effect at all. Some similarity can, however, be found with respect to the point in the row of encoding conditions where variation in encoding starts to influence memory performance. In general knowledge test, this starting point is the semantic encoding. In word fragment completion test priming is present in all encoding conditions — one can argue that the crucial influence is already present at the stage of perceptual encoding, and is included in all further, higher-level encodings as well.

This pattern of results cannot be explained on the basis of predictions from the strong modularity approach. It is more compatible with the hierarchical view of underlying mechanisms supporting the broad idea of multiple levels of processing. We emphasize the word "multiple" in this context as there is a tendency to consider only two possible levels related to processing of physical features of material and semantic information, respectively. A dichotomic interpretation of our data would be that incidental encoding conditions provide a variable amount of semantic information for later retrieval, which increases from perceptual to meta-cognitive encoding. The notion that encoding semantic information can be more or less elaborated (e.g. Craik & Tulving, 1975) is well accepted, but it is not clear why syllable encoding should involve more semantic activity than counting letters, or why judgment of personal relevance should recruit more semantic associations than semantic categorization itself. An unqualified attribution of LOP effects to semantic processing alone is dubious also in light of other aspects of the data. For instance, free recall and recognition benefit from study conditions in different ways. Whereas it might be argued that free recall utilizes conceptual information to a greater degree, it is recognition that shows a steeper increase in performance as a function of the LOP manipulation. In addition, recognition performance deviates from baseline even after perceptual (letter) encoding, although this study condition involves little if any semantic processing.

While the data support the idea of hierarchically related levels, the degree of vertical integration, i.e., the integration across the levels, seems to be dependent on the type of task. This integration is strong in explicit tests where evidence from several levels is accumulated. It is, however, rather weak in implicit tests: The responsibility seems to be taken over here — without interference "from above" — by relatively narrowly defined mechanisms, which can be themselves localized at a low level of the processing hierarchy. In view of such a flexibility, the notion "heterarchy" prompted by Turvey, Shaw and Mace (1978) may be more appropriate for describing the underlying functional architecture as a whole.

     One of our experiments (Challis, Velichkovsky, & Craik, 1996, Experiment 3) provides further support for this interpretation of data from explicit and implicit memory tests. If the typical pattern of flat or step-like LOP functions

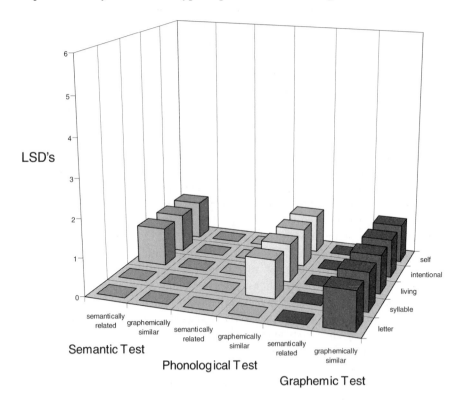

Figure 2. *The number of significant deviations from baseline in three new explicit memory tasks in dependence on 5 encoding conditions (after Challis, Velichkovsky, & Craik, 1996).*

found with implicit tests is connected with activation of relatively narrow mechanisms, then perhaps might it be possible to get the same LOP functions even with explicit tests when the retrieval criteria will be formulated more strictly narrowing down the mechanism accessed to only one level of processing? After studying lists of words under the same 5 encoding conditions, subjects were presented with the test material which consisted of the words 50% graphemically and on the 50% semantically similar to those previously shown. Their tasks were to find words similar to previously presented either graphemically, phonological-ly or semantically. Although these tests were overtly explicit, the results present-ed in Figure 2 demonstrated the whole set of flat and step-like LOP functions that in previous studies were typical for implicit tests. Again, it was the encoding condition where memory performance started to deviate from baseline which was of importance — this starting point shifts for graphemic, phonological, and semantic similarity tests to correspondingly higher levels of encoding.

These examples clearly demonstrate that in its proper domain, psychological investigation of memory, the levels-of-processing approach can produce data which are surprisingly consistent, indeed to a degree which is rare in psychologi-cal research. This consistency is a strong argument against reducing LOP effects to domain-specific phenomena, like transfer appropriate processing. While the results are impressive, they still do not answer the critical question about possible independent (from memory performance) measures of "depth" of a processing, as demanded by some prominent critics of levels of processing. To approach this problem, we shall now consider the discovered gradient from perceptual to meta-cognitive encoding in the context of underlying neurophysiological mechanisms.

2.   Brain imaging and the evoked coherences analysis of EEG

The task of considering data of experiments in memory and cognition from the neurophysiological perspective is not such a speculative adventure as it was a couple of decades ago. In view of critical remarks on circularity in definition of levels, there have been several attempts to find independent measures or correlates of LOP effects in psychophysiological data, such as ERPs (Sanquist, Rohrbaugh, Syndulko, & Lindsley, 1980) and cardiovascular responses (Vincent, Craik, & Furedy, 1993). Particularly interesting and conclusive are recent studies of memory using methods of functional brain imaging.

As the results are rather similar, we shall limit ourselves mainly with one of the last of such neuroimaging studies, a PET-scan investigation of regional cerebral blood flow in four memory tests by Blaxton and her colleagues

(Blaxton, Bookheimer, Zefiro, Figlozzi, Gaillard, & Theodore, 1996). Memory tasks for the study were chosen in such a way that they represented orthogonally both theoretically important dimensions: perceptual versus conceptual processing and implicit versus explicit testing. The larger topographical changes were related to the difference between perceptual and conceptual tasks. Memory effects for both (implicit and explicit) perceptual fragment completion tests were localized in posterior regions including occipital cortex with some right-side asymmetry. In contrast, the analysis of conceptual tests of semantic cued recall and word association revealed metabolic changes in left medial and superior temporal cortex as well as left frontal cortex. Of course, these differences in neuro-anatomical localization have been found with respect to localization of retrieval processes, so it can be interesting to compare them with results of our studies based on a psychophysiological method known as evoked coherences analysis of EEG - a cheaper but also faster alternative to PET-scan (see Velichkovsky, Klemm, Dettmar, & Volke, 1996).

We investigated in a series of levels-of-processing experiments reproduction of visually and acoustically presented words in dependence on three encoding conditions: perceptive, semantic, and metacognitive (self-referential). Although the database of evoked coherence analysis is completely different from that of PET-scan, the loci of global incoherences in perceptual and semantic orienting tasks have been found in approximately the same regions where Blaxton et al. (1996) discovered significant changes in metabolism for corresponding memory tests.

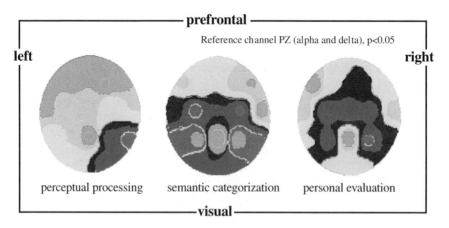

Figure 3. *Typical changes in topography of evoked coherences (darker regions represent areas incoherent with respect to the rest of cortex) in dependence on three types of encoding (after Velichkovsky, Klemm, Dettmar, & Volke, 1996).*

These changes are illustrated by Figure 3. In the perceptive (form-oriented) encoding of visually presented words the major incoherences are localized in the occipital and right occipito-temporal area. In semantic encoding, the incoherences expand to the more anterioraly located region, particularly including left temporal and left frontal areas (cf. also similar data from another investigation of neuro-anatomical correlates of LOP effects by Kapur, Craik, Tulving, Wilson, Houle, & Brown, 1994). In the third condition — self-referential meta-cognitive encoding — even more anteriorely located regions within frontal and right prefrontal lobes are involved. This trend has been confirmed in a later PET investigation of self-referential encoding (Craik, Moroz, Moscovitch, Stuss, Vinokur, Tulving, & Kapur, 1999).

These neuroanatomical changes are not at all astonishing from the point of view of classical neuropsychological and neurophysiological studies (e.g. Luria, 1966). In particular, the gradiental approach to localization of higher cortical functions elaborated by Goldberg (1991) seem to fit exactly with the data reported up to now. In other words, the data suggest that a purely functional interpretation of LOP effects does not go far enough and should be revisited. Of theoretical importance are, in our opinion, not the neuroanatomical changes per se, but their direction: The posterior-anterior gradient corresponds to the main direction of evolutionary growth of the cortex (see also Deacon, 1996). The "deeper" is therefore a particular "level of processing" (that can be evaluated on the basis of memory measurements similar to those described in the first part of the chapter); the more massive is involvement of phylogenetically new brain mechanisms in the solution of task.

The proposed correspondence of functional and structural mechanisms is of course only a heuristic rule — the ideas of perceptual or meta-cognitive process-ing are too vague and as well our knowledge about brain functional evolution is too fragmentary. However the rule may work also in several other cases. We shall try to show this with one additional example. Until now, we discussed the posterior-anterior gradient. There are several other lines of evolutionary develop-ment of brain, for instance, one reflecting differences between sub-cortical and cortical mechanisms (for such an analysis of human motor control see Bernstein, 1996). One of the peculiarities of human cortex is the so-called "Yakovlevian torque", which is related, in particular, to a relatively strongly developed right prefrontal lobe (see Goldberg & Podell, 1995, for new data on individual differences). The role of these structures in autobiographical and episodic remembering is fairly well established (Cimino, Verfaillie, Bowers, & Heilmann, 1991; Tulving, Kapur, Craik, Moscovitch, & Houle, 1994). But it cannot be reduced only to higher forms of memory. The same regions seem to be involved in the control of pragmatic of speech communication, understanding of fresh (not yet lexicalized) metaphors, irony, and humor, as well as the aspects of reflective social behavior known as manifestation of the "theory of mind" (Bihle, Brownell, Powelson, & Gardner, 1986; Deacon, 1997; Velichkovsky, 1994). This list goes well beyond the span of memory phenomena approaching that which could be called "level of metacognitive coordination".

For a further analysis it is important to note that different levels of processing can be dissociated also by temporal parameters of their functioning. This has been shown many times with respect to differentiation of two levels of perceptual processing — localization and identification (e.g. Velichkovsky, 1982) and with respect to differences in perceptual (form-oriented) processing and semantic categorization of the same material (Posner, 1978). In neurophysiology, those are in the first line data on selective dependency of early and late components of ERPs on sensory and semantic characteristics of stimulation, respectively (Kutas & King, 1996; Rugg & Coles, 1995). Our data from evoked coherence analysis of EEG with respect to differences in encoding also demonstrated that a "deep" processing may be differentiated by a functional decoupling of anterioraly located regions of the cortex in the domain of slow rhythms, particularly delta. In contrast, visual and acoustic perceptual encoding is related to faster components of EEG, such as alpha, beta and theta (Velichkovsky, Klemm, Dettmar, & Volke, 1996). A new and practically important *pendant* to these neurophysiological data can be found in temporal parameters of eye movements.

3.   Levels are reflected in the parameters of eye movements

The fast technological progress in the field of video-based eyetracking (e.g. Velichkovsky & Hansen, 1996) made it possible to analyze eye movement in a broad spectrum of situations. This progress leads to revision of data and ideas about the mechanisms of eye movements and their interaction with tasks of different levels. The emerging picture is that behavior of human eye is a common output of several hierarchically related mechanisms. This claim is not only necessary true in view of known facts about neuroanatomy of eye movement control, which is distributed across at least four different levels of brain's organization — from midbrain to frontal cortex (e.g. Gippenreiter, 1978; Kennard, 1989). The new aspect of discussion is that this structural organization is manifested in the temporal parameters of eye movements during a task solution.

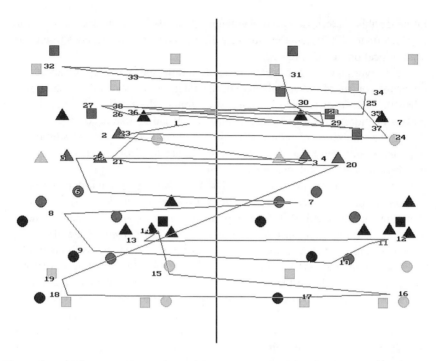

Figure 4. *Typical pattern of saccades and fixations in the search-for-a-difference task (after Velichkovsky, Challis, & Pomplun, 1995).*

Two parameters of eye movements, fixation duration and dwell time, seem to be indeed under selective control of such hierarchical mechanisms. This can be illustrated by some new results from investigation of visual search (Pomplun, 1998; Velichkovsky, Challis, & Pomplun, 1995). In Figure 4 a typical pattern of search eye movements in the task of finding a difference between left and right parts of the display is shown. The solution of this and similar tasks can usually be divided in two phases. The first phase, which is relatively long, is connected with search operations *per se*. The second, shorter phase is one of generation of a hypothesis, its testing and decision to a response. At the first phase, fixation duration is mainly a function of spatial density of objects independent of their identity. Dwell time depends in addition on the variety (entropy) of objects features. Average fixation time is about 150 to 250 ms and the seesaw-pattern of search saccades is a nice illustration of a psychological solution of the classical traveling salesmen problem — how to visit N locations without a return to any of them. One of the possible neurophysiological mechanisms which may influence this pattern of eye movements is the so-called "inhibition of return" (e.g. Hoffman, 1997), whereby directly after a fixation new saccades to the same spatial location are suppressed.

However all these parameters of fixation time and scan-path of saccades are under the control of the actual stage in the solution of task. In the second phase, when the crucial difference is about to be found, the fixation duration rises to 500 ms or more. Repetitive visits to the same location also become possible, as though the "inhibition of return" was not still at work. Obviously, this final phase of visual search can be attributed to some higher level of cognitive processing, which culminates in a conscious decision.

In a quite different experimental setting, we found a similar increase in proportion of such very long fixations (Velichkovsky, 1995; Velichkovsky, Pomplun, & Rieser, 1996). The experiments investigated the natural human ability to take into account information about another person's gaze direction in communication and cooperative problem solving. Early in the development of the face-to-face interaction we learn to coordinate our attentional resources with those of other people, so that the state of "joint attention" becomes possible: we attend the same object at the same time as our partner and the problem of the high referential ambiguity of natural language disappears. Our experimental task consisted of a cooperative solution in a puzzle game. One of the two subjects was an expert, who had solved the task many times before, and the other a novice, who saw the puzzle for the first time but was expected to find a solution in practice. We registered verbal communication of the partner and their eye movements in several modes of communication, for instance, in the "voice and gaze" condition where, in addition to verbal communication, actual position of fixations (either of expert or of novice) were shown on the monitor of the partner. For the present context, the data on the eye movements of experts are of special interest. An explicit intention to support verbal instruction by the gaze leads to a significant rise of the proportion of extremely long fixations — around 500 ms and more. There is also a negative correlation of the number of such fixations in experts and the overall puzzle solution time in novices. In other words, long fixations can be indeed used in a communicative, i.e., meta-cognitive role, as a source of deictic information in a situation of an indirect communication mediated by computer.[2]

On the basis of these results one can expect that higher levels of encoding (i.e. ones emphasizing processes that are predicated to be metacognitive, communicative, involved in conscious decisions, etc.) of visually presented material may be correlated with a higher proportion of longer fixations. Interestingly, there have been no studies of eye movements in LOP tasks, though such studies are a prerequisite of any detailed analysis of encoding processes. What goes on, for instance, when people try to count or process visually presented objects depending on their physical or semantic features? We have recently attempted to answer this and related questions in a series of experiments with verbal and nonverbal visual material.

In the first of the experiments, subjects had to study short biographical sketches, counting either all the words, or all adjectives, or all adjectives that had a self-referential value for them. These three encoding instructions lead to the expected LOP effect, i.e., to a corresponding increase of number of words reproduced in a later free recall test. As to the eye-movement data, they were, on the first sight, rather disappointing from the point of view of our working hypothesis. The longest mean fixation time was obtained with counting words (275 ms), followed by self-referential (216 ms) and categorization (209 ms) conditions. One possible explanation could be that these differences reflect a different involvement of covert counting operations: when we are trying to enumerate similar objects in an homogeneous array by sight, our eyes play the role of an index finger — they continue to fixate an object until a corresponding inner-speech entrance into working memory (in the case of our subjects, they could, at some point, say to themselves something like "sieben-und-zwanzig") is finished. Indeed, when we presented in a control experiment for counting not the words but similarly placed gray bars, this resulted in an even more prolonged average fixation time — obviously because the starring uniform pieces became now the only means to maintaining the correct enumeration (see also Gippenreiter, Romanov & Smirnov, 1969).

There have been however, at least two parameters of eye movements which changed depending on the direction of encoding effects on memory performance. The first parameter was the positive skewness of fixation time distributions: it was least for counting words, more for counting adjectives, and most for counting self-referential adjectives, as shown in Figure 5a (this main effect is highly significant: $F_{(3,17)} = 5.62$, $p < 0.01$). In other words, "deeper" encodings lead to an increase in proportion of relatively long fixations, despite the shifts in average fixation duration caused by the counting. The second parameter was the number of fixations or a correlated parameter of dwell time, i.e., overall time spent in a word area (Figure 5b). Dwell time also monotonically increased with the depth of encoding, but interestingly for the adjectives only (highly significant main effect of LOP and its interaction with the type of material: $F_{(3,17)} = 13.66$, $p < 0.001$ and $F_{(2,16)} = 47.29$, $p < 0.001$, respectively). This difference between skewness and dwell time, which is supported by our further studies, is of obvious theoretical value as illustrating the distinction between two understanding of levels in memory research: as mental set (induced by instruction even in the absense of the appropriate material) and as elaboration activity which is supported only by the relevant material itself (cf. Craik & Tulving, 1975).

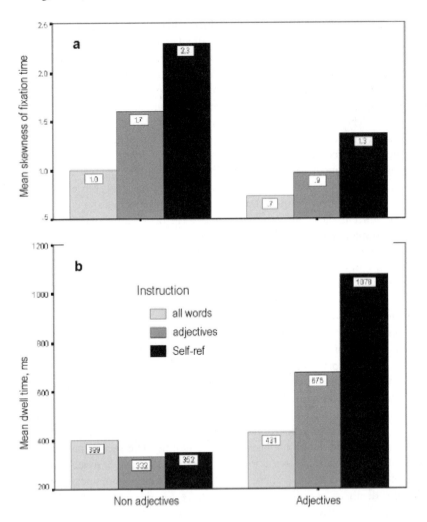

Figure 5. *Skewness of fixation time distributions (a) and mean dwell time (b) in dependence on encoding instruction for non-target and target words (see text for details).*

Unfortunately, the confounding of data by counting operations makes it difficult to say exactly at what segments of fixation duration these changes in skewness, i.e., re-distributions of fixation times in dependence on encoding instruction, take place. In order to obtain a better estimation of the changes inherent to the encoding operation *per se*, we developed a visual memory task with levels of encoding of computer-generated variants of Mooney-faces (cf. Tulving, 1985). Subjects have to estimate the proportion of white and black parts (*qua* perceptual encoding), to decide whether the picture is one of a woman or a man (categorization), or to estimate whether the person in the picture is personally sympathetic to him/her (self-referential encoding). One of the memory tests following the encoding was explicit recognition. As it happened, recognition scores were better for both "deep" encodings than for "shallow" perceptual processing. There was no difference between semantic and self-referential encodings this time, probably because the material was rather arbitrary and unfamiliar to subjects.

These performance data were paralleled by the parameters of fixation-time distributions. Again, all distributions were strongly positively skewed, whereby the distributions for semantic and self-referential encodings were almost identical and deviated from that of perceptual encoding at two temporal segments: from about 120 to 250 ms, where "shallow" encoding produced more fixations, and from 250 to 450 ms, where more fixations were registered with both "deep" encodings. Although only moderately pronounced, these differences were systematic and stable, also with respect to individual variation in fixation duration. They easily reached statistical significance provided that the comparison could be performed on the corresponding segments of the distributions (similarly to the standard analysis of N100 and other components of Evoked Response Potentials in electrophysiology). Of course, one needs serious arguments to consider separate segments of fixation duration as related to qualitatively different mechanisms.

One principal argument supporting this procedure is that the distributions are not unimodal — besides the well-known mode at around 180 ms, high-temporal-resolution eyetracking shows the presence of a second mode, in the diapason of very short fixation durations of less than 100 ms (let us call these fixations "express fixations" — see Velichkovsky, Sprenger, & Unema, 1997). This means that distribution of fixations may be produced by at least two distinct generators in temporal domain or perhaps even by a larger number of generators, though in this last case most of them should produce heavily overlapping data.[3]

In view of the importance of this conclusion, all precautions were made to warrant that express fixations are not an artifact but a genuine oculomotor event.

For example, one could argue that such extremely short fixations are in fact spliced parts of normal fixations divided by occasional blinks. Therefore, all the fixations in an immediate neighborhood of blinks were removed — without any noticeable change for the form of distribution. Another possible explanation is that express fixations may be short pauses preceding corrective saccades (e.g. Yarbus, 1967). Against this explanation one can say that saccades consequent to express fixations can be differentially directed in space from preceding saccades and that their amplitude is even larger than the average amplitude of all other saccades. In controlling possible individual difference, we noticed that in a small subgroup of subjects the proportion of express fixations was indeed excessive, particularly in the self-referential encoding mode. Data of these subjects were also removed from the further consideration.[4]

The clue to the riddle of express fixations is, in our opinion, given when we consider them as stimulus-locked events, i.e., when this subset of data is presented in dependence on the temporal course of visual stimulation, very much as this is done in the case of Evoked Response Potentials studies. In this case, as one can see from Figure 6a, express fixations immediately disclose themselves as manifestations of a fast "ON-OFF" mechanism reacting on any changes in visual display. As their "ON" part demonstrates a center-of-gravity type of spatial localization, express fixations should be considered as a genuine orienting response to the changes in display. Furthermore, their exceptionally short reaction times of 150 ms and less suggests a very low, probably sub-cortical level of corresponding regulatory processes. In all these respects, express fixations have much in common with recently investigated "express saccades" (see Fischer & Weber, 1993).

A rather different, partially reciprocal type of behavior can be observed in the case of longest fixations of 500 to 1000 ms. First of all, they seem to be suppressed during the presentation of pictures as their frequency during the interstimulus interval is much higher. Secondly, the proportion of these long fixations steadily grows to the end of every period of the experiment, i.e., to the end of interstimulus interval and to the end of presentation of a face. This could be a manifestation of expectancy as the temporal structuring of events was in this experiment perfectly predictable. If the expectancy account is supported in further investigation, then a difference between short and long fixations could be summarized in the following simple way: while short fixations react to the changes, long fixations anticipate the changes.

A completely different picture is given by a similar presentation of data of two groups of fixations with middle duration: 120-250 and 300-450 ms (Figure 6b). As the proportion of these fixations was modulated by perceptual and semantic instructions they could be called "perceptual" and "semantic" fixations,

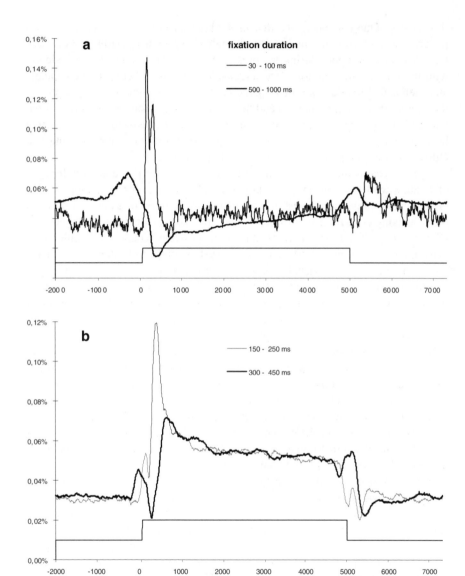

Figure 6. *Relative frequency of fixations from four classes of duration in dependence on a visual event (picture on/picture off): a. Express fixations and very long fixations; b. Fixations from two middle ("perceptual" versus "semantic") classes.*

respectively. One can easily see that in the both cases this is the presence of a picture that mobilizes the processing — indeed the relative frequency of these fixations is much higher during the presentation of a face and it declines slowly with the time of presentation. Two noticeable differences between "perceptual" and "semantic" fixations are that "perceptual" fixations come faster into play at the beginning of the presentation and that they are more pronounced at this initial phase of processing — seemingly even on the cost of "semantic" fixations that become shortly suppressed during the first 200-300 ms after the presentation. Otherwise, both graphics show a very similar dynamic.

Now, what is the deep meaning of these new results? It is that with duration of fixation we have a means to combine the global data on the gradiental LOP effects in two previously investigated domains — memory research as well as in brain imaging — with a more microgenetic perspective of the actual dynamics of processing. There are in particular some possible parallels of oculomotor behavior to the phases of Evoked Response Potentials and other known facts about microgenesis of visual information processing. For instance, the fast automatic response to changes in stimulation which is manifested both in express fixations and express saccades can be similar to the early N100 component of ERPs. Although it may be just a numerical coincidence, differences between our "perceptual" and "semantic" fixations correspond to other well-known aspects of ERPs, namely, that semantic and categorization effects usually are apparent only in such relatively late components as P300 and N400 (see e.g. Kutas & King, 1996). Finally, after 500 ms, processing is no longer connected with information about stimulation itself but more with our "higher-order" expectations, evaluations and intentions to communicate (Rugg & Coles, 1995; Velichkovsky, 1995; Velichkovsky, Pomplun, & Rieser, 1996). Overall, our preliminary conclusion from these results is that human eye may well be a part of human brain not only in anatomical but also in functional aspects.

These functional aspects, in turn, seem to support the idea of a gradiental transition between several levels of processing. Here data on eye movement provide evidence on some additional, early level of processing, preceding that of "physical" (i.e. form-oriented perceptual) encoding from the traditional LOP studies. Its function can be related to detection of the changes in stimulation. Though nothing more is known at this point, such earlier processing could also be connected with the spatial localization of visual events, for instance, in the spirit of the two visual systems distinction of the last decades (Trevarthen, 1968, among many others). In any case, its extraordinary speed and the distinct pick in the otherwise relatively smooth distribution of fixation durations, speak for a possible subcortical localization of corresponding mechanisms, very much like that speculated with respect to substratum of express saccades (see Fischer & Weber, 1993). Within the presumably cortical levels, from perceptual to meta-cognitive encoding, the simplest explanation of increase in proportion of long fixations is, of course, an increase in inhibition of saccades with the progressive involvement of frontal mechanisms. This explanation, however, ignores qualitative aspects of processing at different levels and should be considered only as a preliminary working hypothesis.

4. Conclusions

With the emerging integration of data from hitherto isolated domains of research presented in this chapter, we conclude that in their classical article of 1972 Craik and Lockhart have, earlier than the rest of cognitive community, recognized that there should be something like a basic dimension of the "depth" of processing. From today's perspective, this hypothetical dimension could be identified with the gradients of evolutionary growth of underlying neurophysiological mechanisms. These phylogenetic and ontogenetic gradients determine the functional organization of human cognitive processes and *ipso facto* the organization of our memory. In other words, the second proposition of Craik and Lockhart (1972) can also be basically correct, namely, that memory performance is (at least very often) a byproduct of perceptual and cognitive encoding of the material.

The task of the near future is an attempt to stratify cognitive mechanisms in view of the qualitative differences in the forms of processing at different levels, with respect to their functional, structural and temporal parameters. This strategic task will become much easier if, in addition to brain imaging, levels can be isolated also by analysis of visual fixations, along the lines shown in this chapter. Stratification of cognition might open the way to similar insights about the organization of consciousness, which traditionally was conceptualized in an either-or dichotomic manner. In humans, the phenomenon of consciousness comprises a number of different states from simple vigilance to self-conscious-ness, each of which seems be correlated with the activity of specific cortical and subcortical areas and centers. It is not at all obvious that the low-level forms of processing are automatic, in the sense of being completely deprived of any conscious control (Velichkovsky, 1990). We have seen that even consequences of perceptual processing may be accessed in explicit memory tests if an instruc-tion emphases the retrieval criteria in a sufficiently narrow way, "comprehensive" for the corresponding level. That is, if the instruction is specific enough, even supposedly automatic processes like perceptual form description can be accessed in a explicit (direct) memory test. In a similar vein, it has been demonstrated recently that the classical Stroop effect disappears when the instruction prescribes processing of information on the level of perceptual characteristic of constituent letters and not the word as a lexical unit (Besner, Stoltz, & Boutilier 1997).

The flexibility of the vertical integration in perceptual-cognitive processing and its intertwining with different forms of awareness and conscious control was of course not known 25 years ago when Craik and Lockhart formulated their new framework for memory research. These aspects of human cognition and consciousness, however, have been sparsely investigated until now, partially due to the dominance of the search for double dissociations and presumably isolated modules of processing.

Acknowledgments

I wish to thank David Rosenthal for discussion of issues raised in this chapter and my colleagues in Dresden and Bielefeld — particularly Beata Bauer, Marc Pomplun, Andreas Sprenger, Pieter Unema and Hans-Jurgen Volke — for participation in research. Experiments described in the chapter were in part supported by the German Science Foundation (DFG) and BMW AG.

Notes

1. For the earlier history of similar manipulation of encoding instruction in memory research, see e.g. Velichkovsky, 1988.
2. A similar functional dissociation of visual fixations after their duration is known in the field of gaze-mediated human-computer interaction. The best way to overcome the so-called "Midas touch problem" (i.e. the danger to initiate changes in functioning of the computer by every fixation, even involuntary one) is to build in a "gaze-mouse" software temporal filter with a threshold of about 500 ms (e.g. Reingold & Stampe, 1995).
3. In the literature on eye movements, saccades and not fixations are considered as the oculomotor events, so that the expression "generator of fixations" seems to be unwarranted. However, recent investigation in the physiological conditions of fixations show that their biomechanical complexity competes with and overcomes that of saccadic movements (Seung, 1996). From a functional perspective, the emphasis on fixations can be supported by the increasing evidence that their duration reflects the time of corresponding processing operations (Bridgeman, Van der Heijden & Velichkovsky, 1994; Gippenreiter, 1978; Sanders, 1993).
4. The fact that the proportion of express fixations in these few subjects grows with self-referential, metacognitive encoding may be related with the loading prefrontal mechanisms that otherwise would inhibit low-level forms of behavior. Meanwhile, there have been reports that express saccades too, firstly, could be observed only in a part of an adult population (Fischer & Weber, 1993) and, secondly, are more pronounced in early and in late phases of ontogenesis (Galley, 1997). Obviously, this last fact can be explained by a relatively low inhibitive control on the part of prefrontal structures (cf. Dempster, 1992).

References

Baddaley, A. D. (1978). The trouble with levels: A re-examination of Craik and Lockhart's framework for memory research. *Psychological Review, 85,* 139–152.

Bernstein, N. A. (1996). *Dexterity and its development.* Mahwah, NJ: LEA.

Besner, D., Stoltz, J. A., & Boutilier. C. (1997). The Stroop effect and the myth of automacity. *Psychonomic Bulletin & Review, 4(2),* 221–225.

Bihle, A. M., Brownell, H. H., Powelson, J. A., & Gardner, H. (1986). Comprehension of humorous and nonhumorous materials by left and right brain damaged patients. *Brain and Cognition, 5,* 399–411.

Blaxton, T. A. (1989). Investigating dissociations among memory measures. *Journal of Experimental Psychology: Learning, Memory, and Cognition, 15,* 657–668.

Blaxton, T. A., Bookheimer, S. Y., Zefiro, Th.A., Figlozzi, C. M., Gaillard, W. D., & Theodore, W. H. (1996). Functional mapping of human memory using PET: Comparisons of conceptual and perceptual tests. *Canadian Journal of Experimental Psychology, 50,* 42–56.

Bower, H. & Gilligan, S. G. (1989). Remembering information related to one's self. *Journal of Research in Personality, 13,* 420–432.

Bridgeman, B., Van der Heijden, A. H. C., & Velichkovsky, B. M. (1996). Saccadic suppression and space constancy. *Behavioral and Brain Sciences, 19,* 551–554.

Cabeza, R. & Ohta, N. (1993). Dissociating conceptual priming, perceptual priming and explicit memory. *European Journal of Cognitive Psychology, 5,* 35–53.

Cimino, C. R., Verfaillie, M., Bowers, D., & Heilmann, K. M. (1991). Autobiographical memory: Influence of right hemisphere damage on emotionality and specificity. *Brain and Cognition, 15,* 106–118.

Challis, B. H. & Brodbeck, D. R. (1992). Level of processing affects priming in word fragment completion. *Journal of Experimental Psychology: Learning, Memory and Cognition, 18,* 595–607.

Challis, B. H., Velichkovsky, B. M., & Craik, F. I. M. (1996). Levels-of-processing effects on a variety of memory tasks: New findings and theoretical implications. *Consciousness & Cognition, 5,* 142–164.

Cosmides, L., Tooby, J., & Velichkovsky, B. M. (1997). Biology and psychology. In P. Weingart et al. (eds.). *Human by nature.* Mahwah, NJ: LEA.

Craik, F. I. M. & Lockhart, R. (1972). Levels of processing: A framework for memory research. *Journal of Verbal Learning and Verbal Behaviour, 11,* 671–684.

Craik, F. I. M., Moroz, T. M., Moscovitch, M., Stuss, D. T., Vinokur, G., Tulving, E. and Kapur, S. (1999). *In search of the self: A PET investigation of self-referential information.* Psychological Science, 10, 26–34.

Craik, F. I. M. & Tulving, E. (1975). Depth of processing and the retention of words in episodic memory. *Journal of Experimental Psychology: General, 104,* 268–294.

Deacon, T. W. (1996). Prefrontal cortex and symbolic learning: Why a brain capable of language evolved only once. In B. M. Velichkovsky & D. M. Rumbaugh (eds.),

Communicating meaning: The evolution and development of language. Mahwah, NJ: LEA.

Deacon, T. W. (1997). *Symbolic species: The brain language co-evolution.* New York: Norton.

Dempster, F. N. (1992). The rise and fall of inhibitory mechanism: Toward a unified theory of cognitive development and aging. *Developmental Review, 12,* 45–75.

Fischer, B. & Weber, H. (1993). Express saccades and visual attention. *Behavioral and Brain Sciences, 16,* 553–610.

Fisher, R. P. & Craik, F. I. M. (1977). The interaction between encoding and retrieval operations in cued recall. *Journal of Experimental Psychology: Human Learning and Memory, 3,* 153–171.

Galley, N. (1997, September). *Personal communication.*

Gippenreiter, J. B. (1978). *Dvizhenija chelovecheskogo glaza [Human eye movements].* Moscow: Moscow University Press.

Gippenreiter, J. B., Romanov, V. J., & Smirnov, S. D. (1969). O dvizhenii ruki i glaza v prozesse scheta elementov test-objekta [On the movements of hand and eye in the process of counting test object's elements]. *Psychological Investigations, Vol.1.* Moscow: Moscow University Press.

Goldberg, E. (1991). Higher cortical functions in humans: The gradiental approach. In E. Goldberg (ed.), *Contemporary neuropsychology and legacy of Luria.* Hillsdale, NJ: LEA.

Goldberg, E. & Podell, K. (1995). Lateralization in the frontal lobes. In H. H. Jasper, S. Riggio, & P. S. Goldman-Rakic (eds.), *Epilepsy and the functional anatomy of the frontal lobe.* New York: Raven Press.

Hamann, S. B. (1990). Level-of-processing effects in conceptually driven implicit tasks. *Journal of Experimental Psychology: Learning, Memory and Cognition, 16,* 970–977.

Hoffman, J. E. (1997). Attention and eye movements. In H. Pashler (ed.). *Attention.* London: University College London Press.

Kapur, S., Craik, F. I. M., Tulving, E., Wilson, A. A., Houle, S., & Brown, G. M. (1994). Neuroanatomical correlates of encoding in episodic memory: Levels of processing effect. *Proceedings of the National Academy of Sciences, USA, 91,* 2008–2011.

Kennard, C. (1989). Hierarchical aspects of eye movement disorders. In C. Kennard & M. Swash (eds.), *Hierarchies in neurology: A reappraisal of a Jacksonian concept.* London: Springer-Verlag.

Kutas, M. & King, J. W. (1996). The potentials for basic sentence processing: Differentiating integrative processes. In I. Toshio & J. L. McClelland (eds.), *Attention and performance XVI.* Cambridge, MA: MIT Press.

Lockhart, R. & Craik, F. I. M. (1990). Levels of processing: A Retrospective commentary on a framework for memory research. *Canadian Journal of Psychology, 44,* 87–112.

Loftus, E. F., Green, E., & Smith, K. H. (1980). How deep is meaning of life. *Bulletin of Psychonomic Society, 15,* 282–284.

Luria, A. R. (1966). *Higher cortical functions in man.* London: Tavistock.

Nyberg, L. & Tulving, E. (1996). Classifying human long-term memory: Evidence from converging dissociations. *European Journal of Cognitive Psychology, 8,* 163–184.

Posner, M. (1978). *Chronometric exploration of the mind.* Hillsdale, NJ: LEA.

Pomplun.M. (1998). *Analysis and models of comparative visual search.* Göttingen: Cuvillier.

Roediger, H. L. (1992). Learning and memory: Progress and challenge. In D. Meyer & S. Kornblum (eds.), *Attention and performance XIV.* Cambridge, MA: MIT Press.

Roediger, H. L., Weldon, M. S., Stadler, M. L., & Riegler, G. L. (1992). Direct comparison of two implicit memory tests. *Journal of Experimental Psychology: Learning, Memory and Cognition, 18,* 1251–1269.

Rugg, M. D. & Coles, M. G. H. (1995). *Electrophysiology of mind: Event related brain potentials and cognition.* New York: Oxford University Press.

Sanders, A. F. (1993). On the output of a visual fixation. In A. D. Baddeley and L. Weiskrantz (eds.), *Attention: Selection, awareness, and control.* Oxford, UK: Claredon Press.

Sanquist, T. F., Rohrbaugh, J. W., Syndulko, K., & Lindsley, D. B. (1980). Electrocortical signs of levels of processing: Perceptual analysis and recognition memory. *Psychophysiology, 17,* 568–576.

Seung, H. S. (1996). How the brain keeps the eye still. *Proceedings of the National Academy of Sciences, USA, 93,* 1339–1344.

Stampe, D. M. and Reingold, E. (1994). Eye movement as a response modality in psychological research. In *Proceedings of the 7th European conference on eye movements,* Durham, University of Durham.

Trevarthen, C. (1968). Two visual systems in primates. *Psychologische Forschung, 31,* 321–337.

Tulving, E. (1985). How many memory systems are there? *American Psychologist, 40,* 385–398.

Tulving, E., Kapur, S., Craik, F. I. M., Moscovitch, M., & Houle, S. (1994). Hemispheric encoding/retrieval asymmetry in episodic memory. *Proceedings of the National Academy of Sciences, USA, 91,* 2016–2020.

Tulving, E. & Schacter, D. L. (1990). Priming and human memory systems. *Science, 247,* 301–305.

Turvey, M. T., Shaw, R. E., & Mace, W. (1978). Issues in the theory of action. In J. Requin (ed.), *Attention and performance VII.* Hillsdale, NJ: LEA.

Vincent, A., Craik, F. I. M., & Furedy, J. J. (1993). Sensitivity of heart rate and T-wave amplitude to effort and processing level in a memory task. *Journal of Psychophysiology, 7(3),* 202–208.

Velichkovsky, B. M. (1982). Visual cognition and its spatial-temporal context. In F. Klix, J. Hoffmann, & E. Van der Meer (eds.). *Cognitive research in psychology.* Amsterdam: North Holland.

Velichkovsky, B. M. (1988). *Wissen und Handeln [To know and to act].* Berlin: VCH Verlagsgesellschaft.

Velichkovsky, B. M. (1990). The vertical dimension of mental functioning. *Psychological Research, 52,* 282-289.

Velichkovsky, B. M. (1994). The levels endeavour in psychology and cognitive science. In P. Bertelson, P. Eelen, & G. d'Ydewalle (eds.), *International perspectives in psychological sciences: Leading themes.* Howe, UK: LEA.

Velichkovsky, B. M. (1995). Communicating attention: Gaze position transfer in cooperative problem solving. *Pragmatics and Cognition, 3(2),* 199–222.

Velichkovsky, B. M. (1997). On the variety of "deictic codes". *Behavioral and Brain Science, 20(4),* 237.

Velichkovsky. B. M., Challis, B. H., & Pomplun, M. (1995). Arbeitsgedächtnis und Arbeit mit dem Gedächtnis: Visuell-räumliche und weitere Komponenten der Verarbeitung [Working memory and work with memory: Visual-spatial and further components of processing]. *Zeitschrift für experimentelle Psychologie, 42(4),* 672–701.

Velichkovsky, B. M. & Hansen, J. P. (1996). New technological windows into mind. In *CHI-96: Human factors in computing systems.* NY: ACM Press.

Velichkovsky, B. M., Klemm, T., Dettmar P., & Volke, H.-J. (1996). Evozierte Kohärenz des EEG II: Kommunikation der Hirnareale und Verarbeitungtiefe [Evoked coherence of EEG II: Communication of brain areas and depth of processing]. *Zeitschrift für EEG-EMG, 27,* 111–119.

Velichkovsky, B. M., Pomplun, M., & Rieser, H. (1996). Attention and communication: Eye-movement-based paradigms. In W. H. Zangemeister, S. Stiel, & C. Freksa (eds.), *Visual attention and cognition.* Amsterdam/New York: Elsevier.

Velichkovsky, B. M., Sprenger, A., & Unema, P. (1997). Collecting solutions of the "Midas touch problem". In S. Howard, J. Hammond, & G. Lindgaard (eds.), *Human-Computer Interaction: INTERACT'97* (Sydney, July 14–18th). London: Chapman & Hall.

PART III

Levels of retrieval experience

PREFACE

Retrieval experience
A new arena of psychological study

Henry L. Roediger, III

In a famous chapter in the Annual Review of Psychology in 1970, Tulving and Madigan lamented the lack of progress made by students in the field of verbal learning and memory in understanding their subject matter. In fact, they began their chapter with the claim that "The domain of psychological research known today under the bifurcated title of verbal learning and memory has suffered through a long and dull history" (page 437). Much of their chapter was an attempt to address why this was the case, concluding with the thought that "the broad picture we have of human memory in 1970 does not differ from that in 1870" (page 477). They then went on to ask "What is the solution to the problem of lack of genuine progress in understanding memory?" While claiming not to know conclusively, they suggested that one promising direction might be for psychologists to examine some of the remarkable phenomena of the human memory system in its knowledge of its own capabilities. They initially endorsed the study of how people can monitor their own experiences, the type of study now known as metamemory and studied by feeling-of-knowing judgments, feeling-of-learning judgments, source judgments, and many others (see Nelson, 1992).

Since 1970, researchers interested in memory in all its various manifestations have heeded Tulving and Madigan's call and probably gone well beyond what they might have imagined for the future of the field in 1970. Metamemory studies have boomed, but so have many other types of investigation. The field has been opened to all kinds of influences, from neuropsychological studies of brain-damaged patients (which were generally ignored by mainstream memory researchers in 1970), to the everyday memory movement, to issues in the clinic of repressed/recovered/induced memories, to modern studies of neuroimaging, a technique undreamt of in 1970. And this list includes only a few more prominent new topics.

One of the other remarkable new trends in the psychological study of memory is reflected in the two chapters in this section: the issue of how people may retrieve information in different ways and with different states of awareness. The basic idea is that "responding" on a memory test may reflect different underlying states of awareness, with correspondingly different processes or systems effecting the response. The idea of studying retrieval experience is relatively recent, dating perhaps to Tulving's (1985) introduction of the remember/know paradigm and his claim that remembering reflected an autonoetic (self-knowing) type of awareness, whereas knowing reflected noetic (knowing) awareness. In addition, autonoetic consciousness was attributed to output from an episodic memory system, whereas noetic consciousness was said to arise from retrieval from semantic memory. Remembering reflects mental time travel, the sense of reliving in some form events in one's past. Knowing reflects the more general knowledge of one's past. I know I traveled to several professional meetings in 1977, but I cannot remember any one of the trips.

The two chapters in this section reflect the development of the remember/know paradigm and raise many puzzles for students of human memory. Before discussing these puzzles, however, we might first do well to reflect on the remarkable success of the remember/know paradigm itself in elucidating retrieval experience. The distinction seems an elusive one when first described, perhaps more so to experimental psychologists than to their subjects. Some tough-minded experimentalists bridle at the use of such experiential measures. After all, in the good old days of verbal learning, a response was a response. If subjects wrote down an item on a free recall or cued recall test, that meant they had recalled the item. Similarly, if subjects checked off an item or circled it on a recognition test, that meant the item was recognized. There was no need to ask further questions or pose further problems for the subject. The idea that one and the same response (recalling an item or recognizing it) could arise from different but equally valid types of processes, which would mean that the "same" response could mean different things, was never seriously considered. Of course, everyone knew about the problem of "guessing," the idea being that some responses in recall and in recognition might arise because subjects did not really know the answer but just guessed. However, the idea that different kinds of retrieval experience might underlie responding (of the non-guessing variety) was not contemplated.

The closest technique in the empirical study of memory to capturing experience was asking subjects to rate the confidence of their memories. The relation of confidence to remembering and knowing is not straightforward, but it does seem clear (as described in both the chapters by Gardiner and Conway and by Rajaram in this section) that the remember/know technique does more than simply capture different levels of confidence of subjects, as Donaldson (1996) and others have claimed. Donaldson (1996) argued that the remember/know distinction may simply reflect two states of confidence, with more confident responses being called remembered and less confident old responses being called known. This idea seems wrong, because remember/know and sure/unsure responses can be dissociated. However, theorists may have the relation backwards. Rather than differing levels of confidence explaining remember/know responses, it may well be that the study of retrieval experience through the remember/know technique may help explain why subjects feel more or less confident. Remember responses, with their strong feeling that the event is being re-experienced, might provide a strong basis for high confidence responses. Know responses may reflect high confidence or low confidence. As argued by Yonelinas (1994), only responding based on familiarity or fluency might be modelled by a signal detection process assuming systematic variations in some quantity (trace strength in the theory of signal detectability, fluency of processing in other models). Remember responses, which are almost always made with high confidence, cannot be so modelled.

The remember/know procedure invokes the idea of "the same" response being effected by two different states of awareness that accompany retrieval arising from different sets of processes or systems, just as does two-process recognition theory (Jacoby, 1991; Mandler, 1980). But how to interpret remember/know data? Can they be equated with the two processes postulated in the two process recognition theories? After all, the remember/know technique has also been used for free and cued recall (Tulving, 1985). The relation between remember/know responses and two-process theory is discussed in the ensuing chapters.

I have heard complaints about the remember/know technique, although these are voiced more in person than in print. The remember/know procedure seems soft to most hard-headed experimentalists. After all, isn't the remember/know technique a return to introspectionism, with all its faults? The researcher trusts the subject to report on ineffable experience; unlike standard measures, there is no way to verify that the subject's report is right or wrong. Can these data provide valid and reliable measures of experiential states underlying behavior?

These qualms and questions may have been worth raising fifteen years ago, when Tulving (1985) first introduced the remember/know distinction and procedure, but in my opinion they can now be laid to rest, at least to those of us who have followed the literature on this topic. Despite the seeming impalpability of remember/know judgments, the distinction makes sense to subjects when they are carefully instructed. They use the technique with little problem. Further, a sizable body of evidence now attests to the usefulness of the distinction and the procedure. Systematic patterns of results from experiments using the remember/ know procedure have been readily replicated across labs and the wee bit of inconsistency that sometimes arises may be due to slightly different sets of instructions being used. As is well summarized in the two chapters in this section and in other chapters by the same authors (Gardiner & Java, 1993; Rajaram & Roediger, 1997), the remember/know procedure has produced an interesting body of literature on retrieval experience. Further, the use of remember/know measures have produced sensible and orderly data when related to neural processing (e.g., Blaxton, & Theodore, 1998; Düzel, Yonelinas, Mangun, Heinze, & Tulving, 1997). The procedure captures a real, meaningful distinction both for subjects and for psychologists: two different means of accessing the personal past.

All this is not to say that there are not problems and perplexities galore in the study of retrieval experience via the remember/know technique. There are. Gardiner and Conway and Rajaram mention several puzzles in their chapters and the state of the field is one of exciting ferment. One interesting implication of the remember/know distinction within Tulving's (1985) memory systems theory, in which remembering is thought to reflect episodic memory and knowing semantic memory, is that there are no longer any pure tests of episodic memory. It used to be said that there were "episodic memory tasks," such as free recall, recognition, cued recall, paired associate learning, and so on. That idea can no longer be defended. Rather, episodic memory is now thought to be reflected only by remember responses that occur in one of these tasks. Know responses reflect retrieval from semantic memory, so one can have retrieval from semantic memory in "episodic memory tasks." Perhaps so. However, Rajaram's distinctiveness/fluency framework presented in this volume and elsewhere provides an alternative account of many of the remember/know phenomena. Rajaram's account focuses on the processes by which remember and know responses arise, although it is compatible with Tulving's (1985) ideas, too.

The remember/know procedure also provides a new purchase on some old problems. Take the case of false remembering, a phrase often used to refer to the production of intrusions in recall tests and false alarms on recognition tests. Such false responding is usually held to reflect the false remembering of these events. However, if we accept the idea that false responding, like true responding, can arise from different processes or systems and can reflect either remembering or knowing, then it is clear that the evidence on false memory needs to be reassessed. False responding (producing intrusions or false alarms) does not necessarily indicate false remembering. In fact, within the two process recognition theory (Mandler, 1980; Jacoby, 1991), the usual assumption is that false alarms arise from an integration or fluency process in which an item on a recognition test is processed easily ("jumps off the page") and is judged to be old on this basis. Because such fluency is usually assumed to be reflected in know responses when the remember/know procedure is used, the fact that false alarms are typically accompanied by know responses, not remember responses, seems consistent with this theory. However, if this is so, false alarms or intrusions do not necessarily implicate false remembering, in Tulving's (1985) sense.

Therefore, use of the remember/know distinction permits a different take on the concept of false memory. If this distinction is adopted, there can be more than one experiential basis for both true and false responding in either recall or recognition tests. Subjects could make an error and claim to remember the occurrence of the falsely recollected item. On the other hand, the subject might just know the event occurred, but not remember it. False remembering, then, would refer only to the case of errors that were also given remember judgments.

Although in standard recognition memory paradigms false alarms are often judged to be events that are known, not remembered, Roediger and McDermott (1995) reported a dramatic exception. After studying lists of related words, all of which were associates to a common word that was not presented, subjects falsely recognized the associate at very high rates. In addition, for about 75% of the false alarms to the associates of the list items, subjects reported that they remembered its occurrence when assessed by the remember/know procedure, even though the associate had never been presented. This outcome represents true false remembering, not just false responding (which is what is usually assessed in false memory paradigms). In addition, the level of remember responses for the false alarms in the Roediger and McDermott (1995) study was about the same as the level for actually studied items. Roediger, Jacoby, and McDermott (1996) also reported reasonably high levels of false remembering of misleading information in the Loftus (1991) misinformation paradigm.

In an ensuing chapter, Rajaram grapples with the issue of how data such as those produced by Roediger and McDermott (1995) might be interpreted within her fluency/distinctiveness theory. Remember responses are attributed to distinctive processing within her framework, but how can an event that was never even presented become distinctive? (We leave the answer to readers of her chapter). Here we raise a different point: do the Roediger-McDermott (1995) data (now replicated several times) have dire implications for the remember/know procedure itself? Do these data call into question what remembering means in the technique? Do they invalidate the paradigm's assumptions? After all, how can people claim to experience the remembering of an event that never actually occurred? In my opinion, the remembering of events that never happened, although a fascinating phenomenon in its own right, does not call the remember/know paradigm into question. People can have the illusion of remembering events just as they can have the illusion of perceiving events (as in the phenomena of subjective contours or apparent motion). Perceptual illusions and memory illusions may turn out to have much in common, at a broad level of analysis (Roediger, 1996). Both implicate constructive processes in cognition.

The study of retrieval experience is relatively young. Human memory has been studied for 115 years and retrieval experience has been studied for only the last 15 years. The chapters by Gardiner and by Rajaram serve as interesting milestones in what will doubtless prove to be a long, fascinating journey.

References

Blaxton, T. A. & Theodore, W. H. (1998). The role of the temporal lobes in recognizing visuospatial materials: Remembering versus knowing. *Brain and Cognition, 35,* 5–25.

Donaldson, W. (1996). The role of decision processes in remembering and knowing. *Memory & Cognition, 24,* 523–533.

Düzel, E., Yonelinas, A. P., Mangun, G. R., Heinze, H. J., & Tulving, E. (1997). Event-related brain potential correlates of two states of conscious awareness in memory. *Proceedings of the National Academy of Sciences, 94,* 5973–5978.

Gardiner, J. M. & Java, R. I. (1993). Recognizing and remembering. In A. Collins, S. Gathercole, M. Conway, & P. Morris (eds.). *Theories of memory,* (pp. 163–188). Hillsdale: Erlbaum.

Jacoby, L. L. (1991). A process-dissociation framework: Separating automatic from intentional uses of memory. *Journal of Memory and Language, 30,* 513–541.

Loftus, E. F. (1991). Made in memory: Distortions in recollection after misleading information. In D. L. Medin (ed.), *The Psychology of Learning and Motivation, 27,* 187–215. New York: Academic Press.

Mandler, G. (1980). Recognizing: The judgment of previous occurrence. Psychological Review, 87, 252–271.

Nelson, T. O., Ed. (1992). *Metacognition: Core readings*. Boston: Allyn & Bacon.

Rajaram, S. & Roediger, H. L. III (1997). Remembering and knowing as states of consciousness during recollection. In J. D. Cohen & J. W. Schooler (eds.), *Scientific approaches to the question of consciousness* (pp. 213–240). Hillsdale: Erlbaum.

Roediger, H. L. (1996). Memory illusions. *Journal of Memory and Language, 35,* 76–100.

Roediger, H. L. & McDermott, K. B. (1995). Creating false memories: Remembering words not presented in lists. *Journal of Experimental Psychology: Learning, Memory, and Cognition, 21,* 803–814.

Roediger, H. L., Jacoby, D., & McDermott, K. B. (1996). Misinformation effects in recall: Creating false memories through repeated retrieval. *Journal of Memory and Language, 35,* 300–318.

Tulving, E. (1985). Memory and consciousness. *Canadian Psychologist, 26,* 1–12.

Tulving, E., Madigan, S. A. (1970). Memory and verbal learning. *Annual Review of Psychology, 21,* 437–484.

Yonelinas, A. P. (1994). Receiver-operating characteristics in recognition memory: Evidence for a dual process model. *Journal of Experimental Psychology: Learning, Memory and Cognition, 20,* 1341–1354.

CHAPTER 8

Levels of awareness and varieties of experience

John M. Gardiner   Martin A. Conway

The theme of this book is consciousness and cognition, with an emphasis on stratification. Our contribution is to discuss in this chapter some recent developments in one popular though controversial approach to studying consciousness in relation to memory. The approach is an *experiential* one, introduced by Tulving (1985) with his distinction between remember and know responses. Remember and know responses are subjective reports of the kinds of experiences that occur during memory retrieval. Experiences that are characterized by the specific recollection of contextual details involving one's self at a particular time, in a particular place, are defined as remembering. Experiences of memory that lack these characteristics but are characterized instead by a more abstract awareness of familiarity are defined as knowing. In Tulving's (1983, 1985) theory, these two kinds of experience reflect two kinds of consciousness, autonoetic and noetic consciousness, which in turn reflect distinct episodic and semantic memory systems.

1.   Remember and know responses

Since Tulving (1985) introduced remember and know responses a great many studies have included them, especially conventional laboratory studies of recognition memory. The most important discovery that has been made in these studies is that the two states of awareness, remembering and knowing, appear to be functionally independent in the sense summarized in Table 1. Such functional independence provides important support for this experiential approach.

Table 1. *Functional independence in effects of experimental manipulations on remembering and knowing*

Empirical dissociation or association	Examplar studies
Variable influences remember responses and not know responses	Shallow versus deep level of processing (Gardiner, 1988); divided versus undivided attention (Gardiner & Parkin, 1990)
Variable influences know responses and not remember responses	Unrelated versus repetition test prime (Rajaram, 1993); same versus different study and test mode following a highly perceptual orienting task (Gregg & Gardiner, 1994)
Variable has opposite effects on remember responses and know responses	Nonwords versus words (Gardiner & Java 1990); massed versus spaced repetition (Parkin & Russo, 1993)
Variable has similar effects on remember responses and know responses	Retention intervals longer than a day (Gardiner & Java, 1991); repeated study trials with highly unfamiliar music (Gardiner, Kaminska, Dixon & Java, 1996b)

Various subject variables have also been shown to dissociate remembering and knowing. Among such variables are age, not only when older adults are compared with young adults (Parkin & Walter, 1992) but also when young children are compared with older children and with adults (Toplis, 1997); schizophrenia (Huron, Danion, Giacomoni, Grange, Robert, & Rizzo, 1995); Alzheimer's disease (Dalla Barba, 1997); and autism (Bowler, Gardiner, & Grice, 1998). These subject variables are all associated with decreased remembering and some, under some circumstances, are also associated with increased knowing. The situation with respect to amnesia is less clear-cut. In an experiment by Knowlton and Squire (1995) amnesic patients showed decreased knowing, as well as decreased remembering. But amnesic patients in other experiments by Schacter, Verfaellie, and Anes (1997) did not show much evidence of decreased knowing. Differences between remembering and knowing across the life span, and in different clinical populations, provide equally important support for the experiential approach.

There continues to be healthy theoretical debate about the interpretation of remembering and knowing. Consider remembering first. Among influential theories are Tulving's (1983, 1985) original proposal that remembering is associated with a distinct mind/brain system, episodic memory (see too, Wheeler, Stuss, & Tulving, 1997), a proposal that has recently been reinforced by physiological evidence from an event-related potentials study (Düzel, Yonelinas, Mangun, Heinze, & Tulving, 1997). Remembering has also been identified with recollection in Jacoby's (1991) process dissociation procedure (Jacoby, Yonelinas, & Jennings, 1997). In an extension of the transfer appropriate processing approach, it has been argued that remembering depends on either conceptual or perceptual distinctiveness (Rajaram, 1996). And, in a revision of the classic signal detection model, remembering has been mapped on to a single dimension of trace strength in which remember responses correspond with stronger memory traces and a more stringent response criterion (Donaldson, 1996).

In these same theories, knowing has been associated with another mind/brain system, semantic memory (Tulving, 1983, 1985); with familiarity in the process dissociation procedure (Jacoby et al., 1997); with processing fluency, either perceptual or conceptual, in an extension of the transfer appropriate processing approach (Rajaram, 1996); and with weaker memory traces and a more lenient response criterion in a signal detection model (Donaldson, 1996).

Though these theories, among others, offer quite different kinds of interpretation of remembering and knowing, there has been relatively little controversy about the basic meaning of remember responses at an experiential level. In marked contrast, the basic meaning of know responses has proved more controversial, even at the experiential level.

Partly as a consequence of this concern, in a number of recent studies know responses have been partitioned into additional response categories, notably "guessing", in addition to knowing (e.g., Gardiner, Java, & Richardson-Klavehn, 1996a), and "just knowing", in addition to "familiarity" or "feeling" (e.g., Conway, Gardiner, Perfect, Anderson, & Cohen, 1997; Kihlstrom, Kim, & Dabady, 1996).

Our primary goal in the remainder of this chapter is to briefly review some of this new evidence and to discuss its theoretical implications. We first review and discuss evidence with respect to the guess response category, and then evidence with respect to the just know response category.

2.   Guessing

Allowing subjects to report guesses as such has at least two obvious methodological advantages. First, guesses become the default response category. Second, any contribution that such guesses might otherwise make to know responses is removed.

Of course, there is a sense in which both know and guess responses can be thought of as guessing, because both know and guess responses are attributional (at least in this context, a point we return to later), unlike remember responses, which are not. Know responses indicate awareness of a recent encounter that is not remembered, and this awareness is attributed to the study list encounter. Guess responses involve various other judgmental strategies for believing or suspecting that the selected item might have occurred in the study list (see Gardiner, Ramponi, & Richardson-Klavehn, 1998), and so they also involve attribution to the study list encounter. But studies that have measured guess responses in addition to know responses have revealed at least two important differences between these two kinds of responses (Gardiner et al., 1996a; Gardiner, Kaminska, Dixon, & Java, 1996b; Gardiner, Richardson-Klavehn, & Ramponi, 1997; see too, Mantyla, 1993, 1997).

The first important difference is that when subjects report guesses they generally do not show any ability to select studied items in preference to unstudied items. At City University we have recently analysed a database of forty different experimental conditions from twelve, mostly unpublished, experiments in which remember, know, and guess responses were measured (Gardiner & Ramponi, 1997). As one would expect, in all forty experimental conditions, there were more remember responses to studied than to unstudied items (means of .33 and .04 respectively). However, in all forty experimental conditions, there were also more know responses to studied than to unstudied items (means of .21 and .09 respectively). No such outcome occurred with guess responses. In twenty-four out of thirty-seven cases in which the individual experimental conditions differed, there were more guesses for unstudied than for studied items (means of .14 and .12 respectively). The higher proportion of guesses to unstudied items largely reflects greater response opportunity, and it is particularly pronounced when subjects adopt a more lenient response criterion. These main features of the database are readily apparent from a scatterplot of the data which is shown in Figure 1, where the diagonal represents equal proportions of responses to studied and unstudied items.

There is therefore a sharp behavioral discontinuity between knowing and guessing states of awareness in the sense that one state shows memory for the study list and the other state does not. At the experiential level, subjects are presumably not aware of this discontinuity, a presumption supported by a more detailed analysis of subjects' explanations of recognition decisions accompanied with know or guess responses (see Gardiner et al., 1998). And presumably too, if subjects were aware of their inability to discriminate studied from unstudied items when they were guessing, they would not bother to guess.

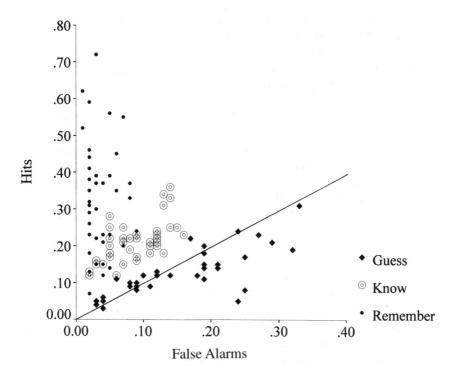

Figure 1. *Proportions of hits versus false alarms for remember, know, and guess responses in forty different experimental conditions.*

There are, however, other circumstances where guess responses do show memory, as we discuss in the next part of this chapter. The circumstances are in more naturalistic studies, in which studied and unstudied items cannot be counterbalanced and therefore are not pre-experimentally equiprobable. If subjects are aware that guesses sometimes succeed in everyday life, then they may not unreasonably imagine that guesses may sometimes succeed in the memory laboratory too.

The second important difference between know responses and guess responses is that there is at least some evidence that when response criteria are explicitly manipulated, the effect of the manipulation falls largely on guessing, rather than on knowing, or, indeed, on remembering (see Gardiner et al., 1997; cf. Strack & Forster, 1995). But there are some contrary indications (e.g., Kihlstrom et al., 1996) and more evidence is needed to resolve this issue. Its resolution may prove tricky because it will depend on a clear separation between know and guess responses. One other point to note, in this connection, is that the kinds of dissociation previously obtained between remembering and knowing in yes/no recognition tests do generalize to forced-choice tests (Gardiner et al., 1996a).

For most theoretical accounts of remembering and knowing, guess responses are critical only insofar as allowing subjects to report them cleans know responses up. Guess responses are, however, of more fundamental importance to the signal detection model proposed by Donaldson (1996; see too, Hirshman & Master, 1997; Inoue & Bellezza, 1998).

According to this model, remember and know responses reflect stronger and weaker trace strengths, with two response criteria, a more stringent one for remember, and a more lenient one for know (Donaldson, 1996). The model could easily be revised to accommodate the guess response category and add a third, even more lenient response criterion. According to this model, the data depicted in Figure 1 merely reflect quantitative differences in trace strength and different response criteria.

The most important prediction of the model is not to do with differences in response criteria, however. As Donaldson (1996) made clear, the most important prediction of the model is that estimates of memory strength will be the same when derived only from remember responses, or from remember and know responses. This raises the question of what kind of estimate should be used. Donaldson (1996) argued in favor of A′ estimates rather than d′ estimates, on the grounds that although both estimates are theoretically bias free, in practice, A′ is less affected by differences in response criteria. Such differences clearly exist, and they are essential to the model. A′ estimates normally vary between .5, which represents chance, and 1. They are given by the formula:

$$A' = .5 + \frac{(\text{HITS} - \text{FALSE ALARMS})(1 + \text{HITS} - \text{FALSE ALARMS})}{4 \times \text{HITS}(1 - \text{FALSE ALARMS})}$$

Gardiner and Gregg (1997) showed that both in meta-analyses of some eighty different experimental conditions in a database described by Donaldson (1996), and in analyses of individual subject data, A′ estimates were significantly greater when derived from remember and know responses than when derived only from remember responses. The individual subject data were from conditions initially developed by Gregg and Gardiner (1994) with a view to preventing much remembering and instead have recognition largely based on knowing. The conditions involve a very rapid study phase combined with a highly perceptual orienting task. For example, in one of four cases reported by Gardiner and Gregg (1997), these conditions resulted in a hit rate of only .11, for remember responses, compared with a hit rate of .52 for know responses. The corresponding

A' estimates were .66, for remember responses, and .80, for remember and know responses (see Gardiner & Gregg, 1997). Nearly every one of a total of fifty-two individual subjects who contributed to the four reported cases showed this effect. Such findings refute the main prediction of the detection model. They show that know responses do not merely reflect a more lenient response criterion; know responses reflect an additional source of memory, even as tested by the assumptions of the model.

If guess responses are additionally measured, then it becomes possible to derive three A' estimates of memory strength, one based only on remember responses, one based on remember and know responses, and one based on remember, know, and guess responses. When this is done for the data summarized in Figure 1, the three A' estimates are .79, for remembering, .80, for remembering and knowing, and .78. for remembering, knowing, and guessing. These three A' estimates are numerically very close, but they nonetheless differ significantly. The A' estimate for remembering and knowing reliably exceeds the A' estimate for remembering [t(39) = 3.68, SE = .004, p < .001]. And the A' estimate for remembering and knowing reliably exceeds the A' estimate for remembering, knowing, and guessing [t(39) = 6.08, SE = .004, p < .001]. The difference between the A' estimates for remembering, knowing, and guessing, and for remembering, was of only marginal significance [t(39) = 1.61, SE = .005, p < .10 > .05]. It appears to be a property of A' estimates that numerically small differences can be significant statistically, which presumably in part reflects their rather restricted range.

These differences make good sense looking at the data in Figure 1. Hits for know responses increase at an appreciably greater rate than false alarms for know responses, so that with these responses discriminability continues to increase. For guess responses, the tendency is reversed. Responses fall away from the diagonal, indicating reduced discriminability. The effect of this, for example, in the most extreme difference in the data-base, was that an A' estimate of .73 for remembering and knowing was reduced to an A' estimate of .63 for remembering, knowing, and guessing.

This kind of negative discriminability can occur in know responses if guesses are not reported as such and response criteria are relatively lenient. Jacoby et al. (1997, see their Figure 2) have data showing what they call this unreasonable outcome, an outcome they claim to have obtained before. They suggested that it leads to the conclusion that new items have become more familiar than old items! The more appropriate conclusion, of course, is that if subjects use know responses in this way then the responses cease to be valid measures of noetic awareness. To the extent that a signal detection model involves manipulating response criteria, then unless guesses are reported separately, as such, the model may invalidate the very responses it seeks to explain.

Table 2. *Proportions of responses to nonwords in Gardiner & Java (1990, Exps. 2 & 3)*

Response proportions	Test items		A' estimates
	Studied	Unstudied	
Remember	.19	.03	.75
Know	.30	.12	
Overall	.49	.15	.77
Sure	.39	.07	.79
Unsure	.27	.23	
Overall	.66	.30	.76

A similar point is made by the data summarized in Table 2, which are taken from two experiments by Gardiner and Java (1990). All conditions in these two experiments were the same except the instructions given to subjects in the recognition tests. In one experiment, subjects made remember and know responses. In the other experiment, subjects instead made binary confidence judgements, "sure" and "unsure". Subjects had studied mixed lists of words and nonwords, but the data shown in Table 2 are for the nonwords only, which elicited higher proportions of know responses. It is quite clear that the different test instructions were not equivalent. The A' estimates are greater for high confidence judgements than they are for remember responses. The overall A' estimate for remember and know responses is greater than that for remember responses, but the overall A' estimate for high and low confidence judgements is less than that for high confidence judgements.

Similar effects were found in a study by Curran, Schacter, Norman, and Galluccio (1997). This study included a total of ten experimental conditions in which A' estimates of the performance of BG, a patient with a right frontal lobe infarction, were compared with those of normal control subjects. These A' estimates are reproduced in Table 3. For normal control subjects, overall A' estimates were greater than A' estimates for remember responses in all ten conditions (cf. Donaldson, 1996). For the patient BG, overall A' estimates were less than A' estimates for remember responses in eight out of the nine conditions that show a difference. Curran et al. (1997) did not remark on the significance of the overall pattern of these results. The reason for this pattern of results is that whereas know responses for the control subjects reflect an additional source of memory, know responses for the patient BG included an exceptionally high false alarm rate. His use of that response category appears to resemble the way normal adults may use guess responses, or make low confidence judgements.

Table 3. *A' estimates from ten comparisons in Curran, Schacter, Norman, & Galluccio (1997, Tables 1 & 2)*

A' estimates	Control subjects	Patient BG
1. Remember	.92	.85
Overall	.93	.82
2. Remember	.96	.86
Overall	.98	.79
3. Remember	.85	.77
Overall	.88	.72
4. Remember	.93	.89
Overall	.96	.85
5. Remember	.80	.77
Overall	.86	.80
6. Remember	.85	.77
Overall	.86	.73
7. Remember	.87	.81
Overall	.88	.78
8. Remember	.83	.42
Overall	.88	.42
9. Remember	.95	.96
Overall	.97	.95
10. Remember	.93	.96
Overall	.95	.83

We draw two conclusions. The first is that guess responses do not normally reflect any consciousness of memory for studied items and in that respect they differ from know responses. Because know responses may sometimes include responses more properly reported as guesses, it will probably be advisable in most future studies routinely to allow guesses to be reported as such. For most theories, guess responses have no other implications.

Guesses are more important theoretically for Donaldson's (1996) signal detection model (see too Hirshman & Master, 1997; Inoue & Bellezza, 1998).

Our second conclusion is that, even accepted on its own terms, this model does not fare well. The model has no way of accounting for differences in the estimated "strength of the signal" depending on whether estimates are derived from remembering, from remembering and knowing, or from remembering, knowing, and guessing. The evidence from these estimates simply does not support a purely quantitative theory.

3.   Just knowing

Even in standard laboratory experiments subjects occasionally report that instead of attributing a feeling of familiarity to the experimental context they "just know" that a particular item occurred in the study list (see Gardiner et al., 1998). In long term learning, just knowing is the natural state that accompanies the use of knowledge and which characterizes a semantic memory system. Just knowing is like remembering in that it is not attributional. One just knows who is President of the United States, or Prime Minister of Great Britain; there is no question of attribution. Like familiarity used in an attributional sense, however, just knowing does not entail remembrance of any contextual details involving one's self at a particular time, in a particular place.

Conway et al. (1997) described a very large-scale naturalistic study of changes in awareness during the acquisition of knowledge by psychology undergraduate students. In this study, just knowing, and feelings of familiarity, were separate response categories. The students took multiple-choice tests featuring three-alternative forced-choice questions about knowledge they should have acquired in a series of six-week lecture courses. The correct alternatives involved information that had been presented directly in a lecture. The incorrect alternatives involved other information presented in the same lecture and were plausible alternatives. For example, one question read: In Pavlov's famous experiments hungry dogs learned to salivate in the presence of a light. In these studies, what was the unconditioned response (a) food; (b) the light; (c) salivation? For each question students were required to indicate whether an answer had been selected because they a) remembered a learning episode in which they had encountered the knowledge, for example, remembered the lecturer saying it or remembered reading it in a book; b) just knew that this was the correct answer, had a strong feeling of knowing and did not remember a learning episode; c) neither remembered the learning episode or knew the answer, but felt the chosen alternative was more familiar; or d) felt they were guessing, for example, choosing the alternative that looked least unlikely. Here we focus on only one of several interesting findings that emerged from this study (see Conway, et al., 1997, for full details), the results of an initial test at the end of an introductory course, compared with the results when some of the same students retook the test some six months later at the end of the academic year.

Table 4. *Proportions of correct responses in Conway, Gardiner, Perfect, Anderson, & Cohen (1997, Table 1)*

Response proportions	Test	
	Initial test	Retest
Remember	.39	.14
Know	.19	.43
Familiar	.25	.26
Guess	.17	.17

Note. These proportions sum to 1.00

These results are summarized in Table 4. Unlike data shown previously, the proportions shown in Table 4 are those for *correct* answers, in forced-choice tests. On the first test correct performance was dominated by remember responses. For most of the questions students answered correctly, they remembered a specific learning episode. For most of the questions students answered correctly in the retest, they just knew the answers, and did not remember any specific learning episode. The relative proportions of correct answers chosen on other grounds, feelings of familiarity or guessing, remained much the same in each test. These results indicate that there is a remarkable remember-to-know shift in the awareness that accompanies the acquisition of knowledge, a shift that presumably occurs gradually, over protracted periods of learning.

The results shown in Table 4 are collapsed over students who obtained both high and moderately high grades. Though all students showed the effect, it was far more marked in those who attained the highest grades. Interestingly, unlike initial tests of lecture courses, in all of which remember responses predominated, in initial tests of research methods courses the predominant response was just knowing (Conway et al., 1997). One possibility is that a remember-to-know shift can occur comparatively rapidly following tuition involving more practical, non-lecture based learning. Another possibility is that the more abstract kind of conceptual information acquired in research methods courses, compared with that acquired in lecture courses, might give rise to less remembering in the first place.

The remember-to-know shift occurred not merely with respect to the relative proportions of correct responses, but in their accuracy too, at least for students with higher grades. Conway et al. (1997) also analyzed their results using accuracy measures provided by a posteriori proportions (see Koriat & Goldsmith, 1994). A posteriori proportions are given simply by dividing the proportion correct, by the total proportion, for each kind of response. They indicate the likelihood, given a particular kind of response, that it will be correct. Some of these results are shown in Table 5, for the same students whose data featured in Table 4, but here partitioned further into an additional factor, degree class, which reflects the grades attained (from highest to lowest).

Table 5. *A posteriori proportions of responses in Conway et al. (1997, Table 2)*

Response proportions	Degree class		
	First	Upper second	Lower second
Initial test:			
Remember	.88	.88	.73
Know	.83	.74	.81
Familiar	.69	.66	.57
Guess	.62	(.48)	(.44)
Retest:			
Remember	.77	.66	.77
Know	.92	.91	.81
Familiar	.81	.66	.63
Guess	.66	.51	(.43)

Note. Proportions in parentheses do not differ significantly from chance, which is .33

These results show that for students with higher grades, remember responses tend to be more accurate than know responses, in the initial test, and know responses tend to be more accurate than remember responses in the retest. Moreover, it is the know responses in the retest that show the highest accuracy of all. Answers selected on the grounds of familiarity and guessing also show some accuracy, but for these responses the level of accuracy declines more in students with lower grades. Guesses were often not (significantly) above chance for students with low grades. These students may have acquired insufficient knowledge for them to be able to make an educated guess at the least unlikely alternative (see too, Conway, Collins, Gathercole, & Anderson, 1996).

Other research (Henrichs & Conway, 1997) has investigated the remember-to-know shift under more controlled laboratory conditions. In these studies participants learn novel definitions of nonwords (e.g., a type of undersea lava formation — *Pelstisteron*). The number of learning sessions is systematically varied and tests are given initially and again following various delays. This research showed rather similar results to those from the naturalistic study of student learning, although the remember-to-know shift was less dramatic.

Unlike the guess responses reviewed in the previous section of the chapter, just know responses have important implications for all theoretical accounts, and they raise the issue of how these responses relate to other judgements of familiarity, as used previously in remember/know studies.

To begin with, it seems clear that the remember-to-know shift lies outside the range of signal detection models that assume differences in awareness can be accounted for by variations in trace strength. Following the remember-to-know shift, remembering, which according to these models reflects stronger memory traces, is in fact the weaker form of memory, measured either in terms of quantity or accuracy. Note that much the same kind of outcome occurred in the very different situation described by Gregg and Gardiner (1994; Gardiner & Gregg, 1997). Also, confidence ratings of remember and just know responses are always very high and do not differ reliably. Moreover the false alarm rates for the two types of response do not differ, and therefore they cannot be distinguished by trace strength. If trace strength models cannot be used to distinguish memory performance accompanied by different states of awareness then the inescapable conclusion must be that this is because the different states of awareness do not depend on trace strength.

It is also hard to see how some other theories devised originally to account for performance in standard laboratory recognition memory tasks, such as the process dissociation procedure (Jacoby, 1991) and Rajaram's (1996) transfer-appropriate-processing account, can readily be extended to explain changes in awareness during protracted periods of learning. The explanation suggested by Conway et al. (1997) was that the remember-to-know shift reflects the schematization of conceptual knowledge in semantic memory. Initially, gaining access to newly acquired knowledge depends largely on episodic memory, but with repeated encounters knowledge becomes more abstract, more schematized, and gaining access to it no longer involves remembering specific learning episodes. It is significant, in this account, that the shift is most marked in students with the highest grades. The role of episodic memory is to facilitate conceptual learning. Superior episodic memory results in a greater ability to remember a variety of specific learning episodes and so to reflect upon them, relate them, and make connections between them — and hence develop more schematized knowledge. Poorer episodic memory makes this more difficult, though not impossible — conceptual learning can occur even in amnesia (see e.g., Tulving, Hayman, & Macdonald, 1991).

According to Tulving's (1983, 1985) multiple systems model, just know responses clearly reflect the semantic system, but so too do familiarity responses. Both responses reflect awareness of memory in the absence of remembering, and are therefore manifestations of noetic, not autonoetic consciousness. The idea that just knowing must be associated with knowledge in semantic memory seems relatively uncontroversial, compared with the idea that awareness of a recent encounter that cannot be remembered also reflects semantic memory. It is tempting to think that knowing of a recent encounter that cannot be remembered is likely to reflect some form of decayed episodic memory, rather than semantic memory. Yet the notion of trace decay is intimately related to that of trace strength, and trace strength models do not seem appropriate. There are other possibilities. Knowing of a recent encounter that cannot be remembered could result from a failure to encode that encounter episodically in the first place, which is exactly the outcome the study procedure devised by Gregg and Gardiner (1994; see too Gardiner & Gregg, 1997) was intended to foster.

There are varieties of knowing, as there are of remembering (Conway, 1987). People not only have feelings of knowing about recent encounters they do not remember, and feelings of just knowing about conceptual knowledge when they gain access to it. People also have feelings of knowing about knowledge they have when they cannot gain access to it (e.g., Koriat, 1993). They have feelings of "knowing not" when they know that they do not know something (see Kolers & Palef, 1976). And some feelings of knowing reflect certain kinds of those illusory memories that give rise to false recognition effects (see Dewhurst & Hitch, 1997; Schacter et al., 1997).

All these experiences of knowing differ in a number of ways. For example, they differ with respect to the kinds of knowledge that they relate to, and they differ with respect to whether they involve making attributions or not. Such differences are not unimportant, and can often be expressed subjectively in finer-grained judgements, but the more fundamental question is whether they are appropriately conceived as varieties of experience or whether they are distinct states of awareness in the sense that they reveal more than one type of consciousness.

This is as much a problem of classification as it is of theory, and here we simply raise the issue rather than attempt to solve it. Its resolution is likely to depend on many converging sources of evidence, not least on further evidence from neuroimaging studies (e.g., Düzel et al., 1997). So far as the difference between just know and familiar responses is concerned, our point is simply that this difference alone does not compel a reclassification of consciousness, any more than guess responses do. For all the differences between various experiences of knowing, they also have in common one overriding similarity. All of them involve consciousness of memory, and none of them reflect autonoetic consciousness.

A full typology of consciousness in relation to memory will have to distinguish between states of awareness, contents of awareness, and the uses to which awareness is put. Consciousness of memory is stratified in terms of levels of awareness which subsume varieties of experience. Awareness of memory is in turn distinct from awareness of task goals and of strategies for fulfilling task goals (see e.g., Richardson-Klavehn, Gardiner, & Java, 1996). One fundamental problem facing the cognitive system as a whole is apprehending the state that it is in. Perhaps these different levels of awareness have a role in overcoming this problem. They might facilitate certain operations, and even inhibit others.

Those comments aside, we also draw two conclusions to sum up this section of the chapter. The first is that important changes in memory awareness during protracted periods of conceptual learning — the remember-to-know shift — fall completely outside the range of trace-strength models and they also seem beyond the scope of several other current interpretations of remembering and knowing. Our second conclusion is that these changes in awareness seem likely to reflect the development of schematized conceptual knowledge in semantic memory.

4.   Concluding remarks

Remember and know responses measure two functionally independent states of awareness that reflect two kinds of consciousness of memory. In this chapter we have concentrated on knowing, and discussed the implications of partitioning know responses to allow reports of guesses, and of just knowing. In so doing we have gone to some lengths to appraise the plausibility of a trace strength account of patterns of memory awareness following a variety of experimental manipulations and following extended learning in a more naturalistic setting. In some respects, a trace strength account has several desirable features. Theoretically it is simple and parsimonious and it is amenable to analysis by signal detection models (e.g. Donaldson, 1996). If such an approach could be made to fit the data then it might well be the preferred approach. Yet even were these conditions to be fulfilled a trace strength model would still have nothing to contribute to understanding the *nature* of different states of memory awareness, of their different qualities, and functions. But, as we have shown in this chapter, it now seems clear that trace strength models cannot even account for the data that is currently available. That being so, and given that trace strength models will always fall far short of providing anything approaching a full theoretical understanding of states of memory awareness, it seems to us that it makes sense to turn to other approaches.

Acknowledgments

The authors' research is supported by Grants R000–23–6225 and R000–23–1158 from the Economic and Social Research Council (ESRC) of Great Britain and we thank them for their support. We also thank Cristina Ramponi for her help in the preparation of this chapter.

References

Bowler, D. M., Gardiner, J. M., & Grice, S. (1998). *Episodic memory and remembering in high-functioning individuals with autism.* Manuscript under review.

Conway, M. A. (1987). Verifying autobiographical facts. *Cognition, 25,* 39–58.

Conway, M. A., Collins, A. F., Gathercole, S. E., & Anderson, S. J. (1996). Recollections of true and false autobiographical memories. *Journal of Experimental Psychology: General, 125,* 69–95.

Conway, M. A., Gardiner, J. M., Perfect, T. J., Anderson, S. J., & Cohen, G. (1997). Changes in memory awareness during learning: The acquisition of knowledge by psychology undergraduates. *Journal of Experimental Psychology: General, 126,* 393–413.

Curran, T., Schacter, D. L., Norman, K. A., & Galluccio, L. (1997). False recognition after a right frontal lobe infarction: Memory for general and specific information. *Neuropsychologia, 35,* 1035–1049.

Dalla Barba, G. (1997). Recognition memory and recollective experience in Alzheimer's disease. *Memory, 5,* 657–672.

Dewhurst, S. A. & Hitch, G. J. (1997). Illusions of familiarity caused by cohort activation. *Psychonomic Bulletin & Review, 4,* 566–571.

Düzel, E., Yonelinas, A. P., Mangun, G. R., Heinze, H.-J., & Tulving, E. (1997). Event-related brain potential correlates of two states of conscious awareness in memory. *Proceedings of the National Academy of Science USA, 94,* 5973–5978.

Donaldson, W. (1996). The role of decision processes in remembering and knowing. *Memory & Cognition, 24,* 523–533.

Gardiner, J. M. (1988). Functional aspects of recollective experience. *Memory & Cognition, 16,* 309–313.

Gardiner, J. M. & Gregg, V. H. (1997). Recognition memory with little or no remembering: Implications for a detection model. *Psychonomic Bulletin & Review, 4,* 474–479.

Gardiner, J. M. & Java, R. I. (1990). Recollective experience in word and nonword recognition. *Memory & Cognition, 18,* 23–30.

Gardiner, J. M. & Java, R. I. (1991). Forgetting in recognition memory with and without recollective experience. *Memory & Cognition, 19,* 617–623.

Gardiner, J. M., Java, R. I., & Richardson-Klavehn, A. (1996a). How level of processing really influences awareness in recognition memory. *Canadian Journal of Experimental Psychology, 50,* 114–122.

Gardiner, J. M., Kaminska, Z., Dixon, M., & Java, R. I. (1996b). Repetition of previously novel melodies sometimes increases both remember and know responses in recognition memory. *Psychonomic Bulletin & Review, 3,* 366–371.

Gardiner, J. M. & Parkin, A. J. (1990). Attention and recollective experience in recognition memory. *Memory & Cognition, 18,* 579–583.

Gardiner, J. M., Ramponi, C. (1997). [Meta-analysis of remembering, knowing, and guessing]. Unpublished raw data.

Gardiner, J. M., Ramponi, C., & Richardson-Klavehn, A. (1998). Experiences of remembering, knowing, and guessing. *Consciousness and Cognition, 7,* 1–26.

Gardiner, J. M., Richardson-Klavehn, A., & Ramponi, C. (1997). On reporting recollective experiences and "direct access to memory systems". *Psychological Science, 8,* 391–394.

Gregg, V. H. & Gardiner, J. M. (1994). Recognition memory and awareness: A large effect of study-test modalities on "know" responses following a highly perceptual orienting task. *European Journal of Cognitive Psychology, 6,* 137–147.

Henrichs, C. & Conway, M. A. (1997, September). *Changes in memory awareness during and after repeated learning.* Paper presented to the 14th Annual Meeting of the Cognitive Section of the British Psychology Society, Bristol.

Hirshman, E. & Master, S. (1997). Modeling the conscious correlates of recognition memory: Reflections on the remember-know paradigm. *Memory & Cognition, 25,* 345–351.

Huron, C., Danion, J.-M., Giacomoni, F., Grange, D., Robert, P., & Rizzo, L. (1995). Impairment of recognition memory with, but not without, conscious recollection in schizophrenia. *American Journal of Psychiatry, 152,* 1737–1742.

Inoue, C. & Bellezza, F. S. (1998). The detection model of recognition using know and remember judgements. *Memory & Cognition, 26,* 299–308.

Jacoby, L. L. (1991). A process-dissociation framework: Separating automatic from intentional uses of memory. *Journal of Memory and Language, 30,* 513–541.

Jacoby, L. L., Yonelinas, A. P., & Jennings, J. M. (1997). The relation between conscious and unconscious (automatic) influences: A declaration of independence. In J. D. Cohen & J. W. Schooler (eds.), *Scientific approaches to the question of consciousness,* (pp. 13–47). Hillsdale: Erlbaum.

Kihlstrom, J. F., Kim, M., & Dabady, M. (1996, November). *Remembering, knowing, and feeling in episodic recognition.* Paper presented at the 37th Annual Meeting of the Psychonomic Society, Chicago.

Knowlton, B. J. & Squire, L. R. (1995). Remembering and knowing: Two different expressions of declarative memory. *Journal of Experimental Psychology: Learning, Memory, and Cognition, 21,* 699–710.

Kolers, P. A. & Palef, S. R. (1976). Knowing not. *Memory & Cognition, 4,* 553–558.

Koriat, A. (1993). How do we know that we know? The accessibility model of the feeling of knowing. *Psychological Review, 100,* 609–639.

Koriat, A. & Goldsmith, M. (1994). Memory in naturalistic and laboratory contexts: Distinguishing the accuracy-oriented and quantity-oriented approaches to memory assessment. *Journal of Experimental Psychology: General, 123,* 297–315.

Mantyla, T. (1993). Knowing but not remembering: Adult age differences in recollective experience. *Memory & Cognition, 21,* 379–388.

Mantyla, T. (1997). Recollections of faces: Remembering differences and knowing similarities. *Journal of Experimental Psychology: Learning, Memory, and Cognition, 23,* 1203–1216.

Parkin, A. J. & Russo, R. (1993). On the origin of functional differences in recollective experience. *Memory, 1,* 231–237.

Parkin, A. J., Walter, B. M. (1992). Recollective experience, aging, and frontal dysfunction. *Psychology and Aging, 7,* 290–298.

Rajaram, S. (1993). Remembering and knowing: Two means of access to the personal past. *Memory & Cognition, 21,* 89–102.

Rajaram, S. (1996). Perceptual effects on remembering: Recollective processes in picture recognition memory. *Journal of Experimental Psychology: Learning, Memory, and Cognition, 22,* 365–377.

Richardson-Klavehn, A., Gardiner, J. M., & Java, R. I. (1996). Memory: Task dissociations, process dissociations, and dissociations of consciousness. In G. Underwood (ed.), *Implicit cognition,* pp. 85–158, Oxford: Oxford University Press.

Schacter, D. L., Verfaillie, M., & Anes, M. D. (1997). Illusory memories in amnesic patients: Conceptual and perceptual false recognition. *Neuropsychology, 11,* 331–342.

Strack, F. & Forster, J. (1995). Reporting recollective experiences: Direct access to memory systems? *Psychological Science, 6,* 352–358.

Toplis, R. (1997). *Recollective experiences in children and adults: A comparative study.* Unpublished PhD thesis. University of East London, England.

Tulving, E. (1983). *Elements of episodic memory.* New York: Oxford University Press.

Tulving, E. (1985). Memory and consciousness. *Canadian Psychology, 26,* 1–12.

Tulving, E., Hayman, C. A. G., & Macdonald, C. A. (1991). Long-lasting perceptual priming and semantic learning in amnesia: A case study. *Journal of Experimental Psychology: Learning, Memory, and Cognition, 17,* 595–617.

Wheeler, M. A., Stuss, D. T., & Tulving, E. (1997). Towards a theory of episodic memory: The frontal lobes and autonoetic consciousness. *Psychological Bulletin, 121,* 331–354.

CHAPTER 9

Assessing the nature of retrieval experience
Advances and challenges

Suparna Rajaram

The study of consciousness has taken many forms in the philosophical and empirical inquiries of our times. This pervasive and endless interest attests to the widespread acknowledgment that consciousness permeates mental life. At the same time, fierce debates about the very definition of consciousness, its nature, and its role in cognition continue to surround this enterprise. The role of consciousness in memory has been studied in several domains such as conscious and nonconscious processing, subliminal perception, recovery of the so-called repressed memories, implicit and explicit memory, deficits of conscious awareness as in amnesia, and experiential states that accompany the retrieval of information from the past. The psychological research on this last topic, that is, the subjective states of awareness that accompany retrieval, forms the topic of discussion in the present chapter.

The empirical focus on the nature of conscious experience was enabled by the introduction of a new paradigm by Tulving (1985). The success and the popularity of this paradigm may be attributed to the fact that it provided a way to quantify an inherently qualitative experience. This paradigm draws a distinction between two types of experience that characterize the access to past information, Remembering and Knowing. When we think about events from our past, the memories for that event may be vivid and come to mind with great clarity. It can seem as if one has traveled mentally to that point in time and space and is now re-living that moment. In such instances, the sensory aspects of the events such as sights, sounds, and smell, the thoughts that accompanied the events, or other such details may also come to mind. This type of conscious experience during retrieval is termed Remembering. Not all memories possess such qualities. Sometimes, we retrieve events from the past that are facts or pieces of knowledge rather than vivid experiences. These memories may or may not be anchored in space and time, and the information about the space and time is also available as a fact. Such memories are marked by the certainty of their occurrence but lack the properties that enable one to mentally re-experience the event. This type of conscious experience is termed Knowing.

At least at the experiential level, the experience of Knowing can be contrasted with implicit memory. Implicit memory influences performance without entering the realm of conscious experience (Roediger, 1990). In contrast, when one claims to Know that an event occurred, this experience is very much a part of a conscious past. The critical point to bear in mind is that Remembering and Knowing capture two different types of conscious experience that accompany explicit memory.

An impressive body of evidence gathered in the last decade documents a variety of variables that give rise to these different experiential states. The effects of these variables have been theoretically organized in more than one way by different researchers. The flurry of empirical investigations and theoretical developments has both advanced our understanding of the factors and processes that influence conscious experiences, and posed new challenges. In this chapter, a selective review of studies will be presented to describe these advances and challenges.

1.   The appeal of the Remember/Know distinction

As mentioned earlier, the Remember/Know paradigm (Tulving, 1985) has come to be used widely by various researchers because it provides an elegant tool to quantify at least two different types of conscious experience. Tulving originally introduced this distinction to measures two states of awareness, autonoetic (Remembering) and noetic (Knowing) consciousness. Tulving conceptualized these forms of consciousness to represent the output of the episodic memory system and the semantic memory system, respectively (Tulving, 1983, 1985; 1989, 1994; Nyberg & Tulving, 1996; Wheeler, Stuss, & Tulving, 1997). In his seminal study, Tulving (1985) gave subjects three different explicit memory tasks in succession, free recall, category cued recall, and category plus the initial letter (of the target) recall. As expected, the recall performance rose predictably across tasks as more cues were provided. Interestingly, subjects gave fewer Remember responses as the number of retrieval cues increased across tasks. Based on this finding, Tulving concluded that increase in retrieval support reduced the need for subjects to rely on autonoetic consciousness.

Although Tulving employed various recall tasks, the majority of subsequent studies have used the recognition memory paradigm to partition the retrieval experience. There are several reasons why the Remember/Know paradigm caught the imagination of memory researchers. First, this paradigm demonstrates that many of the standard measures of explicit memory such as free recall, cued recall, and recognition are not faithful indicators of conscious recollection. Instead, Remember responses, by definition, provide such a measure. Second, a variety of experimental manipulations produce systematic dissociations between Remember and Know judgments. Although the theoretical interpretations of these dissociations vary, the orderliness of the data continues to propel research on this issue. Third, this paradigm has enabled researchers to capture the subjective experience associated not only with true memories but also with false memories. Fourth, the widespread use of this paradigm has provided a framework to evaluate other subjective states that may be associated with retrieval.

1.1 Dissociations and explanations

At least four types of effects of independent variables have been reported on Remember and Know judgments. Detailed discussions of these dissociations have been presented in a number of reviews (Gardiner & Java, 1993a, 1993b; Gardiner & Richardson-Klavehn, in press; Rajaram & Roediger, 1997; Richardson-Klavehn, Gardiner, & Java, 1996; Roediger, Wheeler, & Rajaram, 1993). Therefore, only the representative examples will be provided here. The early studies using this paradigm reported large effects of experimental manipulations on Remember responses whereas Know responses remained unaffected. For example, Gardiner and his colleagues reported the levels of processing effect (Gardiner, 1988), the generation effect (Gardiner, 1988), and an advantage for words studied under full rather than the divided attention (Gardiner & Parkin, 1990) for Remember responses in the recognition memory task. Know responses remained largely unaffected (but see Rajaram, 1993). Similarly, Jones and Roediger (1995) reported serial position effects on Remember responses, not Know responses.

Some variables produce opposite effects on Remember and Know responses. For example, studying pictures at study enhances Remember responses in a word recognition memory task whereas studying words increases Know responses (Rajaram, 1993). Lexical status of the items also produces opposite effects such that studied words are given more Remember responses whereas studied nonwords are given more Know responses (Gardiner & Java, 1990; see also Gardiner, Gawlik & Richardson-Klavehn, 1994).

There are other instances where the effects of the independent variables have been observed on Know responses but not on Remember responses. For example, preceding a test word with a masked presentation of itself compared to an unrelated word, increases Know judgments but does not affect Remember judgments (Rajaram, 1993). Similarly, maintaining compared to varying the modality of presentation across study and test selectively increases Know judgments (Gregg & Gardiner, 1994; Gardiner & Gregg, 1997). Certain manipulations of divided attention increase Knowing while leaving Remembering unaffected (Mantyla & Raudsepp, 1996). A fourth pattern of results produced by the manipulation of independent variables concerns parallel effects on Remember and Know judgments. For example, three presentations of folk songs compared to one presentation increased both Remember and Know responses in a test of recognition memory (Gardiner, Kaminska, Dixon, & Java, 1996b).

Several theoretical accounts have been advanced to interpret these dissociations and what they might tell us about the relationship between subjective states and the processes that give rise to them. As mentioned earlier, the earliest account was a systems account proffered by Tulving (1985). In this account, Remember responses were associated with the output of the episodic memory system and Know responses were associated with the output of the semantic memory system. Gardiner and his colleagues (e.g., Gardiner, 1988; Gardiner & Java, 1990) modified this systems account based on the striking similarities in the dissociations between Remember and Know judgments on one hand, and explicit memory tasks and implicit memory tasks (particularly data-driven tasks such as the word fragment completion task) on the other. Based on the consistent effects of perceptual variables on Know responses, these responses were considered to be a product of the procedural memory system in this modified account. A large body of data, including the studies discussed earlier, supports this classification scheme.

Rajaram (1993, 1996) offered a processing account of the dissociations between Remember and Know judgments. Based on the type of evidence described thus far, Rajaram argued that conceptual processes mediate Remember responses and perceptual processes mediate Know responses. This orientation was not so much an alternate framework but a complementary one to the systems account (see also Gardiner & Richardson-Klavehn, in press, for similar ideas).

However, a series of studies subsequently proved problematic for the conceptual/perceptual dichotomy. Specifically, Rajaram (1996) reported 3 experiments in which perceptual manipulations produced strong effects on Remember responses, not Know responses. In one experiment, subjects studied pictures and words, and later performed a recognition memory test consisting of studied and nonstudied items presented in the pictorial form. Even though the perceptual overlap between the study and the test picture was perfect compared to studied word and its pictorial counterpart at test, studied pictures received a higher proportion of Remember responses, not Know responses. Similarly, Remember responses were adversely affected when the perceptual overlap between study and test stimuli was reduced by either changing the size of objects (Experiment 2) or the left-right orientation (Experiment 3) across study and test. A conceptual/perceptual dichotomy cannot readily handle these perceptual effects on Remember judgments (see also Dewhurst & Conway, 1994). In light of these findings, Rajaram (1996; see also Rajaram & Roediger, 1997) proposed the distinctiveness/fluency framework. According to this modified version of the processing account, processing of the distinctive or salient attributes of the stimuli, either conceptual or perceptual, will give rise to the Remember experience. In contrast, fluency of processing, regardless of whether it arises from conceptual or perceptual sources, should mediate the experience of Knowing.

Rajaram (1998) tested one aspect of this theory by examining the effects of conceptual salience and perceptual distinctiveness of Remember judgments. Previous research documented the effects of conceptual factors on Remember judgments in designs where the effect of a conceptual manipulation was typically contrasted with that of a perceptual manipulation. For example, Gardiner (1988) and Rajaram (1993) reported the levels of processing effect on Remembering judgments where the effects of semantic processing were compared with that of phonemic processing. In order to test the idea that it was not conceptual processing per se, but the salience of conceptual information that gives rise to Remembering, Rajaram (1998) contrasted the effects of encoding the salient or dominant meaning (money-bank) with the encoding of the nondominant meaning (river-bank) on later subjective experience. In a recognition memory test, Rajaram found that subjects gave more Remember responses to homographs that were encoded for their salient or dominant meaning compared to homographs that were encoded for their nondominant meaning (see Table 1). These results

Table 1. *The mean proportions of hits and false alarms as a function of homographs encoded for their dominant and nondominant meanings (Rajaram, 1998).*

	Dominant hits	Nondominant hits	False alarms
Recognition	.79	.66	.12
Remember responses	.64	.49	.02
Know responses	.15	.17	.10

demonstrate the need to differentiate between salient and nonsalient encoding within the conceptual dimension.

Rajaram (1998) also tested the role of salience or distinctiveness along the perceptual dimension. This experiment involved the presentation of orthographically distinctive (e.g., subpoena) or orthographically common (e.g., sailboat) words for study. The words from both groups were equated for frequency, length, and the initial letter. In a recognition memory test, subjects gave more Remember judgments to studied items that were orthographically distinctive than items that were orthographically common (see Table 2). Know judgments did not differ across this manipulation.

The specialized role of fluency of processing in mediating Know responses comes from a number of studies. In a study described earlier (Rajaram, 1993), the perceptual fluency engendered by the masked repetition of items clearly increased only Know responses (see Table 3). Evidence for conceptual fluency effects on Knowing come from at least two different studies. In one study, Mantyla (1997) showed that grouping similar faces into conceptual categories, a task that likely requires the use of conceptual schemas, subsequently increased Know responses, not Remember responses. In another study, Conway, Gardiner, Perfect, Anderson, and Cohen (1997) reported that subjects' correct answers to questions from a research methods course were accompanied largely with the Know experience rather than the Remember experience. The nature of the material in a research methods course requires development of schematized knowledge that clearly relies of conceptual processes. On the assumption that such conceptually based information comes to mind at the time of retrieval without effortful retrieval operations, these results support the role of conceptual fluency in mediating Know responses.

There is considerable agreement between the systems account and the processing account in explaining the nature of dissociations obtained for Remember and Know judgments. The two accounts also share a common purpose that involves the organization of variables that produce dissociations or parallel

Table 2. *The mean proportions of hits and false alarms as a function of orthographically distinctive and orthographically common words (Rajaram, 1998).*

	Hits		False alarms	
	Distinctive	Common	Distinctive	Common
Recognition	.90	.78	.12	.06
Remember responses	.61	.49	.04	.02
Know responses	.29	.29	.08	.04

Table 3. *The design and results for proportions of hits and false alarms (FA) and the RT data (in milliseconds) as a function of masked repetition of words (Rajaram, 1993, Experiment 3). Copyright 1993 by Psychonomic Society. Adapted with permission.*

Study items (targets) - table, plate.

	Targets		Lures	
	Masked repetition	Unrelated prime	Masked repetition	Unrelated prime
Mask	&&&&&&&&&	&&&&&&&&&	&&&&&&&&&	&&&&&&&&&
Prime	table	scale	glass	chalk
Test word	TABLE	PLATE	GLASS	SHIRT
Response required	"Yes"	"Yes"	"No"	"No"
RT data	1,296	1,275	1,354	1,293
Recognition	"Yes"	"Yes"	"Yes" (FA)	"Yes" (FA)
	.67	.60	.23	.18
Remember responses	.43	.42	.05	.05
Know responses	.24	.18	.18	.13

effects. Furthermore, both approaches aim to understand the nature of the subjective experience through a first-person account. That is, the assessment of subjective experience in these accounts is based on the reports provided by the subjects rather than on the estimates that may be derived from using a model (e.g., Jacoby et al., 1997).

In their current formulations, these two accounts differ in their theoretical interpretation of Knowing. In the systems account, the experience of Knowing is a product of the semantic (Tulving, 1985) or the procedural (Gardiner, 1988) memory system. One can partition the extant data into two groups based on the factors that affect Knowing. Some studies have shown effects of conceptual manipulations (e.g., Conway et al., 1997; Mantyla, 1997; Gardiner et al., 1996a). These findings support the notion that Knowing is associated with the semantic memory system. Other studies have documented effects of perceptual manipulations (e.g., Gardiner, & Java, 1990; Gardiner & Gregg, 1997; Gregg & Gardiner, 1994; Rajaram, 1993). These effects are consistent with the idea that Knowing is mediated by the procedural memory system. However, in their most recent formulations, Gardiner and colleagues (e.g., see Gardiner & Gregg, 1997; Gardiner et al., 1996a) have retained the original association drawn by Tulving (1985) between the experience of Knowing and the semantic memory system.

The processing account (Rajaram, 1996) already contains the assumptions to accommodate both perceptual and conceptual effects on Knowing. The assumption that fluency of processing, or the ease with which information comes to mind, may be mediated by perceptual or conceptual factors comfortably explains the extant data on Knowing. The fluency with which a stimulus is processed can arise from a single previous encounter with that stimulus (Gardiner & Java, 1990; Gardiner & Gregg, 1997; Gregg & Gardiner, 1994; Rajaram, 1993). Thus, a highly perceptual encoding of a once-presented stimulus may increase the perceptual fluency with which that stimulus will be processed in its second presentation. Fluency may also arise from the development of a schematic representation of that stimulus. That is, developing an integrated representation of a stimulus may cause the details of the episode to fade, but the conceptual knowledge thus acquired may come to mind with relative ease (Conway et al., 1997).

In addition to these two theoretical approaches, Jacoby et al. (1997) have developed an "Independence Remember/Know (IRK)" model to measure the underlying processes that influence memory. The assumptions of this model are derived from the process dissociation procedure developed by Jacoby (1991) to separate the independent and opposing influences of controlled (or conscious) and automatic (or unconscious) processes on memory. In the IRK model, the goal is to measure the contributions of the recollective processes (or the conscious or controlled processes) and the familiarity processes (or the unconscious or automatic processes). Jacoby et al. considered Remember judgments to be an appropriate measure of recollective processes. Furthermore, the assumption of independence implies that some memories may be mediated by both recollective and familiarity processes. Such responses will be given Remember judgments due to the operation of recollective processes. On this argument, the contribution of the familiarity processes to memory is underestimated by Know responses in the standard Remember/Know paradigm. Therefore, the contribution of familiarity in the IRK model is estimated by using a correction (Familiarity = Know/1 – Remember). This correction increases the proportion of Know responses. With this correction, Jacoby et al. (1997) found a good agreement between the estimates of recollection and familiarity in the Remember/Know paradigm and the process dissociation procedure.

Detailed discussions of the strengths and problems associated with the IRK model have been already provided (see Jacoby et al., 1997; Parkin, Gardiner, & Rosser, 1995; Richardson-Klavehn & Gardiner, 1995, 1996; Richardson-Klavehn, Gardiner, & Java, 1996), and therefore, will not be discussed here. Instead, an additional issue that pertains to the third-person account used in the IRK model, and is at the heart of studying the nature of retrieval experience per se, is discussed here. The process dissociation procedure provides a powerful tool to estimate the contributions of different processes to memory performance. However, the proposal that such processes operate independently (or for that matter, in a redundant fashion, see Joordens & Merikle, 1993) is somewhat orthogonal to the issue of unraveling the nature of these different subjective experiences. Specifically, the Remember experience arises from the unique operation of one type of process. Thus, even if a particular memory is guided by an additional, say familiarity process, it is the recollective process that uniquely leads to Remembering. In contrast to Remembering, the Know experience is uniquely the outcome of the fluency or the familiarity process. That the operation of the familiarity process on memory may be underestimated to some extent (on the independence assumption) or to a large extent (on the redundancy assumption) does not clarify the nature of Knowing itself. The assumption that two processes jointly operate on some memories may help us estimate the proportion of Remember responses that could turn into Know responses under certain circumstances such as passage of time. These estimates can then be tested against the estimates provided by other models such as the redundancy model (see Knowlton & Squire, 1996, for such an analysis). This goal is quite different from the one intended in theories (e.g., Rajaram, 1996; Rajaram & Roediger, 1997) that attempt to organize the nature of experimental, neural, pharmacological, and age-related variables that are responsible for creating different conscious experiences at any given point in time. In other words, the attempt in these theories is to determine a priori the nature of the independent variables to predict their influence on different retrieval experiences.

A fourth and final description of the data obtained with the Remember/ Know paradigm comes in the form of signal-detection models (Donaldson, 1996; Hirshman & Master, 1997; Inoue & Bellezza, 1998). Unlike the systems account of Gardiner and colleagues, the processing account of Rajaram, and the IRK model of Jacoby and colleagues, all of which posit the operation of at least two processes in memory, the signal-detection models assume the operation of a single process. According to this latter group of models, all responses in a retrieval situation lie on a single continuum. On this continuum, subjects set two thresholds, one for making recognition responses, and a more stringent one for making Remember responses. This model can account for different patterns of dissociations by shifting the placement of the two decision criteria. Thus, the model can fit the data from studies where Remember responses increase but Know responses remain the same, both Remember and Know responses increase, and Remember and Know responses move in opposite directions.

A strong prediction of a single-process model (e.g., Donaldson, 1996) is that the bias-free estimates of memory (either d' or A') should be equivalent for recognition memory and Remember responses. In a detailed analysis, Gardiner and Gregg (1997) have shown that this prediction does not hold because the bias-free estimates of memory have been found to be consistently better for overall recognition (Remember plus Know) than for Remember alone. This class of models also fails to explain how the placement of decision criteria may lead to specific subjective experiences that subjects report. In addition to the problems noted above, the psychological reality of these models also comes into question when we consider the effects of neural factors on reports of awareness. These studies are discussed in the next section.

2.   The neural bases of subjective states: separating subjective states from confidence judgments

The assumption that a single process underlies different mnemonic experiences suggests that Remember and Know judgments simply reflect high and low confidence in one's memory. However, it has been shown that in response to certain experimental manipulations, Remember and Know judgments behave differently from confidence judgments (Gardiner & Java, 1990; Parkin & Walter, 1992; Perfect, Williams, Anderson-Brown, 1995; Rajaram, 1993). For example, Rajaram (1993) reported that masked repetition of test items selectively increased Know responses. But when subjects were required to make confidence judgments instead of experiential judgments, such a selective increase was not observed in the Unsure judgments. Gardiner and Java (1990) examined this issue by present-ing subjects with words and nonwords for study. On later tests of recognition memory, subjects produced more Remember judgments to words but more Know judgments to nonwords. This cross-over interaction was not obtained when subject made Sure/Unsure judgments. Of course, a cross-over interaction can be accounted for by the single-process models (e.g., Donaldon, 1996). But these models cannot explain why subjects treat Remember/Know judgments differently from confidence judgments.

The psychological distinction between experiential judgments and confi-dence judgments was dramatically illustrated in a study we recently conducted in our laboratory with amnesic and control subjects (Rajaram, Hamilton & Bolton, 1999). The amnesic syndrome provides us with a unique situation to study the nature of retrieval experience because the hallmark of this disorder is a deficit in the experiential components of memory. Because of this defining characteristic of amnesia, it is reasonable to expect impairments in the reports of awareness in amnesics relative to matched controls (Knowlton & Squire, 1995; Schacter, Verfaellie, & Anes, 1997; Yonelinas, Kroll, Dobbins, Lazzara, & Knight, 1998). However, confidence judgments do not entail an assessment of one's subjective experience and may simply be based on the strength of familiarity with an item, i.e., on a single continuum. According to the dual-component approaches to memory and retrieval experience (Gardiner et al., in press; Rajaram, 1996; Jacoby et al., 1997), amnesics should exhibit an impairment in performance relative to controls when required to make experiential judgments. However, the amnesics' performance should not differ from that of matched controls on confidence judgments if these judgments are made on the basis of the strength of memory. In contrast, the single-process models should predict a deficit in both Remember and Sure responses of amnesics if experiential judgments arise from the same underlying continuum that mediates confidence judgments. We tested these predictions by adapting Gardiner and Java's (1990) study with words and nonwords. The matched controls in our study produced a similar pattern of results as reported in the Gardiner and Java study; A cross-over interaction was obtained for Remember/Know judgments as a function of the lexical status of the item. Furthermore, a greater proportion of words and nonwords were given Sure responses rather than Unsure responses, thereby producing only a main effect of response type. Amnesic subjects in our study also showed a main effect of response type in their confidence judgments. But interestingly, the lexical status of items did not produce any effect on the Remember/Know judgments made by the amnesic subjects. In other words, the amnesic subjects responded just like the matched controls in making confidence judgments but their performance fell apart when the task required the use of awareness.

Effects of brain damage on Remember/Know responses were also reported by Blaxton and Theodore (1997). In this study, unilateral temporal lobe epileptics (TLEs) were tested for their memory of abstract visuospatial designs. The left TLEs produced more Know responses than Remember responses whereas the right TLEs produced the opposite pattern of responses. Even if the single-process model can predict these opposite patterns of interactions by shifting the decision criteria, it cannot explain why damage to specific loci in the brain would prompt a particular shift in the placement of the criteria. The neural underpinnings of the subjective states have also been investigated with the measure of event-related potentials (ERPs) (Smith, 1993; Düzel, Yonelinas, Mangun, Heinze, & Tulving, 1997). Düzel et al. not only observed distinct patterns of ERP activity for Remember and Know judgments, they also reported that the ERP measure was sensitive to the states of awareness and not to the studied or nonstudied status of the targets.

Other studies have shown that disorders such as the frontal lobe dysfunctions (Dalla Barba, 1993), Alzheimer's disease (Dalla Barba, 1997), and schizophrenia (Huron, Danion, Giacomoni, Grange, Robert, & Rizzo, 1995) produce different patterns of deficits in the two experiential judgments. Various psycho-pharmacological substances that modulate certain brain activities also bring about changes in the states of awareness during retrieval (Curran, Gardiner, Java, & Allen, 1993; Curran & Hildebrandt, 1998). Aging also affects the states of awareness such that the elderly show reduced Remembering, and either no difference in Knowing or an increase in Knowing, compared to younger adults (Mantyla, 1993; Parkin & Walter, 1992; Perfect et al., 1995). Taken together, the relationship between neural changes from brain damage, other diseases and aging, neural changes documented via electrophysiological measures, or revers-ible changes through psychopharmacological substances on one hand, and the changes in awareness on the other, substantiate the distinction between Remem-bering and Knowing. These conclusions are further corroborated by the dissocia-tive performance of amnesics on tasks that require experiential judgments and tasks that require confidence judgments (Rajaram et al., 1999).

3.   Subjective states across different retrieval situations

With the exception of Tulving's original study (1985), the vast majority of published studies have used the recognition memory task to measure Remember and Know responses. The selection of the recognition was memory task was motivated by the dual-bases of recognition proposed in several models (Atkinson & Juola, 1973, 1974; Jacoby, 1983a, 1983b; Jacoby & Dallas, 1981; Mandler, 1980). However, explicit memory does not operate only in the form of recogni-tion. Therefore, an examination of different subjective states that accompany retrieval states in other retrieval situations is timely.

   A small set of studies has included different types of cued recall tasks in the study of subjective states. Lindsay and Kelley (1996) used easy or difficult frag-mented versions of targets at test as cues to aid recall. Mantyla (1994) provided subjects with either self-generated cues at test or someone else's cues to recall target items. Java (1994) reported the use of words stem cues in a cued recall task in which subjects made Remember/Know judgments. In all three studies, subjects provided both Remember and Know responses, and furthermore, the proportions of these responses were found to be sensitive to experimental changes.

   Recently, Rajaram and Hamilton (1999) obtained evidence for different experiential states in a series of experiments by comparing multiple recall tasks. These researchers selected the tasks used in Tulving's (1985) study, i.e., free recall, category cued recall, category plus initial letter recall, and also included a recognition memory task to compare the proportion of Remember and Know judgments across these tasks. Instead of using a successive, within-subject testing paradigm (Tulving, 1985), Rajaram and Hamilton (1999) assigned these four tasks to subjects in a between-subjects design in order to circumvent several confounds that may arise in a successive testing paradigm. Unlike Tulving's findings, in this between-subjects design the proportions of Remember responses increased as the experimental cues increased. Because this increase in cues also increased overall levels of recall across tasks, proportional values (Remember/overall recall) showed that an equivalent proportion of recall responses received Remember judgments. Interestingly, even in free recall, a task considered to be the quintessential measure of conscious recollection, subjects produced a substantial proportion of Know responses (see also Tulving, 1985). Furthermore, Rajaram and Hamilton also reported that Remember responses in cued recall tasks were modulated by conceptual as well as perceptual factors (Rajaram, 1998). Finally, these researchers ruled out the possibility that equivalent proportions of Remember judgments were a function of response bias; A levels of processing effect was obtained in each task even when the overall proportions of Remember responses were equivalent across tasks. That is, the proportions of Remember and Know responses did vary systematically as a function of a theoretically motivated variable.

The results from this series of experiments clearly demonstrate that the measurement of subjective states of awareness across a wide variety of retrieval situations produces systematic findings. Furthermore, these studies highlight the utility of the Remember/Know procedure in measuring experiential states for diverse memory products. This second point is further elaborated in the following section.

4. Remembering and knowing events that did not occur

In a typical recognition memory experiment that includes the Remember/Know procedure, the false alarms rates are typically found to be low. To the extent that subjects do false alarm to nonstudied items, subjects tend to assign Know responses rather than Remember responses to these items. Recently, the Remember/Know procedure has been used to examine the subjective experience that may be associated with false memories or illusions.

Roediger and McDermott (1995) applied the Remember/Know procedure in a false memory paradigm (Deese, 1959). In this false memory paradigm, subjects are presented with a list of conceptually associated words (e.g., thread, pin, eye, sewing, sharp, point, prick, thimble, haystack, thorn, hurt, injection, syringe, cloth, knitting) at study. At test, among various studied and nonstudied words, a critical, highly related, lure (needle) is included. Even though this word was not presented earlier, subjects show high rates of false alarms to it if its associates had been presented at study. Furthermore, subjects largely assigned Remember judgments to these never-presented items (see also Lane & Zaragoza, 1995).

Schacter, Verfaellie, and Anes (1997) also used associated lists with amnesics and matched controls to examine false memories. These researchers examined Remember and Know responses to false alarms not only for conceptually related lists (e.g., funnel, twister, spiral, cyclone, spinning, whirling, typhoon, gusts, windstorm; critical non-presented lure: tornado) but also for perceptually related lists (fade, fame, face, fake, mate, hate, late, date, rate; critical non-presented lure: fate). Amnesics showed low and equal levels of Remember and Know false alarms. More interestingly for present purposes, the false alarms for conceptually associated words were largely accompanied by Remember responses and the false alarms for perceptually associated words were given Know responses. An increase in Know responses for perceptually-based false memories has been shown in other studies as well (Dewhurst & Hitch, 1997; Rajaram, 1993).

Mather, Henkel, and Johnson (1997) carried out a detailed analysis of the contents of Remember experiences associated with studied words as well as the non-presented critical lures. Their results showed that false Remember responses were based on associative information rather than on perceptual details.

In another study, Holmes, Waters, and Rajaram (1998) assessed the subjective states of awareness in the recognition of sentences in an adaptation of Bransford and Franks' (1971) semantic integration paradigm. Three results from this series of experiments are directly relevant here. One, subjects showed high levels of false alarms rates as semantic integration in the sentences increased, and these false alarms were largely accompanied by Remember responses. Two, the high confidence ratings assigned to false alarms were not necessarily associated with Remember judgments. Three, when the semantic integration of sentences was experimentally attenuated, false Remember responses decreased.

Clearly, illusions of memory appear to be powerful enough to give rise to the experience of not just Knowing but also Remembering. Furthermore, conceptual context seems to produce false Remember responses whereas perceptual factors lead to false Know responses. How can we theoretically interpret these findings? Specifically, the distinctiveness-fluency framework (Rajaram, 1996, 1998) postulates that the operations of distinctive processes lead to the experience of Remembering. How can a never-presented item become distinctive in memory? This puzzle can be solved by examining the conditions under which the experiences of false Remembering or false Knowing arise. False remembering has been typically reported in studies where each of the associated items (e.g., funnel, twister, spiral, cyclone, spinning, whirling, typhoon, gusts, windstorm) is individually capable of activating the critical lure (tornado). Thus, the presentation of each of the associated items may bring to mind the critical lure. Roediger and McDermott (1995) have offered a similar explanation for false Remember responses. It is possible that this internal generation of the critical lure may amount to multiple presentations of items. Repeated experimental presentations have been known to increase Remembering as well as Knowing (Gardiner, et al., 1996b). Repetitions can create two effects. Repetitions may increase the activation of an item, thereby increasing the fluency of processing. This process can increase Knowing. However, repetitions also lead to better encoding of details or distinctive features. Thus, effects of repetitions on Remembering could arise from either experimentally arranged multiple presentations (Gardiner et al., 1996b) or repeated, internal generation of the critical lure, as in the case of the tornado list. This repeated activation may make the internally generated critical lure vivid, and thereby lead to false Remembering.

The perceptually associated words give rise to false Knowing, not false Remembering (Schacter et al., 1997). By the account described above, this result is not surprising. While the individual words in the perceptually associated list would activate some orthographic or phonemic constituents of the critical lure (fate), no single word in this list can activate the entire critical lure. Thus, the representation of the critical lure is gradually strengthened with the presentation of various perceptual associations although this strengthening of activation is not the same as repeated internal generation of the critical lure. As a result, the strengthened activation may not lead to a distinct internal representation. These possible mechanisms that lead to false Remembering and Knowing need to be explored further in future studies.

5.   Interpreting the nature of Knowing

A study of the nature of Remembering has proceeded with relatively little controversy. Much of the work has involved specifying the system (Gardiner, 1988; Tulving, 1985) or the processes (Jacoby, et al., 1997; Rajaram, 1996, 1998) that govern these judgments. Researchers have also worked out the similarities between Remember judgments and source monitoring decisions (Johnson, 1988; Johnson, Hashtroudi, & Lindsay, 1993; Donaldson, Mackenzie & Underhill, 1996), and the details that characterize Remember judgments (Mather et al., 1997).

Much of the controversy surrounds the nature of Knowing. Tulving (1985) conceptualized Knowing, or noetic consciousness, as a product of the semantic memory system. Subsequently, Gardiner and colleagues (Gardiner, 1988; Gardiner & Java, 1990; Gardiner & Parkin, 1990) associated Knowing with the functioning of the procedural memory system. In recent works, Gardiner and associates have returned to Tulving's classification system (see Gardiner & Gregg, 1997; Gardiner et al., 1996a; Gardiner, et al., 1996b). In Rajaram's processing framework, it was assumed that perceptual processes mediate Knowing (Rajaram, 1993). In a later version, fluency of processing, conceptual as well as perceptual, is assumed to mediate Knowing (Rajaram, 1996). In addition, some researchers have argued in favor of using different estimates of Knowing (Jacoby et al., 1997).

These debates attest to the difficulty in defining Know responses. The Know response can represent many things. It can represent familiarity (Gardiner, 1988; Jacoby et al., 1997; Rajaram, 1993) or abstract knowledge from semantic memory (Tulving, 1985). In the initial reports, the experience of Knowing was hypothesized to arise from processes that govern perceptual priming (Gardiner, 1988; Gardiner & Java, 1990; Gardiner & Parkin, 1990). However, subsequent research has called this possibility into question (Java, 1994; Kinoshita, 1995; Wagner, Gabrieli, & Verfaellie, 1997; see also Richardson-Klavehn, Gardiner, & Java, 1996).

Attempts are being made to better grasp the nature of Knowing and the varieties of experiences that may be subsumed under this category. In this effort, researchers have contrasted a feeling or an intuition with the abstract knowledge that arises from semantic memory (Kihlstrom, Kim, Dabady, 1996), and familiarity with just Knowing or conceptual knowledge (Conway et al., 1997). Although the exact nature of Knowing remains open for scrutiny, the contention that Know judgments may reflect guesses rather than real awareness (Strack & Forster, 1995) has been refuted in a series of studies by Gardiner and colleagues (Gardiner, Java, & Richardson-Klavehn, 1996a; Gardiner, et al., 1996b; Gardiner, Richardson-Klavehn, & Ramponi, 1997). In future studies, the exact conditions that may lead to different types of Knowing, and the specific processes that may mediate such experiences, remain to be explored.

6.   Conclusions

In 1985, Tulving lamented that consciousness was not an integral aspect of research on memory. In less than 15 years, a large body of evidence on the nature of subjective states has vastly changed the landscape of memory research. We now have some understanding of the experimental, neural, and pharmacological factors that modulate these retrieval experiences. Several theories and models have been developed to account for the processes associated with different states of awareness. However, there are many questions that have been prompted by these advances, particularly about the nature of Knowing. Future research may help us tackle some of these difficult and interesting issues in the study of conscious experience.

Acknowledgments

Preparation of this chapter was supported by grant R29MH57345-01 to Suparna Rajaram. Yoko Yahata's assistance in the preparation of this chapter is acknowledged.

References

Atkinson, R. C. & Juola, J. F. (1973). Factors influencing speed and accuracy of word recognition. In S. Korblum (ed.), *Attention and Performance IV* (pp. 583–612). New York: Academic Press.

Atkinson, R. C. & Juola, J. F. (1974). Search and decision processes in recognition memory. In D. H. Krantz, R. C. Atkinson, R. D. Luce, & R. Suppes (eds.), *Contemporary developments in mathematical psychology (Vol. 1): Learning, memory, and thinking.* (pp. 242–293). San Francsco: Freeman.

Blaxton, T. A. & Theodore, W. H. (1998). The role of the temporal lobes in recognizing visuospatial materials: Remembering versus knowing. *Brain and Cognition, 35,* 5–25.

Conway, M. A., Gardiner, J. M., Perfect, T. J., Anderson, S. J., & Cohen, G. (1997). Changes in memory awareness during learning: The acquisition of knowledge by psychology undergraduates. *Journal of Experimental Psychology: General, 126,* 393–413.

Curran, H. V. & Hildebrandt, M. (1998). *Selective effects of alcohol on recollective experience.* Manuscript under review.

Curran, H. V., Gardiner, J. M., Java, R. I., & Allen, D. (1993). Effects of lorazepam upon recollective experience in recognition memory. *Psychopharmacology, 110,* 374–378.

Curran, T., Schacter, D. L., Norman, K. A., & Galluccio, L. (1997). False recognition after a right frontal lobe infarction: Memory for general and specific information. *Neuropsychologia, 35,* 1035–1049.

Dalla Barba, G. (1993). Confabulation: Knowledge and recollective experience. *Cognitive Neuropsychology, 10,* 10–20.

Dalla Barba, G. (1997). Recognition memory and recollective experience in Alzheimer's disease. *Memory, 5,* 657–672.

Deese, J. (1959). On the prediction of occurrence of particular intrusions in immediate recall. *Journal of Experimental Psychology, 58,* 17–22.

Dewhurst, S. A. & Conway, M. A. (1994). Pictures, images, and recollective experience. *Journal of Experimental Psychology: Learning, Memory, and Cognition, 20,* 1088–1098.

Dewhurst, S. A. & Hitch, G. J. (1997). Illusions of familiarity caused by cohort activation. *Psychonomic Bulletin & Review, 4,* 322–328.

Düzel, E., Yonelinas, A. P., Mangun, G. R., Heinze, H. J., & Tulving, E. (1997). Event-related brain potential correlates of two states of conscious awareness in memory. *Proceedings of the National Academy of Science, 94,* 5973–5978.

Donaldson, W. (1996). The role of decision processes in remembering and knowing. *Memory & Cognition, 24,* 523–533.

Donaldson, W., MacKenzie, T. M., & Underhill, C. F. (1996). A comparison of recollective memory and source memory. *Psychonomic Bulletin & Review, 3,* 186–192.

Gardiner, J. M. (1988). Functional aspects of recollective experience. *Memory & cognition, 16,* 309–313.

Gardiner, J. M., Gawlik, B., & Richardson-Kalvehn, A. (1994). Maintenance rehearsal affects knowing, not remembering; elaborative rehearsal affects remembering, not knowing. *Psychonomic Bulletin & Review, 1,* 107–110.

Gardiner, J. M. & Gregg, V. H. (1997). Recognition memory with little or no remembering: Implications for a detection model. *Psychonomic Bulletin & Review, 4,* 474–479.

Gardiner, J. M. & Java, R. I. (1990). Recollective experience in word and nonword recognition. *Memory & Cognition, 18,* 23–30.

Gardiner, J. M. & Java, R. I. (1993a). Recognising and remembering. In A. Collins, S. Gathercole, M. Conway, & P. Morris (eds.). *Theories of memory* (pp. 163–188). Hillsdale: Erlbaum.

Gardiner, J. M. & Java, R. I. (1993b). Recognition memory and awareness: An experiential approach. *European Journal of Cognitive Psychology, 5,* 337–346.

Gardiner, J. M., Java, R. I., & Richardson-Klavehn, A. (1996a). How level of processing really influences awareness in recognition memory. *Canadian Journal of Experimental Psychology, 50,* 114–122.

Gardiner, J. M., Kaminska, Z., Dixon, M., & Java, R. I. (1996b). Repetition of previously novel melodies sometimes increases both remember and know responses in recognition memory. *Psychonomic Bulletin & Review, 3,* 366–371.

Gardiner, J. M. & Parkin, A. J. (1990). Attention and recollective experience in recognition memory. *Memory & Cognition, 18,* 579–583.

Gardiner, J. M. & Richardson-Klavehn, A. (in press). Remembering and Knowing. In E. Tulving & F. I. M. Craik (eds.), *Handbook of memory*. Oxford University Press.

Gardiner, J. M., Richardson-Klavehn, A., & Ramponi, C. (1997). On reporting recollective experiences and "direct access to memory systems". *Psychological Science, 8,* 391–394.

Gregg, V.H. & Gardiner, J.M. (1994). Recognition memory and awareness: A large effect of study-test modalities on "know" responses following a highly perceptual orienting task. *European Journal of Cognitive Psychology, 6,* 137–147.

Hirshman, E. & Masters, S. (1997). Modeling the conscious correlates of recognition memory: Reflections on the remember-know paradigm. *Memory & Cognition, 25,* 345–351.

Holmes, J.B., Waters, H.S., & Rajaram, S. (1998). The phenomenology of false memories: Episodic content and confidence. *Journal of Experimental Psychology: Learning, Memory, and Cognition, 24,* 1026–1040.

Huron, C., Danion, J.M., Giacomoni, G., Grange, D., Robert, P. & Rizzo, L. (1995). Impairment of recognition memory with, but not without, conscious recollection in schizophrenia. *American Journal of Psychiatry, 152,* 1737–1742.

Inoue, C. & Bellezza, F.S. (1998). The detection model of recognition using know and remember judgements. *Memory & Cognition, 26,* 299–308.

Jacoby, L.L. (1983a). Perceptual enhancement: Persistent effects of an experience. *Journal of Experimental Psychology: Learning, Memory, and Cognition, 9,* 21–38.

Jacoby, L.L. (1983b). Analyzing interactive processes in reading. *Journal of verbal Learning and Verbal Behavior, 22,* 485–508.

Jacoby, L.L. (1991). A process-dissociation framework: Separating automatic from intentional uses of memory. *Journal of Memory and Language, 30,* 513–541.

Jacoby, L.L. & Dallas, M. (1981). On the relationship between autobiographical memory and perceptual learning. *Journal of Experimental Psychology: General, 110,* 306–340.

Jacoby, L.L., Yonelinas, A.P., & Jennings, J.M. (1997). The relation between conscious and unconscious (automatic) influences: A declaration of independence. In J.D. Cohen & J.W. Schooler (eds.), *Scientific approaches to the question of consciousness* (pp. 13–47). Hillsdale: Erlbaum.

Java, R.I. (1994). States of awareness following word stem completion. *European Journal of Cognitive Psychology, 6,* 77–92.

Johnson, M.K. (1988). Reality monitoring: An experimental phenomenological approach. *Journal of Experimental Psychology: General, 117,* 390–394.

Johnson, M.K., Hashtroudi, S., & Lindsay, D.S. (1993). Source monitoring. *Psychological Bulletin, 114,* 3–28.

Jones, T.C. & Roediger, H.L. (1995). The experiential basis of serial position effects. *European Journal of Cognitive Psychology, 7,* 65–80.

Joorderns, S. & Merikle, P.M. (1993). Independence or redundancy? Two models of conscious and unconscious influences. *Journal of Experimental Psychology: General, 122,* 462–467.

Kinoshita, S. (1995). The word frequency effect in recognition memory versus repetition priming. *Memory & Cognition, 23,* 569–580.

Kihlstrom, J.F., Kim, M., & Dabady, M. (1996, November). *Remembering, knowing, and feeling in episodic recognition.* Paper presented at the 37th annual meeting of the Psychonomic Society, Chicago.

Knowlton, B.J. & Squire, L.R. (1995). Remembering and knowing: Two different expressions of declarative memory. *Journal of Experimental Psychology: Learning, Memory, and Cognition, 21,* 699–710.

Lane, S.M. & Zaragoza, M.S. (1995). The recollective experience of cross-modality errors. *Memory & Cognition, 23,* 607–610.

Linsay, S.D. & Kelley, C.M. (1996). Creating illusions of familiarity in a cued recall Remember/Know paradigm. *Journal of Memory and Language, 35,* 197–211.

Mandler, G. (1980). Recognizing: The judgment of previous occurrence. *Psychological Review, 87,* 252–271.

Mantyla, T. (1993). Knowing but not remembering: Adult age differences in recollective experience. *Memory & Cognition, 21,* 379–388.

Mantyla, T. (1994). Components of recollective experience in cued recall. *Scandinavian Journal of Psychology, 35,* 263–270.

Mantyla, T. (1997). Recollections of faces: Remembering differences and knowing similarities. *Journal of Experimental Psychology: Learning, Memory, and Cognition, 23,* 1203–1216.

Mantyla, T. & Raudsepp, J. (1996). Recollective experience following suppresion of focal attention. *European Journal of Cognitive Psychology, 8,* 195–203.

Mather, M., Henkel, L.A., & Johnson, M.K. (1997). Evaluating characteristics of false memories: Remember/know judgments and memory characteristics compared. *Memory & Cognition, 25,* 826–837.

Nyberg, L. & Tulving, E. (1996). Classifying human long-term memory: Evidence from converging dissociations. *European Journal of Cognitive Psychology, 8,* 163–183.

Parkin, A.J., Gardiner, J.M., & Rosser, R. (1995). Functional aspects of recollective experience in face recognition. *Consciousness and Cognition, 4,* 387–398.

Parkin, A.J. & Walter, B. (1992). Recollective experience, normal aging, and frontal dysfunction. *Psychology and Aging, 7,* 290–298.

Perfect, T.J., Williams, R.B., & Anderson-Brown, C. (1995). Age differences in reported recollective experience are due to encoding effects, not response bias. *Memory, 3,* 169–186.

Rajaram, S. (1993). Remembering and knowing: Two means of access to the personal past. *Memory & Cognition, 21,* 89–102.

Rajaram, S. (1996). Perceptual effects on remembering: Recollective processes in picture recognition memory. *Journal of Experimental Psychology: Learning, Memory, and Cognition, 22,* 365–377.

Rajaram, S. (1998). The effects of conceptual salience and perceptual distinctiveness on conscious recollection. *Psychonomic Bulletin & Review, 5,* 71–78.

Rajaram, S., Hamilton, M. & Bolton, A. (1999). *Separating conscious recollection from confidence: Evidence from cognitive neuropsychology.* Manuscript in preparation.

Rajaram, S. & Hamilton, M. (1999). *The phenomenology of retrieval across multiple memory tasks: Determining a "pure" measure of conscious recollection.* Manuscript under review.

Rajaram, S. & Roediger, H.L. III (1997). Remembering and knowing as states of consciousness during recollection. In J.D. Cohen & J.W. Schooler (eds.), *Scientific approaches to the question of consciousness* (pp. 213–240). Hillsdale: Erlbaum.

Richardson-Klavehn, A. & Gardiner, J.M. (1995). Retrieval volition and memorial awareness in stem completion: An empirical analysis. *Psychological Research, 57,* 166–178.

Richardson-Klavehn, A. & Gardiner, J.M. (1996). Cross-modality priming in stem completion reflects conscious memory, but not voluntary memory. *Psychonomic Bulletin & Review, 3,* 238–244.

Richardson-Klavehn, A., Gardiner, J.M., & Java, R.I. (1996). Memory: Task dissociations, process dissociations, and dissociations of consciousness. In G. Underwood (ed.), *Implicit cognition* (pp. 85–158). Oxford: Oxford University Press.

Roediger, H.L. (1990). Implicit memory: Retention without remembering. *American Psychologist, 45,* 1043–1056.

Roediger, H.L. & McDermott, K.B. (1995). Creating false memories: Remembering words not presented in lists. *Journal of Experimental Psychology: Learning, Memory, and Cognition, 21,* 803–814.

Roediger, H.L., Wheeler, M.A., & Rajaram, S. (1993). Remembering, knowing, and reconstructing the past. In D.L. Medin (ed.), *The psychology of learning and motivation* (pp. 97–134). Academic Press.

Schacter, D.L., Verfaillie, M., & Anes, M.D. (1997a). Illusory memories in amnesic patients: Conceptual and perceptual false recognition. *Neuropsychology, 11,* 331–342.

Smith, M.E. (1993). Neuropsychological manifestations of recollective experience during recognition memory judgements. *Journal of Cognitive Neuroscience, 5,* 1–13.

Strack, F. & Forster, J. (1995). Reporting recollective experiences: Direct access to memory systems? *Psychological Science, 6,* 352–358.

Tulving, E. (1983). *Elements of episodic memory.* Oxford: Oxford University Press.

Tulving, E. (1985). Memory and consciousness. *Canadian Psychologist, 26,* 1–12.

Tulving, E. (1989). Memory: Performance, knowledge, and experience. *European journal of Experiemntal Psychology, 1,* 3–26.

Tulving, E. (1994). Varieties of consciousness and levels of awareness in memory. In A. Baddeley & L. Weiskrantz (eds.). *Attention: Selection, awareness, and control. A tribute to Donald Broadbent* (pp. 283–299). Oxford: Oxford University Press.

Wagner, A.D., Gabrieli, J.D.E., & Verfaellie, M. (1997). Dissociations between familiarity processes in explicit recognition and implicit perceptual memory. *Journal of Experimental Psychology: Learning, Memory, and Cognition, 23,* 305–323.

Wheeler, M.A., Stuss, D.T., & Tulving, E. (1997). Towards a theory of episodic memory: The frontal lobes and autonoetic consciousness. *Psychological Bulletin, 121,* 331–354.

Yonelinas, A.P., Kroll, N.E.A., Dobbins, I., Lazzara, M., & Knight, R.T. (1998). Recollection and familiarity deficits in amnesia: Convergence of Remember/Know, process dissociation, and ROC data. *Neuropsychology, 12,* 323–339.

Index of Subjects

Index of Names